# CONTENDING
# PERSPECTIVES
# IN
# INTERNATIONAL
# POLITICAL
# ECONOMY

# CONTENDING PERSPECTIVES IN INTERNATIONAL POLITICAL ECONOMY

**NIKOLAOS ZAHARIADIS**

*State University of New York—New Paltz*

**HARCOURT BRACE COLLEGE PUBLISHERS**

Fort Worth   Philadelphia   San Diego   New York   Orlando   Austin   San Antonio
Toronto   Montreal   London   Sydney   Tokyo

| | |
|---:|:---|
| PUBLISHER | Earl McPeek |
| ACQUISITIONS EDITOR | David Tatom |
| PRODUCT MANAGER | Laura Brennan |
| PROJECT EDITOR | Sandy Walton Mann |
| ART DIRECTOR | Candice Johnson Clifford |
| PRODUCTION MANAGER | Linda McMillan |

Cover image credit: Tony Stone Images, Reza Estakhrian

Address for Editorial Correspondence: Harcourt Brace College Publishers, 301 Commerce Street, Suite 3700, Fort Worth, TX 76102

Address for Orders: Harcourt Brace College Publishers, 6277 Sea Harbor Drive, Orlando, FL 32887-6777
1-800-782-4479
Web Site Address: http://www.hbcollege.com

ISBN: 0-15-508261-2

Library of Congress Catalog Card Number: 98-71174

Printed in the United States of America

8  9  0  1  2  3  4  5  6  7     039     9  8  7  6  5  4  3  2  1

Harcourt Brace College Publishers

*To Ellen and Lucy*
*For just being themselves*

———————————■———————————

# ACKNOWLEDGMENTS

This book is a product of many people. Although they all deserve thanks, they are too numerous to mention by name here. But one stands out more than others. Ken Fuller provided considerable assistance with the logistics of the project, particularly the process of contacting publishers. My students at the State University of New York—New Paltz deserve my gratitude for providing valuable feedback on the selections included in this volume. I would also like to thank the political science editor at Harcourt Brace, David Tatom, for valuable support and encouragement throughout the project. Finally, I wish to express appreciation to my wife, Ellen, for being so understanding with my academic pursuits and the time they take to complete.

# INTRODUCTION

The term political economy has been used for over three hundred years to denote the management of the economic affairs of the state. It emerged first, as a framework to bridge the old notion of *oikonomia*—the Greek word for household management—to the new notion of capitalism—the satisfaction of individual desires by industrial production—and second, as a response to the mercantile practice of wealth acquisition and management prevalent since the Italian city states of the thirteenth century and the discovery of the New World. Mercantilism, and its recent incarnation as economic realism, involves the subordination of all economic activity to the pursuit of state power. Wealth accumulates when exports are encouraged and imports are discouraged with state support in both tariff or subsidy form. Political economy as a field of study, in Adam Smith's sense, reverses the relationship, suggesting that the state should support rather than subordinate economic activity. This new way of thinking provided at the time the medium for connecting the individual to society at large, bypassing the need to study familial management. It facilitated the study of new institutions of production and distribution of wealth, such as the textile factory; gave rise to intriguing new questions, such as the role of the state in facilitating or inhibiting the capitalist process; and served as a framework with which individuals could better understand and cope with the dramatic consequences of the industrial revolution.

The study of political economy, however, had one more objective that is often forgotten in contemporary discourse. It legitimized the pursuit of individual interests and aimed at designing institutions that promoted human happiness. It is important to highlight this moral dimension of political economy for two reasons.

First, it helps us understand the transition from a Christian tradition that deprecated the pursuit of the material in favor of focusing on "the next world." Even as late as the 1700s, there were fervent disputes over the "just" prices of commodities. Job mobility as well as that of persons were severely restricted. Advertising was not allowed for the most part. The pursuit of human happiness in terms of earthly possessions was not merely restricted on the basis of state or church prohibitions but also on the basis of social norms and values. As Albert Hirschman (1977) maintains, up until then individual interests were thought to involve the pursuit of honor and glory, not material advantage.

The field of political economy provided an intellectual agenda to ennoble individual wealth acquisition.

Second, the study of political economy has a normative objective. This point has been lost in contemporary discourse because the modern disciplines of economics and political science have adopted a positive outlook becoming more concerned with questions of "what is" rather than "what should be." Examined from this angle, the study of political economy acquires a distinct advantage over the separate study of either politics or economics. It not only sensitizes the student to the interconnections between the two, but it also serves as a normatively good and analytically useful guide in times of dramatic change. It is normatively good because it forces analysts to question their assumptions and values. For example, accepting globalization as *de facto* reality and exploring the constraints it places on the state are important issues to address, but equally important is the question whether the state has a role in promoting the welfare of its citizens and whether such restrictions undermine this role. No matter what the answer may be, asking such a normative question forces the analyst to think about the direction of human evolution. The first political economists, including Adam Smith, as well as Karl Marx, were also moralists. Such a conception of political economy is an analytically useful guide to policy because it challenges analysts to think of ways to adapt, create, or discard institutions should the need arise. Political economy is not simply an intellectual agenda that helps us understand what is happening in specific areas of human life. It is also a way of forcing us to think of ways to make things better.

The book has two aims. First, it serves as a survey of theoretical approaches to international issues of political economy. Good surveys, in theory, must be both comprehensive and coherent. In practice there is a trade-off where coherence, that is, a complete illumination of all aspects of a perspective, stands in the way of the need for comprehensive coverage of all perspectives. This anthology of readings leans on the side of coherence. It is guided by the very practical limitation of space to provide adequate coverage of several major, but not all, strands of thought. Second, the book aims to introduce students to the separate and sometimes distinct logic of economic and political ways of thinking about the same issues. It is all too common for students of political science to have limited exposure to economic concepts and theories. Similarly, students of economics are usually unaware of the political dimensions and consequences of economic decisions. The aim is to show the distinctiveness between the two disciplines, but it is also hoped that students will be able to judge for themselves whether, how, and in what areas there are interconnections.

**WHAT IS INTERNATIONAL POLITICAL ECONOMY?** There is no widely accepted definition of the term. Some analysts try to separate the field from either of its core constituent disciplines—political science or economics—and present it as a distinct, new approach. Others try to integrate the two fields into one coherent framework.

Some analysts view the term as distinct and separate from economics or politics. Robert Cox (1995, 32), for example, defines it as the study of "the historically constituted frameworks or structures within which political and economic activity takes place" on a global level. The focus is not on the present or on actors operating under fixed assumptions, but on history and structures, that is, actor-reproduced pictures of reality. The question the field asks, according to Cox, is how these structures came about and how they may be changed. This definition is too narrow. It imposes a particular methodology (dialectic), time frame (past), and analytical framework (critical theory). Why should international political economy (IPE) not be concerned with problem-solving or with the present? What good is historically derived knowledge if not to be utilized to better humans? And why should an entire field be confined to only one theoretical framework? It is certainly a good way to dismiss competing explanations, but it is an inefficient and inappropriate way to accumulate knowlege because academic discourse ends up being a monologue rather than a dialogue.

Most analysts, including the present author, proceed in a different direction. IPE is understood as the interconnection between politics and economics in the domain of international economic relations. The trick is to determine how this connection is defined. That's no easy task because there are many different conceptualizations of the constituent terms.

One important assumption underlies the above definition for IPE. What distinguishes IPE from mainstream international economics is the fact that the world economy does not and cannot exist without some political framework to stabilize it. The state needs the market to function properly. As Robert Gilpin (1987, 8) remarks,

> [W]ithout both state and market there would be no political economy. In the absence of the state, the price mechanism and market forces would determine the outcome of economic activities; this would be the pure world of the economist. In the absence of the market, the state or its equivalent would allocate economic resources; this would be the pure world of the political scientist.

Obviously, neither is true, so IPE must involve some combination of both.

One implication is the search for a unified framework that transcends disciplinary boundaries. Some analysts view this as a fruitful attempt to reconstitute social science and to overcome artificial disciplinary distinctions. Since the disciplinary divide allows us to specialize into observing only parts of a complex social reality, disciplinary explanations are incomplete. It follows that attempts at integration can only permit a fuller explanation. Other analysts deplore political economy as an example of "muddying the waters." This is because knowledge gained through specialization is based on simplifying assumptions, for example, the economic man or political man. Because the two are very different, any attempt to combine them will only confuse not clarify. Regardless of where one comes down on this debate, the fact is that attempts at unified frameworks have been made. One clear example is dependency theory (Chilcote, 1994, Chapter 4), but there are others, such as hegemonic theory inspired by the writings of Antonio Gramsci (Gill and Law, 1988), or world-systems theory (Wallerstein, 1979).

To help us cut through the maze of definitions, assumptions, and implications, we divide the definition into three parts and examine each separately. Our definition necessitates a clear conceptualization of politics, economics, and the term international. We examine each in turn and then we explore their interconnections.

**WHAT IS POLITICS?** While there are many ways to conceive of politics, they can be usefully classified in two distinct groups. This classification scheme has been inspired by the work of Caporaso and Levine (1992). Politics can be seen as a mode and as a locus of inquiry. Each conception examines different kinds of politics and leads to dramatically different implications for the study of political economy.

Politics as a mode of inquiry refers to the use of power to capture and control the allocation of resources. This definition comes close to David Easton's (1981) celebrated definition of politics as the authoritative allocation of values, but it is more specific to resources than to the wide array of nebulous values. This is appropriate in our case, not simply because of the difficulty of defining values, but also because of the subject matter of our inquiry into material well-being. What is noteworthy about this way of conceptualizing politics is that the focus is on activities—not institutions—and on some kind of coercion or authority—not simply a voluntary exchange.

The focus of inquiry is on exploring how the process of allocating resources is being made. This takes politics away from the formal study of institutions or the state in that politics may take place outside the limits of "government." For example, the media play a significant role in shaping the government's agenda even though newspapers, magazines, radio, and television are not part of the government. Political activities, therefore, take place through a variety of institutions, some of which may involve state agencies. Politics provides us with a way of thinking about such activities.

The allocation of resources depends on the ability of individuals or groups to control the process. Capital accumulation does not occur spontaneously but rather takes place within a hierarchy of individuals or groups—some of whom have greater influence over the others. Sources of influence may include group characteristics such as information. For example, some entrepreneurs know the results of geological surveys and, consequently, can ask for exclusive rights on contracts for oil extraction much earlier than other entrepreneurs and at much lower prices. One of the most frequently cited advantages of multinational corporations (MNCs) is managerial know-how and access to technology. Consequently, MNCs always have the intitial advantage in negotiating contracts with host governments involving the extraction, processing, and distribution of raw materials. Other sources of influence may be access, that is, some entrepreneurs have access to governing officials so that they can negotiate better terms on contracts to, say, supply the government with computers. Still others simply have more money and can buy off opponents. All in all, the activities of individuals and groups are considered political if they are involved in holding, making, or trying to influence the authoritative allocation of resources.

Politics as a locus of inquiry stresses the need to study formal institutions. Attention is directed at the state and its ability to function properly. For example, analysts may examine congressional legislation or elections, domains traditionally associated with "government" and its functions. They may, however, analyze the constitutional make-up of a particular government and its historical development. In contrast to the previous conceptualization, politics is viewed as a particular domain or area of study.

**WHAT IS ECONOMICS?**   In a similar way, conceptions of economics can be divided into two groups of conceptualizations—as a mode and as a locus of inquiry. Each examines different aspects and has different consequences for the study of IPE.

Economics as a mode of inquiry refers to the efficient allocation of resources. Just as in the political definition, the focus is on resources but the key concern is on efficiency, not on power. Efficiency has positive and normative implications. On the positive side, it refers to finding ways to increase net benefits, that is, maximizing benefits and minimizing the costs of specific allocation schemes. This in turn creates greater wealth. On the normative side, greater wealth is viewed as something that is desirable. A more efficient allocation of resources implicitly increases human happiness.

Resources are, of course, not allocated automatically. The process is conducted by individuals within a system of free will. Hence economics focuses on individuals and requires the making of assumptions about their behavior. Individuals are assumed to be utility maximizers, that is, seeking to satisfy their desires by pursuing certain available means. Economic calculation entails the efficient utilization of means so that more can be accomplished with less. This means that individual behavior is conditioned by constraints to which it is exposed. Changes in behavior are not attributed to shifts in preferences. Preferences are assumed to be stable, consistent, and exogenously determined. Instead, changes in behavior are attributed to changes in environmental constraints and the systematic evaluation of alternative available options. For example, our decision not to buy a car but purchase a television set is not based on the fact that we changed our minds and now we want the set more than the car. Rather, it is the result of constraints and rational calculus telling us that we need the television set more than the car given the utilization rates of each, our lifestyles, and our funds. Such a way of thinking has been characterized by Max Weber (1978) as "instrumental rationality." Modern man understands the world by reducing it to a series of means-ends calculations. Of course, such a way of thinking need not be restricted to what are traditionally thought of as economic activities, such as the production and sale of typewriters or automobiles. Nobel laureate Gary Becker (1976) has expanded it to a wide array of activities and institutions, such as voting, suicide, and the family.

Economics as a locus of inquiry refers to what is commonly alluded to as the market. It is distinguished in two ways: as a particular type of activity and as a distinct set of institutions. Economists influenced by older traditions of economics refer to the realm of the economic as the production and distribution of goods and services (Caporaso and Levine, 1992, 24). In other words, economic activities are those that provide or satisfy material desires. This is certainly compatible to earlier conceptions of the economy as household management. How these wants can be satisfied and who should produce or consume lead us to the second conceptualization of the market as an institution.

Economics is usually identified with the market. It is defined as "a system of exchanges in which supply and demand interact to determine prices for both resources and products" (Clark, 1991, 6). Implicit in this definition are the basic tenets of a competitive market, which involves many small buyers and sellers with undifferentiated tastes. Not all markets need be competitive, but competition in the form of voluntary exchange is held to be the key image of the ideal market. In addition, a central tenet of the market is private property. Markets cannot exist without private individuals owning portions, or ideally all, of the means of production. It is the right of individuals who own property to sell or buy other property that differentiates the market from the polity. Individuals pursue their objectives apart from those of the state and it is precisely this separation that makes the market work well. It is no surprise that one of the first things that all former communist countries established during the transition period from command economies was the legal notion of private property.

Such a conception of the market requires a clear differentiation of it from other social and political institutions. One of the biggest contributions of Adam Smith was his ability to clearly articulate the logic of the self-regulating or free market. His aim was to differentiate commercial transactions from state authority and to show that such a system guided by the "invisible hand" would bring greater prosperity to the nation and the sovereign. Indeed, it was this transformation of the organization of production that leads Polanyi (1957, 71) to argue that "a self-regulating market demands nothing less than the institutional separation of society into an economic and political sphere." Conceptualizing a free market requires a clear and distinct separation of the processes of production from the vagaries of governance and diplomacy. However, to be separate does not mean to be independent. Adam Smith, as well as most economists, accepts a significant amount of state involvement in what are commonly referred to as public goods, such as public works or defense.

**WHAT IS INTERNATIONAL?** The term "international" refers to issues going beyond any national boundaries. This means that although national boundaries are important, they do not represent a different order of reality. They are simply one of the parts of the complex mosaic of issues, problems, and actors that have a role to play in international affairs.

Such a definition is different from others in the literature. The term has a standard definition in international relations as referring to issues and actions between countries and not within them. But "unlike stylized versions of 'international' (that is, interstate) politics," Keohane (1997, 150) boldly asserts, "political economy cannot be encompassed solely by the interactions of states." The definition provided here accepts that some issues may involve actors in domestic and international politics. In other words, the conception of "international" refers to a locus of inquiry, not a type of explanation. International is the domain within which the present study on political economy is situated. Some analysts prefer to differentiate this conception by using the term "global." This seems redundant.

We are now ready to begin putting the parts of our definition together. We have argued that the political can be viewed in two ways: as a mode and as a locus of inquiry. The same is true for the economic. Combining the two gives us a matrix with four cells. Using one as a method and the other as a locus of inquiry permits us to offer two different ways of looking at political economy. The first is the neo-economic way, or public choice, that uses economic concepts, assumptions, and methods to examine politics as an area of inquiry. The chapter by Bruno Frey illustrates this approach. The second approach is the neo-political approach. One uses political methods and concepts, such as hegemony, to examine traditionally economic activities, such as trade or foreign investment. Keohane (1984, 21) illustrates this approach well in his definition of IPE: It is "the intersection of the substantive area of economics—production and exchange of marketable means of want satisfaction—with the process by which power is exercised that is central to politics." The chapter by Krasner is a good example of the political approach. There are also two more cells in the matrix. The first has to do with traditional economic analysis. Decisions on whether to trade with another country and how much trade there should be have as much to do with factor endowments (traditional economic analysis) as they have to do with the balance of self-interested pressure groups and their ability to influence decision makers (neo-economic or neo-political approaches, depending on assumptions). The chapter by Coughlin, Chrystal, and Wood demonstrates the strength of traditional economic analysis. The last cell includes traditional political analysis. It is not illustrated in this book because the focus is on economic activities.

Analysts employ different criteria when examining each institution separately—the state or the market—depending on their disciplinary orientation. This has serious consequences for the study of political economy. Economists value primarily efficiency, growth, and stability, while political scientists are more interested in freedom, equity, and order (Clark, 1991). Hence, economists view institutions, such as the state or the market, in terms of their ability to foster or inhibit such goals. For example, looking at the state as an economic institution, economists conclude that relative to the market the state is a poor allocator of resources, and an institution that fosters less wealth accumulation. The usual policy advice of such a perspective, with some exceptions and refinements, is to shrink the state in favor of the market. Examining the market as a political institution, political scientists are more interested in freedom, equity, and order. The market, they argue, limits choice through consumption power, subordinates some individuals to others because resources are distributed unevenly, and promotes social dislocation and disorder through periods of economic recession. The usual policy advice is to subordinate the market to the state. Regardless of which side of the debate one advocates, the point is that the objectives of inquiry differ depending on the lens or mode of inquiry that is employed. All this serves to buttress our argument that we may not collapse completely politics into economics and vice versa. The two contain important differences that must be illuminated.

The book illustrates the variety of perspectives contained within the three approaches mentioned above by including several works from each. Traditional economic analysis is merged with public choice under the rubric of the economic approach. It is contrasted with the political approach. To keep the anthology focused and manageable, stress is put on international issues, such as trade, the role of multinational companies, or capital flows. However, the anthology also includes other topics such as the relationship between capitalism and democracy, as well as the role of the state in an increasingly globalized economy. These are important issues in IPE that are not given proper attention in traditional anthologies.

Such a way of framing the study of IPE has distinct advantages. First, it is more complete than other attempts that present one-sided views. For example, the field of international political economy is defined by some analysts primarily as the economic view of international politics. Frey (1984, 10), for example, utilizes public choice theory to explore "those areas most grossly neglected by the traditional theory of international trade." This anthology transcends Frey's attempt by including illustrations of traditional international economic analysis. Still other analysts expand the field of IPE to any attempts employing economic methods in noneconomic areas. The collection of essays by Sandler (1980), for example, uses the externalities paradigm to examine *inter alia* arms control issues. The present anthology expands the theoretical diversity, but limits the issues to traditional economic activities. IPE is considered in this book to be a field of study, not a theoretical perspective (Staniland, 1985).

Second, the present work moves away from the traditional theoretical focus on liberal, realist, and radical, or some form of Marxist perspectives. While such a classification scheme served Gilpin (1975) and others after him well, it is no longer analytically useful. Marxism has been delegitimized with the fall of communism, and realism or neo-mercantilism appears to be in retreat. An exclusive or even predominant focus on the state seems no longer to be an appropriate analytical strategy in IPE. This classification scheme needs to be replaced by one that is more appropriate and more useful. The scheme presented here captures the diversity in the field and permits a direct comparison between political and economic approaches to IPE. Although the economic method is far more developed than the political, it is important to highlight the differences. Each has important insights to offer and one has no primacy over the other. They are just different ways of looking at the same thing.

**PLAN OF THE BOOK.** We begin with the classics. This first section informs the contemporary debates and sets the parameters upon which others have built. The next four sections deal with specific issues of international economic relations—multinationals, trade, money, and development. The final section explores the role of the democratic state in the new global economy. Each section is divided into two subsections, one illustrating the economic and the other the political approaches. Each subsection contains one or more selections designed to illuminate the particular approach on a given issue. To further shed light, each approach was written by specialists in their disciplines. Selections elaborating on the economic approach were written mostly by economists and the ones dealing with politics were written largely by political scientists. All in all, the selections should give students a complete understanding of contending perspectives in international political economy.

# REFERENCES

Becker, Gary. *The Economic Approach to Human Behavior.* Chicago: University of Chicago Press, 1976.

Caporaso, James A., and David P. Levine. *Theories of Political Economy.* Cambridge: Cambridge University Press, 1992.

Chilcote, Ronald H. *Theories of Comparative Politics: The Search for a Paradigm Reconsidered.* Boulder, CO: Westview Press, 1994.

Clark, Barry. *Political Economy: A Comparative Approach.* New York: Praeger, 1991.

Cox, Robert W. "Critical Political Economy." In *International Political Economy: Understanding Global Disorder,* edited by Björn Hettne. London and New Jersey: Zed Books, 1995.

Easton, David. *The Political System: An Inquiry into the State of Political Science.* Chicago: Chicago University Press, 1981 [1953].

Frey, Bruno S. 1984. *International Political Economics.* Oxford: Basil Blackwell.

Gill, Stephen, and David Law. *The Global Political Economy: Perspectives, Problems, and Politics.* Baltimore: Johns Hopkins University Press, 1988.

Gilpin, Robert. *The Political Economy of International Relations.* Princeton: Princeton University Press, 1987.

———. *U.S. Power and the Multinational Corporation.* New York: Basic Books, 1975.

Hirschman, Albert O. *The Passions and the Interests.* Princeton: Princeton University Press, 1977.

Keohane, Robert O. *After Hegemony.* Princeton: Princeton University Press, 1984.

———. "Problematic Lucidity: Stephen Krasner's 'State Power and the Structure of International Trade.'" *World Politics,* 50 (1997): 150–170.

Polanyi, Karl. *The Great Transformation.* Boston: Beacon Press, 1957 [1944].

Sandler, Todd, ed. *The Theory and Structures of International Political Economy.* Boulder, CO: Westview Press, 1980.

Staniland, Martin. *What Is Political Economy? A Study of Social Theory and Underdevelopment.* New Haven: Yale University Press, 1985.

Wallerstein, Immanuel. *The Capitalist World Economy.* Cambridge: Cambridge University Press, 1979.

Weber, Max. *Economy and Society.* 4th ed. Berkeley: University of California Press, 1978 [1956].

# CONTENTS

# DEMOCRACY AND THE FREE MARKET 167

## THE ECONOMIC APPROACH

## THE POLITICAL APPROACH

# Contending Perspectives in International Political Economy

# THE CLASSICS

Although writings on economics go back quite a few centuries, the modern foundations of political economy were laid by a Scottish professor, Adam Smith. His main argument was that individuals pursuing their self-interest are also benefiting society at large. The selection included here from his seminal work, *The Wealth of Nations*, deals with the effects of tariffs and other prohibitive measures on the domestic production of goods. The question Smith seeks to answer is whether such restraints are advantageous for the society as a whole. It is self-evident that the pursuit of gainful employment benefits an individual. But does this mean that such pursuit benefits society as well? Adam Smith's main contribution was to show that the not-so-obvious answer is a convincing "yes." Eliminating protection of domestic industry helps consumers by lowering prices of goods. According to Smith, not only is the free market desirable from the individual's point of view, but it is also the most efficient allocation of resources. From society's point of view, therefore, it generates the most wealth.

Many decades later, a Russian revolutionary, V. I. Lenin, qualified this statement by arguing that such pursuit of self-interest actually benefits only a few people while creating poverty and unhappiness for others. Referring to countries rather than to individuals and building on the seminal ideas proposed by Karl Marx, Lenin argues that such a system actually leads to exploitation and conflict. The policy of imperialism—the territorial expansion of great powers—is caused by the need to accumulate more capital. The system serves only the needs of the capitalist class of a powerful country, which includes banks, multinational companies, and others. Because there are several powerful countries each trying to promote the interests of its own capitalists, international conflict is inevitable. While the need to accumulate capital is infinite, the number of new territories and markets to be conquered is limited. Sooner or later, capitalist powers will have to confront each other for the same land. Indeed, the late nineteenth and early twentieth centuries were the golden age of imperialism.

It is very interesting to note Lenin's critique of, as he terms it, the global interlocking economy. This raises two points: First, contemporary interdependence between countries is not a new phenomenon, nor is the debate over its consequences. Second, Lenin's criticism of interdependence as exploitation in disguise may be as relevant today as it was seventy years ago. There are significant inequalities within and among countries today that continue to grow. The logic of interdependence (or globalization) is couched in terms of a struggle between countries for national dominance and market share. The means of fighting the struggle may have changed, but its end or potential consequences has not.

A sharp contrast to these economic views is Alexander Hamilton's perspective on the promotion of industry. Hamilton exemplifies the political view of trade. Defending mercantilist policies against Smith's liberal critique, Hamilton argues that protectionism is beneficial to the imposing nation. In Hamilton's America of the 1700s, there was little industry. As he saw it, there can be no competition between industries or economic development if there is no domestic industry to compete. Nascent industries need time and protection to grow. Hence protectionism is good for society and government must lead the way. According to Hamilton, in a world of politics one must not be fooled by the liberal talk of philosophers. It would be nice if other countries (Hamilton referred to European countries at the time) did not protect their domestic industry or promote their exports, but that is not the case. So not only does a country gain from protectionism but it also stands to lose industry if it does not practice it.

The debate primarily between Smith and Hamilton is as relevant today as it was over three centuries ago. Some of the arguments espoused by these writers resemble those advocated by proponents and opponents of the free trade debate regarding NAFTA and disputes in the World Trade Organization. The arguments, which vividly illustrate the differences between the economic and political approaches, set the parameters for the debates to follow later in this anthology.

# THE WEALTH OF NATIONS

## OF RESTRAINTS UPON THE IMPORTATION FROM FOREIGN COUNTRIES OF SUCH GOODS AS CAN BE PRODUCED AT HOME

Adam Smith

By restraining, either by high duties, or by absolute prohibitions, the importation of such goods from foreign countries as can be produced at home, the monopoly of the home market is more or less secured to the domestic industry employed in producing them. Thus the prohibition of importing either live cattle or salt provisions from foreign countries secures to the graziers of Great Britain the monopoly of the home market for butcher's meat. The high duties upon the importation of corn, which in times of moderate plenty amount to a prohibition, give a like advantage to the growers of that commodity. . . .

That this monopoly of the home-market frequently gives great encouragement to that particular species of industry which enjoys it, and frequently turns towards that employment a greater share of both the labour and stock of the society than would otherwise have gone to it, cannot be doubted. But whether it tends either to increase the general industry of the society, or to give it the most advantageous direction, is not, perhaps, altogether so evident.

Every individual is continually exerting himself to find out the most advantageous employment for whatever capital he can command. It is his own advantage, indeed, and not that of the society which he has in view. But the study of his own advantage naturally, or rather necessarily leads him to prefer that employment which is most advantageous to the society.

First, every individual endeavours to employ his capital as near home as he can, and consequently as much as he can in the support of domestic industry; provided always that he can thereby obtain the ordinary, or not a great deal less than the ordinary profits of stock. . . .

Secondly, every individual who employs his capital in the support of domestic industry, necessarily endeavours so to direct that industry, that its produce may be of the greatest possible value.

The produce of industry is what it adds to the subject or materials upon which it is employed. In proportion as the value of this produce is great or small, so will likewise be the profits of the employer. But it is only for the sake of profit that any man employs a capital in the support of industry; and he will always, therefore, endeavour to employ it in the support of that industry of which the produce is likely to be of the greatest value, or to exchange for the greatest quantity either of money or of other goods.

But the annual revenue of every society is always precisely equal to the exchangeable value of the whole annual produce of its industry, or rather is precisely the same thing with that exchangeable value. As every individual, therefore, endeavours as much as he can both to employ his capital in the support of domestic industry, and so to direct that industry that its produce may be of the greatest value; every individual necessarily labours to render the annual revenue of the society as great as he can. He generally, indeed, neither intends to promote the public interest, nor knows how much he is promoting it. By preferring the support of domestic to that of foreign industry, he intends only his own security; and by directing that industry in such a manner as its produce may be of the greatest value, he intends only his own gain, and he is in this, as in many other cases, led by an invisible hand to promote an end which was no part of his intention. Nor is it always the worse for the society that it was not part of it. By pursuing his own interest he frequently promotes that of the society more effectually than when he really intends to promote it. I have never known much good done by those who affected to trade for the public good. It is an affectation, indeed, not very common among merchants, and very few words need by employed in dissuading them from it.

What is the species of domestic industry which his capital can employ, and of which the produce is likely to be of the greatest value, every individual, it is evident, can, in his local situation, judge much better than any statesman or lawgiver can do for him. The statesman, who should attempt to direct private people in what manner they ought to employ their capitals, would not only load himself with a most unnecessary attention, but assume an authority which could safely be trusted, not only to no single person, but to no council or senate whatever, and which would no-where be so dangerous as in the hands of a man who had folly and presumption enough to fancy himself fit to exercise it.

To give the monopoly of the home-market to the produce of domestic industry, in any particular art or manufacture, is in some measure to direct private people in what manner they ought to employ their capitals, and must, in almost all cases, be either a useless or a hurtful regulation. If the produce of domestic can be brought there as cheap as that of foreign industry, the regulation is evidently useless. If it cannot, it must generally be hurtful. It is the maxim of every prudent master of a family, never to attempt to make at home what it will cost him more to make than to buy. The taylor does not attempt to make his own shoes, but buys them of the shoemaker. The shoemaker does not attempt to make his own clothes, but employs a taylor. The farmer attempts to make neither the one nor the other, but employs those different artificers. All of them find it for their interest to employ their whole industry in a way in which they have some advantage over their neighbours, and to purchase with a part of its produce, or what is the same thing, with the price of a part of it, whatever else they have occasion for.

What is prudence in the conduct of every private family, can scarce be folly in that of a great kingdom. If a foreign country can supply us with a commodity cheaper than we ourselves can make it, better buy it of them with some part of the produce of our own industry, employed in a way in which we have some advantage. The general industry of the country, being always in proportion to the capital which employs it, will not thereby be diminished, no more than that of the above-mentioned artificers; but only left to find out the way in which it can be employed with the greatest advantage. It is certainly not employed to the greatest advantage, when it is thus directed towards an object which it can buy cheaper than it can make. The value of its annual produce is certainly more or less diminished, when it is thus turned away from producing commodities evidently of more value than the commodity which it is directed to produce. According to the supposition, that commodity could be purchased from foreign countries cheaper than it can be made at home. It could, therefore, have been purchased with a part only of the commodities, or, what is the same thing, with a part only of the price of the commodities, which the industry employed by an equal capital would have produced at home, had it been left to follow its natural course. The industry of the country, therefore, is thus turned away from a more, to a less advantageous employment, and the exchangeable value of its annual produce, instead of being increased, according to the intention of the lawgiver, must necessarily be diminished by every such regulation.

# 2

# IMPERIALISM, THE HIGHEST STAGE OF CAPITALISM

V. I. Lenin

We must now try to sum up, to draw together the threads of what has been said above on the subject of imperialism. Imperialism emerged as the development and direct continuation of the fundamental characteristics of capitalism in general. But capitalism only became capitalist imperialism at a definite and very high stage of its development, when certain of its fundamental characteristics began to change into their opposites, when the features of the epoch of transition from capitalism to a higher social and economic system had taken shape and revealed themselves in all spheres. Economically, the main thing in this process is the displacement of capitalist free competition by capitalist monopoly. Free competition is the basic feature of capitalism, and of commodity production generally; monopoly is the exact opposite of free competition, but we have seen the latter being transformed into monopoly before our eyes, creating large-scale industry and forcing out small industry, replacing large-scale by still larger-scale industry, and carrying concentration of production and capital to the point where out of it has grown and is growing monopoly: cartels, syndicates and trusts, and merging with them, the capital of a dozen or so banks, which manipulate thousands of millions. At the same time the monopolies, which have grown out of free competition, do not eliminate the latter, but exist above it and alongside it, and thereby give rise to a number of very acute, intense antagonisms, frictions and conflicts. Monopoly is the transition from capitalism to a higher system.

If it were necessary to give the briefest possible definition of imperialism we should have to say that imperialism is the monopoly stage of capitalism. Such a definition would include what is most important, for, on the one hand, finance capital is the bank capital of a few very big monopolist banks, merged with the capital of the monopolist associations of industrialists; and, on the other hand, the division of the world is the transition from a colonial policy which has extended without hindrance to territories unseized by any capitalist power, to a colonial policy of monopolist possession of the territory of the world, which has been completely divided up.

But very brief definitions, although convenient, for they sum up the main points, are nevertheless inadequate, since we have to deduce from them some especially important features of the phenomenon that has to be defined. And so, without forgetting the conditional and relative value of all definitions in general, which can never embrace all the concatenations of a phenomenon in its full development, we must give a definition of imperialism that will include the following five of its basic features:

(1) the concentration of production and capital has developed to such a high stage that it has created monopolies which play a decisive role in economic life; (2) the merging of bank capital with industrial capital, and the creation, on the basis of this "finance capital," of a financial oligarchy; (3) the export of capital as distinguished from the export of commodities acquires exceptional importance; (4) the formation of international monopolist capitalist associations which share the world among themselves, and (5) the territorial division of the whole world among the biggest capitalist powers is completed. Imperialism is capitalism at that stage of development at which the dominance of monopolies and finance capital is established; in which the export of capital has acquired pronounced importance; in which the division of the world among the international trusts has begun, in which the division of all territories of the globe among the biggest capitalist powers has been completed. . . .

We have seen that in its economic essence imperialism is monopoly capitalism. This in itself determines its place in history, for monopoly that grows out of the soil of free competition, and precisely out of free competition, is the transition from the capitalist system to a higher socio-economic order. We must take special note of the four principal types of monopoly, or principal manifestations of monopoly capitalism, which are characteristic of the epoch we are examining.

Firstly, monopoly arose out of the concentration of production at a very high stage. This refers to the monopolist capitalist associations, cartels, syndicates and trusts. We have seen the important part these play in present-day economic life. At the beginning of the twentieth century, monopolies had acquired complete supremacy in the advanced countries, and although the first steps towards the formation of the cartels were taken by countries enjoying the protection of high tariffs (Germany, America), Great Britain, with her system of free trade, revealed the same basic phenomenon, only a little later, namely, the birth of monopoly out of the concentration of production.

Secondly, monopolies have stimulated the seizure of the most important sources of raw materials, especially for the basic and most highly cartelised industries in capitalist society: the coal and iron industries. The monopoly of the most important sources of raw materials has enormously increased the power of big capital, and has sharpened the antagonism between cartelised and noncartelised industry.

Thirdly, monopoly has sprung from the banks. The banks have developed from modest middleman enterprises into the monopolists of finance capital. Some three to five of the biggest banks in each of the foremost capitalist countries have achieved the "personal linkup" between industrial and bank capital, and have concentrated in their hands the control of thousands upon thousands of millions which form the greater part of the capital and income of entire countries. A financial oligarchy, which throws a close network of dependence relationships over all the economic and political institutions of present-day bourgeois society exception—such is the most striking manifestation of this monopoly.

Fourthly, monopoly has grown out of colonial policy. To the numerous "old" motives of colonial policy, finance capital has added the struggle for the sources of raw materials, for the export of capital, for spheres of influence, i.e., for spheres for profitable deals, concessions, monopoly profits and so on, economic territory in general. When the colonies of the European powers, for instance, comprised only one-tenth of the territory of Africa (as was the case in 1876), colonial policy was able to develop by methods other than those of monopoly—by the "free grabbing" of territories, so to speak. But when nine-tenths of Africa had been seized (by 1900), when the whole world had been divided up, there was inevitably ushered in the era of monopoly possession of colonies and, consequently, of particularly intense struggle for the division and the redivision of the world.

The extent to which monopolist capital has intensified all the contradictions of capitalism is generally known. It is sufficient to mention the high cost of living and the tyranny of the cartels. This intensification of contradictions constitutes the most powerful driving force of the transitional period of history, which began from the time of the final victory of world finance capital.

Monopolies, oligarchy, the striving for domination and not for freedom, the exploitation of an increasing number of small or weak nations by a handful of the richest or most powerful nations—all these have given birth to those distinctive characteristics of imperialism which compel us to define it as parasitic or decaying capitalism. More and more prominently there emerges, as one of the tendencies of imperialism, the creation of the "rentier state," the usurer state, in which the bourgeoisie to an ever-increasing degree lives on the proceeds of capital exports and by "clipping coupons." It would be a mistake to believe that this tendency to decay precludes the rapid growth of capitalism. It does not. In the epoch of imperialism, certain branches of industry, certain strata of the bourgeoisie and certain countries betray, to a greater or lesser degree, now one and now another of these tendencies. On the whole, capitalism is growing far more rapidly than before; but this growth is not only becoming more and more uneven in general, its unevenness also manifests itself, in particular, in the decay of the countries which are richest in capital (Britain). . . .

From all that has been said in this book on the economic essence of imperialism, it follows that we must define it as capitalism in transition, or, more
precisely, as moribund capitalism. It is very instructive in this respect to note
that bourgeois economists, in describing modern capitalism, frequently employ catchwords and phrases like "interlocking," "absence of isolation," etc.;
"in conformity with their functions and course of development," banks are
"not purely private business enterprises; they are more and more outgrowing
the sphere of purely private business regulation." And this very Riesser, whose
words I have just quoted, declares with all seriousness that the "prophecy" of
the Marxists concerning "socialisation" has "not come true."!

What then does this catchword "interlocking" express? It merely expresses
the most striking feature of the process going on before our eyes. It shows
that the observer counts the separate trees, but cannot see the wood. It slav-
ishly copies the superficial, the fortuitous, the chaotic. It reveals the observer
as one who is overwhelmed by the mass of raw material and is utterly inca-
pable of appreciating its meaning and importance. Ownership of shares, the
relations between owners of private property "interlock in a haphazard
way." But underlying this interlocking, its very base, are the changing social
relations of production. When a big enterprise assumes gigantic proportions,
and, on the basis of an exact computation of mass data, organises according
to plan the supply of primary raw materials to the extent of two-thirds, or
three-fourths, of all that is necessary for tens of millions of people; when the
raw materials are transported in a systematic and organised manner to the
most suitable places of production, sometimes situated hundreds or thousands of miles from each other; when a single centre directs all the consecu-
tive stages of processing the material right up to the manufacture of finished
articles; when these products are distributed according to a single plan
among tens and hundreds of millions of consumers (the marketing of oil in
America and Germany by the American oil trust)—then it becomes evident
that we have socialisation of production, and not mere "interlocking"; that
private economic and private property relations constitute a shell which no
longer fits its contents, a shell which must inevitably decay if its removal is
artificially delayed, a shell which may remain in a state of decay for a fairly
long period (if, at the worst, the cure of the opportunist abscess is protracted),
but which will inevitably be removed.

# REPORT ON MANUFACTURES

Alexander Hamilton

For the purpose of this vent, a domestic market is greatly to be preferred to a foreign one; because it is in the nature of things, far more to be relied upon. . . .

To secure such a market, there is no other expedient, than to promote manufacturing establishments. . . .

It merits particular observation, that the multiplication of manufactories not only furnishes a Market for those articles which have been accustomed to be produced in abundance in a country, but it likewise creates a demand for such as were either unknown or produced in inconsiderable quantities. The bowels as well as the surface of the earth are ransacked for articles which were before neglected, Animals, Plants and Minerals acquire a utility and a value which were before unexplored.

The foregoing considerations seem sufficient to establish, as general propositions, that it is the interest of nations to diversify the industrious pursuits of the individuals who compose them—that the establishment of manufactures is calculated not only to increase the general stock of useful and productive labour; but even to improve the state of Agriculture in particular, certainly to advance the interests of those who are engaged in it. . . .

If the system of perfect liberty to industry and commerce were the prevailing system of nations, the arguments which dissuade a country, in the predicament of the United States, from the zealous pursuit of manufactures, would doubtless have great force. It will not be affirmed, that they might not be permitted, with few exceptions, to serve as a rule of national conduct. In such a state of things, each country would have the full benefit of its peculiar advantages to compensate for its deficiencies or disadvantages. If one nation were in a condition to supply manufactured articles on better terms than another, that other might find an abundant indemnification in a superior capacity to furnish the produce of the soil. And a free exchange, mutually beneficial, of the commodities which each was able to supply, on the best terms, might be carried on between them, supporting in full vigour the industry of each.

But the system which has been mentioned, is far from characterising the general policy of Nations. The prevalent one has been regulated by an opposite spirit. The consequence of it is, that the United States are to a certain extent in the situation of a country precluded from foreign Commerce. They can indeed, without difficulty obtain from abroad the manufactured supplies, of which they are in want; but they experience numerous and very injurious impediments to the emission and vent of their own commodities. Nor is this the case in reference to a single foreign nation only. The regulations of several countries, with which we have the most extensive intercourse, throw serious obstructions in the way of the principal staples of the United States.

In such a position of things, the United States cannot exchange with Europe on equal terms; and the want of reciprocity would render them the victim of a system which should induce them to confine their views to Agriculture, and refrain from Manufactures. A constant and increasing necessity, on their part, for the commodities of Europe, and only a partial and occasional demand for their own, in return, could not but expose them to a state of impoverishment, compared with the opulence to which their political and natural advantages authorise them to aspire.

The remaining objections to a particular encouragement of manufacturers in the United States now require to be examined.

One of these turns on the proposition, that Industry, if left to itself, will naturally find its way to the most useful and profitable employment: whence it is inferred that manufactures without the aid of government will grow up as soon and as fast, as the natural state of things and the interest of the community may require.

Against the solidity of this hypothesis, in the full latitude of the terms, very cogent reasons may be offered. These have relation to—the strong influence of habit and the spirit of imitation—the fear of want of success in untried enterprises—the intrinsic difficulties incident to first essays towards a competition with those who have previously attained to perfection in the business to be attempted—the bounties premiums and other artificial encouragements, with which foreign nations second the exertions of their own Citizens in the branches, in which they are to be rivalled.

Experience teaches, that men are often so much governed by what they arc accustomed to see and practise, that the simplest and most obvious improvements, in the most ordinary occupations, are adopted with hesitation, reluctance, and by slow gradations. The spontaneous transition to new pursuits, in a community long habituated to different ones, may be expected to be attended with proportionably greater difficulty. When former occupations ceased to yield a profit adequate to the subsistence of their followers, or when there was an absolute deficiency of employment in them, owing to the superabundance of hands, changes would ensue; but these changes would be likely to be more tardy than might consist with the interest either of individuals or of the Society. In many cases they would not happen, while a bare support could be insured by an adherence to ancient courses; though a resort to a more profitable employment might be practicable. To produce the desireable changes as early as may be expedient, may therefore require the incitement and patronage of government.

The apprehension of failing in new attempts is perhaps a more serious impediment. There are dispositions apt to be attracted by the mere novelty of an undertaking—but these are not always the best calculated to give it success. To this, it is of importance that the confidence of cautious sagacious capitalists, both citizens and foreigners, should be excited. And to inspire this description of persons with confidence, it is essential, that they should be made to see in any project, which is new, and for that reason alone, if, for no other, precarious, the prospect of such a degree of countenance and support from government, as may be capable of overcoming the obstacles, inseparable from first experiments.

The superiority antecedently enjoyed by nations, who have prcoccupied and perfected a branch of industry, continues a more formidable obstacle, than either of those, which have been mentioned, to the introduction of the same branch into a country in which it did not before exist. To maintain between the recent establishments of one country and the long matured establishments of another country, a competition upon equal terms, both as to quality and price, is in most cases impracticable. The disparity, in the one or in the other, or in both, must necessarily be so considerable as to forbid a successful rivalship, without the extraordinary aid and protection of government.

But the greatest obstacle of all to the successful prosecution of a new branch of industry in a country, in which it was before unknown, consists, as far as the instances apply, in the bounties premiums and other aids which are granted, in a variety of cases, by the nations, in which the establishments to be imitated are previously introduced. It is well known (and particular examples in the course of this report will be cited) that certain nations grant bounties on the exportation of particular commodities, to enable their own workmen to undersell and supplant all competitors in the countries to which those commodities are sent. Hence the undertakers of a new manufacture have to contend not only with the natural disadvantages of a new undertaking, but with the gratuities and remunerations which other governments bestow. To be enabled to contend with success, it is evident that the interference and aid of their own governments are indispensable.

# II

# MULTINATIONAL CORPORATIONS

The issue of foreign direct investment and its agent, the multinational corporation (MNC), has received considerable attention in international political economy. The selections included here summarize some of the causes and the consequences of the global expansion of MNCs.

The first selection by three economists reviews the consequences of multinationals in the context of the contemporary global economy. The authors reach a dramatic conclusion: Despite the many benefits that multinationals can bring to the host nation, such as managerial know-how, technology, and additional income, on balance, MNCs hurt recipient countries. This has as much to do with the current economic conditions of the host nation as it does with the advantages that MNCs have in renegotiating new and better deals with host governments.

Many countries around the world are experiencing serious budgetary problems and shortages of high-paying jobs. MNC investment can significantly alleviate both problems, but it will do so only under optimal conditions. For example, if host governments threaten to impose new taxes on MNCs or make it more difficult to lay off workers (all politically very attractive policies under present conditions), MNCs will move production elsewhere. Indeed, the mere threat of leaving will probably win labor concessions and more tax subsidies. As a result, the very things that make countries attractive to MNCs—a well-educated labor force, high aggregate demand, good infrastructure—are destroyed by increasingly mobile capital as more and more concessions on the part of the host country lead to a loss of its ability to invest in those activities. In short, MNCs have a mostly negative impact on host countries. This is likely to be most evident in developed countries where the ease of exit is greatest, such as the United States. Although many economists do not agree with this pessimistic conclusion, the point of this selection is to give students a good understanding of the logic behind the economic analysis of MNCs.

The selection by the political scientist Robert Gilpin proceeds in a different direction. While he does not dispute the economic reasons behind the spread of MNCs, he maintains that the primary reason for their expansion is the power of the U.S. government. MNCs have been allowed to flourish because they serve the political interests of the U.S. While it made more sense to talk solely about the U.S. in the early 1970s when Gilpin was writing, one may today include Japan and major European powers as well. Nevertheless, the main point of the political framework—namely that politics is of paramount importance—remains valid. Domestic and international politics play a significant role in maintaining, fostering, or precluding the expansion of MNCs. As long as major countries find it advantageous to maintain a system of relatively unrestricted foreign investment, MNCs will flourish. However, the spread of industry and demands for the redistribution of wealth and power will eventually undermine the system and most likely lead to fragmentation until a new dominant power establishes itself. In contrast to most economic analyses which operate in a political vacuum, Gilpin's arguments underscore the impact that politics can have in elucidating international economic relations.

# WINNERS AND LOSERS
# IN THE GLOBAL ECONOMICS GAME

Gerald Epstein, James Crotty, and Patricia Kelly

Is globalization "a bunch of globaloney," as some have suggested? Or is it a significant phenomenon, one that hurts workers and communities while dramatically reducing a nation's ability to pursue independent policies? If the latter, what, if anything, can be done to control this process and create a framework for viable progressive policies?

Here we look at one aspect of globalization: the role of multinational corporations and foreign direct investment.[1] How might MNCs and FDI affect our standard of living in the long run? In discussing this question, we identify five views of the effect these phenomena might have on the trajectory of the world economy.

The first view is "the race to the bottom." Over 15 years ago, two widely read books, *The New International Division of Labor* and *Global Reach*, claimed that multinational corporate mobility had reached extreme levels.[2] These books gave life to the view of stateless corporations roaming the globe,

---

[1] Foreign direct investment refers to an equity investment outside a parent corporation's home country that implies some control by the parent corporation over economic activity, usually a greater than 10 percent stake. Multinational corporations generally refer to companies that have significant economic operations in more than one country. FDI and MNCs will be used interchangeably despite the fact that multinational corporations undertake significant economic activities outside their home countries independent of foreign direct investment, especially licensing and outsourcing activities.

[2] Folker Froble, J. Heinrichs, and O. Kreye, *The New International Division of Labor* (Cambridge: Cambridge University Press, 1980); Richard Barnet and Ronald E. Mueller, *Global Reach* (New York: Simon and Schuster, 1975).

reconfiguring capital and communities beyond the reach of any government. According to this perspective, capital will increasingly be able to play workers, communities, and nations off one another as it demands tax, regulatory, and wage concessions while threatening to move. The increased mobility of MNCs benefits capital while workers and communities lose. A modified version of this view is that the winners in the race to the bottom will include highly educated (or skilled) workers, or workers in particular professions (for example lawyers), along with the capitalists.

The second view, "the climb to the top," suggests that multinational corporations are attracted less by low wages and taxes than by highly educated workers, good infrastructure, high levels of demand, and synergistic effects arising from the existence of other companies that have already located in a particular place. Competition for foreign direct investment will lead countries in the North and the South to try to provide well-educated labor and high-quality infrastructure. Thus, "footloose" capital and competition, far from creating a race to the bottom will instead induce a climb to the top around the world.

This "climb to the top" could lead to the outcome represented by the third view: "neoliberal convergence." This is the mainstream view that the mobility of multinational corporations, made possible by deregulation and free trade, will produce increased living standards in all countries. This process will, moreover, transfer capital and technology abroad, thereby raising the standard of living in the poorer countries at a faster rate than in the wealthier ones, eventually generating a worldwide convergence in living standards.

These same processes could, however, lead to the outcome envisaged in the fourth view, "uneven development." This view holds that one region of the world grows at the expense of another. The idea of uneven development has a long and, now, ironic history: for decades the dominant version of this view was the theory of imperialism, which held that if the South integrated with the North, the North would grow at the expense of the South. Today the fear seems to be the opposite: by having to compete with cheap southern labor, an integrated world economy will help the South grow, but this time at the expense of the North.

Two of these views, race to the bottom and uneven development, hold that FDI and MNCs are significant causes of unemployment, inequality, and wage stagnation in the North. The other two, climb to the top and neoliberal convergence, hold that MNCs and FDI and other aspects of global integration actually ought to be helping the North and South to grow and that problems such as increases in economic inequality and unemployment in the industrialized countries are caused by other factors, the most important of which is rapid technological change.

We have not mentioned the fifth and most popular view: "much ado about nothing." The other views differ greatly but have at least one thing in common: a conviction that FDI and MNCs have a big impact. "Much ado about nothing" indicates that FDI and MNCs play a much more modest role than the others suggest. Adherents argue that:

1. International economic integration is currently not much greater than it was at the turn of the century;

2. FDI is still a relatively small percentage of gross domestic products;

3. Most FDI is between the rich countries and therefore can generate neither convergence nor a race to the bottom;

4. Of the FDI that does go to the developing countries, most flows to a handful of nations, with 80 percent of developing country FDI going to fewer than 10 countries.

5. Moreover, these few countries attract FDI on the basis of their large markets and modern infrastructure rather than cheap labor. Given these circumstances, the role of FDI for good or ill has been highly exaggerated.

## INVESTMENT IN CONTEXT

Which of the five views is correct? To answer this, we would first argue that foreign direct investment is neither inherently good nor inherently bad. The effect of capital mobility on nations and communities fundamentally depends on the context within which it occurs. We will focus on three aspects of the overall context that we think are especially important in determining the impact of FDI and MNCs: aggregate demand (that is, total national expenditures); the nature of the domestic and international rules of the game and institutions governing investment; and the nature of domestic and international competition. We argue that these three factors decisively influence how FDI and MNCs affect the economy—especially wages, inequality, and the level of unemployment.

Foreign direct investment made in a context of high levels of aggregate demand and effective rules that limit the destructive aspects of competition may indeed have a positive impact on nations and communities. However, foreign investment made in a context of high unemployment and destructive economic and political competition in the absence of effective rules can have a significantly negative impact on both home and host countries.

This framework leads to the key observation that the same level of FDI can have different effects in different contexts. For example, contrast the effects on workers and communities of outward flows of FDI from the United States in the 1960s with their probable effects today. During the 1960s, outward FDI was at roughly the same level as it is today. In the high-employment, high-growth era of the 1960s, FDI was more likely to increase exports from domestic companies than act as a substitute for them. But even when FDI led to domestic plant shutdown, replacement jobs were relatively easy for workers and communities to find. As a result, companies had much less bargaining power over workers and communities through threats of shutdown, which meant that companies had less leverage to bargain down wages and tax rates.

In the 1990s, with a shortage of high-paying jobs and critical state and local budget problems, workers and governments are much more subject to the bargaining power of companies when they threaten to move abroad. Jobs lost because of plant shutdowns are not easily replaced with jobs at similar wages and tax revenues. And companies are much more likely to substitute foreign production for domestic production, especially for the export market, when they move abroad.

We can now state a central hypothesis: we believe that in the current neoliberal economic regime, FDI and MNCs have more negative than positive effects. The neoliberal regime is composed of strong forces that lead to insufficient levels of aggregate demand and therefore chronic unemployment, coercive competition, and destructive domestic and international rules of the game—that is, precisely those factors that undermine the potentially positive effects of FDI. Some of the most important components include budgetary austerity, financial liberalization, privatization, increased labor market "flexibility," and trade and investment liberalization.

The negative impact of these processes is most evident in the United States. Highly advanced in its adoption of neoliberal precepts and facing serious aggregate demand constraints, it is both the biggest host to and source of FDI, and it faces enormous coordination problems among its state and local governments. In contrast, in Asia, where government controls have been relatively strong and aggregate demand high, the negative impact is currently much less in evidence. In Europe, where protective institutions may be even stronger than in Asia but where the outflows of FDI are greater, the story may be somewhere in between. The point, however, is that as the neoliberal regime widens, so may its negative impact. If Europe and Asia look to the United States in this regard, they may see their future.

Looking at MNCs and FDI within the neoliberal regime helps resolve several puzzling issues. First, it helps explain how the impact of FDI can be much larger than its sheer size would suggest. When corporations threaten to leave, they can win concessions from labor and tax subsidies from governments. This occurs even if they don't move. Such effects can spill over into the community, leading, for example, to lower tax revenues for services such as education.

Second, this framework helps explain why these problems are created even if FDI flows are primarily between the countries of the North rather than between the North and the South: it is the mobility and the threat of mobility that generate many of the problems, even if that mobility is between similar nations or even similar states or provinces. Workers and communities may be harmed even if a country such as the United States has both large inward and outward flows of FDI; the problem again is the possibly destructive impact of capital mobility in a particular setting. Third, there may be a negative impact even if countries or locales do not (or indeed especially if they do not) receive any FDI. At the behest of promoters of neoliberal ideology, countries and locales may engage in destructive bidding and structural changes to attract FDI, yet may not receive much.

This shift in bargaining power and the destructive competition among nations and locales for capital suggests an important paradox. As we noted earlier, foreign direct investment is attracted by high aggregate demand, high-quality infrastructure, and a highly skilled workforce. Yet foreign direct investment and capital mobility within the neoliberal structure undermine those very factors that attract and sustain MNCs. Short-term capital mobility and austerity undercut demand, and destructive tax competition, wage stagnation, and unemployment constrain government and private investment in infrastructure and human capital. In short, countries will find it increasingly difficult to offer companies the demand, infrastructure, and skills that they need.

## THE OTHER WAR BETWEEN THE STATES

The "War Between the States," as the competition among American states for investment and jobs has come to be called, may well be a microcosm of what could be emerging in the global arena as the neoliberal regime strengthens. As nations sign bilateral and multilateral investment agreements, as aggregate demand continues to stagnate, and as the ideology of attracting FDI as the engine of growth catches hold, global conditions may begin to look more like those found among the states. Of course, given national sovereignty, which is not going to go away, the international risks and enforcement problems for capital will be substantially greater than they are within the United States. But the same tendencies will hold.

In the United States, the increased mobility of capital across geographic regions has brought heightened competition between states to attract and retain corporate investment. This growing competition can be seen in the rush of deals offering multimillion-dollar tax breaks and incentives to large corporations in return for in-state investments, as well as in the proliferation of state tax credit programs for firms looking for new production sites. These corporate tax credits and other financial incentives result in billions of dollars in foregone state revenues each year. The fall in corporate tax collections has put additional pressure on state governments, which have cut public services while struggling to balance budgets. Moreover, with the decline in revenues from corporate tax dollars has come a shifting of the tax burden onto individuals.

Competitive business incentive policies by the states have a natural propensity to expand. As one state institutes a new tax break or subsidy, other states feel compelled to expand their incentive packages; officials fear that otherwise their state would be left behind in the contest to hold onto existing jobs and channel increasingly mobile capital to their communities. The frantic competition between the states in effect rewards firms for relocating. The growth of incentives thus may even further encourage the capital mobility that has driven the proliferation of these competitive programs in the first place.

Ironically, past studies have shown that tax incentives have generally been either ineffective or relatively unimportant in determining the location decisions of firms. One study suggests that these kinds of state incentive programs have now become so widespread that they basically offset each other in attracting new investment. Thus, the last decade's proliferation of "beggar thy neighbor" incentive programs may not have actually generated any significant change in the distribution of production among states. For many states, the end result of corporate tax breaks and subsidies has likely been a "race to the bottom," with little gain in jobs, lower corporate tax revenues, and fewer public services and higher taxes for the public.

Similar problems may be appearing in other countries as the neoliberal regime spreads and deepens. In the South we confront the paradox that while many countries are making large and costly changes in their economies and government policies to attract FDI, most are receiving little. While direct investment flows have increased in recent years, the Organization for Economic Cooperation and Development (OECD) countries continue to claim the lion's share of these flows; 80 percent between 1981 and 1990 and over 50 percent between 1990 and 1995. While these numbers do suggest an increase in flows to less developed countries, capital flows to the developing world are highly concentrated; 10 countries received 70 percent of the flows between 1980 and 1990, a trend that continued into the 1990s. Thus, most developing nations remain nearly shut out of international financial markets.

## FACING THE NEOLIBERAL PARADOX

In this neoliberal environment, international investment coordination problems may well lead to a paradox: while MNCs are attracted to high levels of demand, infrastructure, and human capital, nations and communities are likely to be increasingly prevented from becoming strong in these areas as they engage in a race to the bottom in tax revenues and austerity measures. Many academics and policymakers, though they recognize the potential dangers of capital mobility in combination with technological change and freer trade, are reluctant to place significant constraints on a company's ability to move in and out of a country. Instead, some have called for more skills training and infrastructure investment to attract FDI. We doubt that this is the path that countries, working in decentralized fashion, will be able to follow without some significant changes in their economic and political structure.

A "climb to the top" requires expenditure on infrastructure and education, as well as companies that are committed enough to a locale to incur these costs for the long-term benefits they will yield. But a world of international tax competition and mobility may preclude this climb to the top option. Race-to-the-bottom tactics give an advantage to some countries that are willing to move first to lower taxes. Governments may simply not be able to tax sufficiently to provide the resources necessary to implement the climb to the top option.

Are there policies that can restore the relative bargaining power of workers, communities, and nations and stop the race to the bottom, making the climb to the top more likely? Yes.

The following framework proposes policies that address the three central problems we have identified: insufficient aggregate demand, destructive practices and rules of the game, and coercive competition. We should note at the outset that a distinction must be made between levels of policy implementation as well as between the actors involved. In the first place, we can distinguish among local, national, regional, and international levels of policy implementation. We can also distinguish between actions taken primarily by governments and those taken by workers and citizens.

In making this latter distinction we recognize that a central problem in trying to devise policies to alter the bargaining power between the government and capital is that capital has in many instances become the government. In short, an essential difficulty in devising and implementing progressive policies is the relative lack of power citizens have in determining government economic policy.

Restoring high levels of aggregate demand would help create an environment that would greatly reduce the negative impact of FDI. Of course, there is a chicken and egg aspect to resolving this problem, since FDI, by driving down wages and creating government budget problems, contributes to the aggregate demand deficiency. Standard policies to restore aggregate demand may not be sufficient to correct the bargaining and coordination problems created by FDI within the neoliberal regime. However, if national governments had the will, there is no shortage of feasible institutional mechanisms to coordinate policies to enhance aggregate demand. These could be implemented at the international level (coordinated by the IMF, for example), or by regional groups, such as the European Union.

To remedy the second problem of destructive practices and rules of the game, governments and communities should implement policies to foreclose the race to the bottom. Here action could be undertaken at the international, national, and regional levels in the North and the South.

First, there should be a moratorium on all international agreements promoted by international organizations or countries in the North to liberalize the laws that control FDI. This would include, for example, the comprehensive treaty to protect foreign direct investment currently being negotiated by the OECD, as well as negotiations for an investment treaty with the World Trade Organization (WTO). This moratorium should remain in place until an international set of rules to foreclose the race to the bottom option is put into place. Discussions within the WTO and OECD to further liberalize FDI should end unless they focus on mechanisms to foreclose the "low wage, high wage" option. The same holds true of current negotiations to extend NAFTA.

Second, international organizations such as the World Bank and the IMF should stop pressuring developing and transitional countries to open their economies to FDI as a condition for receiving credit. This simply contributes to the wasteful competition we have described. And third, governments of home countries, including the United States, should stop investing so much diplomatic capital in encouraging countries like China to make it easier for MNCs to operate.

An international agreement forbidding unproductive tax competition should be implemented and enforced by an international organization like the WTO. Some international organizations are investigating voluntary agreements along these lines. Such agreements should also be implemented at regional and national levels.

For the third problem, separate measures to rein in coercive competition may not be required if there is expansionary aggregate demand policy, international tax competition treaties, and a moratorium on new investment agreements. However, in the event that there is not, measures to slow rapid structural change on the trade side may be required. In particular, policies that limit the rate of increase of imports over the medium term may be needed to slow the pace of structural change and allow companies and communities to adjust. Such interferences with trade ought to be used as a last resort, however, since trade between countries can be mutually beneficial.

## A WAY FORWARD

The increased mobility of foreign direct investment and multinational corporations is imposing real and increasingly severe constraints on workers, communities, and states. But it is not the case that, as supporters of neoclassical economics or the globalization thesis argue, these constraints are an inevitable outcome of technological change or an irreversible juggernaut. On the contrary, the effect of FDI depends crucially on the domestic and international context within which it occurs. Different domestic and international contexts governing MNCs and FDI produce different outcomes. As we have shown, the growing neoliberal regime is increasingly creating real constraints on progressive economic policy. Moreover, within that regime, MNCs and FDI have increasingly negative impacts. But other regimes are possible; indeed, they coexist within the neoliberal regime. These regimes include policies to expand aggregate demand, to impose an international set of standards, and to raise domestic standards. Despite the increasing international constraints posed by capital mobility within the neoliberal regime, pessimism is not the order of the day.

# U.S. Power and the Multinational Corporation

Robert Gilpin

The argument of this study is that the modern world economy has evolved through the emergence of great national economies that have successively become dominant. . . .

An economic system, then, does not arise spontaneously owing to the operation of an invisible hand and in the absence of the exercise of power. Rather, every economic system rests on a particular political order; its nature cannot be understood aside from politics. This basic point was made some years ago by E. H. Carr when he wrote that "the science of economics presupposes a given political order, and cannot be profitably studied in isolation from politics." Carr sought to convince his fellow Englishmen that an international economy based on free trade was not a natural and inevitable state of affairs but rather one that reflected the economic and political interests of Great Britain. The system based on free trade had come into existence through, and was maintained by, the exercise of British economic and military power. With the rise after 1880 of new industrial and military powers with contrasting economic interests—namely, Germany, Japan, and the United States—an international economy based on free trade and British power became less and less viable. Eventually this shift in the locus of industrial and military power led to the collapse of the system in World War I. Following the interwar period, a liberal international economy was revived through the exercise of power by the world's newly emergent dominant economy—the United States.

Accordingly, the regime of free investment and the preeminence of the multinational corporation in the contemporary world have reflected the economic and political interests of the United States. The multinational corporation has prospered because it has been dependent on the power of, and consistent with the political interests of, the United States. This is not to deny the analyses of economists who argue that the multinational corporation is a response to contemporary technological and economic developments. The argument is rather that these economic and technological factors have been able to exercise their profound effects because the United States—sometimes with the cooperation of other states and sometimes over their opposition—has created the necessary political framework.

[A]lthough nation-states, as mercantilists suggest, do seek to control economic and technological forces and channel them to their own advantage, this is impossible over the long run. The spread of economic growth and industrialization cannot be prevented. In time the diffusion of industry and technology undermines the position of the dominant power. As both liberals and Marxists have emphasized, the evolution of economic relations profoundly influences the nature of the international political system. The relationship between economics and politics, to restate the theme of this volume, is a reciprocal one.

Although economic and accompanying political change may well be inevitable, it is not inevitable that the process of economic development and technological advance will produce an increasingly integrated world society.

## A Model of International Change

An interdependent economic system—regional, national, or international—is a hierarchical structure composed of dominant core(s) or center(s) and a dependent periphery or hinterland. The core or center constitutes the organizing and controlling component of the system. Whether it is a financial and commercial city such as London or New York or an industrial city such as Manchester or Pittsburgh, the center draws resources (food, raw materials, and manpower) from the periphery and provides goods, services, and markets in return. While the variations of the core-periphery relationships are many, the important point is the dominant role of the core in the administration and governance of the system.

## Domestic Politics and Foreign Investment

In domestic as in international affairs, the political order is a major determinant of the direction of economic activity. Market forces do not operate in a political vacuum; on the contrary, the domestic political order and public policies seek to channel economic forces in one direction or another. Similarly, as in international affairs, over time the evolution of economic, political, and technological forces tends to transform the configurations of domestic interests and undermine the existing political order and public policies. Economic relations become increasingly "politicized" as rising and declining economic interests clash over domestic and international economic policy. The emergent domestic political order and public policies redirect economic forces into new channels. Thus, in domestic as in international affairs, the relationship between politics and economics is a reciprocal and dynamic one.

Behind both British and American heavy reliance upon foreign investment has been the strong commitment to a liberal economic order at home and abroad. The political and economic leadership of both societies have shared this liberal perspective and have projected this vision to the international sphere. They have assumed that a liberal world of self-adjusting free trade, freedom of capital movements, and an efficient international division of labor provides the natural and best economic order, and that all reasonable men share this belief. Confident in their own economic and technological strengths, political leadership and dominant economic interests have desired an open world and asked only access (i.e., an open door) to other economies for their exporters and investors. The rationale behind the expansionism of both economies, to paraphrase an American Secretary of Defense, has been the belief that what was good for General Motors was not only good for the country but was good for the world as well, in terms of economic growth, the diffusion of productive technology, and the spread of the free enterprise doctrine itself. The economic expansion of both societies has embodied the liberal belief that underlying economic intercourse (in contrast to political relations), there is a basic harmony of interests, and that everyone can benefit through the creation of a liberal international economic order.

Specifically, the domestic political order and public policies are important in that they influence the capacity and the propensity to invest abroad. In the cases of Great Britain and the United States (and in contrast to other capitalist economies such as Germany, France, or Japan, which for political and economic reasons have been more reluctant to place their assets abroad), public policies and liberal ideology have operated to encourage massive exports of capital and the ownership of foreign assets. However, as we argue below, the consequence of this emphasis on foreign investment has been to help undermine both the domestic and international political order upon which this foreign investment strategy rested.

The capacity to invest (at home or abroad) is largely a function of the distribution of income in the core. There is a relatively high rate of savings when a large fraction of the national wealth is held by classes or groups which have a propensity to save rather than consume. In nineteenth-century Britain, with its rigid class stratification and relatively docile lower classes, a high proportion of the national wealth was held by a *rentier* class. In the United States, a large fraction of the national wealth has been held by giant corporations. In both cases, this uneven distribution of wealth to the advantage of savers and investors was a consequence of the internal politics of the society. A progressive income or corporate tax which greatly redistributed income would have significantly decreased the core's capacity to invest abroad.

Similarly, the propensity of the core to invest savings at home or abroad is influenced by public policies. Taxation and other policies determine in large measure in whose hands savings will be lodged; whether savings are held by *rentiers,* corporations. or public bodies is highly relevant for investment decisions. Furthermore, public policies profoundly affect the incentives and disincentives for investors to invest in domestic industry, foreign-government bonds, or extractive and manufacturing industries in the periphery or at home. In short, "surplus capital" and capital export are more a function of the domestic political order and public policies than an inherent feature of capitalism.

Liberal students of foreign investment tend to ignore the importance of the domestic political and social order. The reason for this neglect of domestic politics is highly significant; bringing it to light focuses attention on a critical aspect of the whole subject.

In the cases of Great Britain throughout much of the nineteenth century and the United States until the middle 1960s, foreign investment was not an issue of domestic politics. The reason, I believe, was that foreign investment was relatively costless, or perceived to be costless, to the core. To put it another way, there were no powerful groups in the core which regarded foreign investment as detrimental to their interests, or to what they held to be the "national interest." The technical superiority of the core, its high rate of savings, the international role of its currency, and liberal ideology enabled the core to export capital, technology, and other resources at what was perceived by domestic interest groups to be a low cost. With the shift in industrial power from core to periphery, however, the cost to interest groups in the core began to become apparent. Domestic labor began to see its interests adversely affected as jobs moved abroad and imports increased. Others became concerned over the fact of relative industrial decline and the shift in the locus of industrial power. In the American case, apprehension over foreign investment in extractive industries developed with the appreciation of America's growing dependence on politically vulnerable foreign sources of energy and resources. In short, foreign investment became increasingly politicized in a declining industrial power.

With respect to Great Britain, the politicization of foreign investment took place in the last decade of the nineteenth century. For the first time, strong voices were raised which challenged the great outflow of capital. In the United States, the beginnings of this domestic challenge are to be found during the Kennedy administration. The first assault on the tax privileges of multinationals was undertaken in 1962, when the administration became concerned over the export of industry. The lowering of trade barriers proposed by the Trade Expansion Act of 1962 was partially conceived of as a means of decreasing foreign investment in, and increasing trade with, the European Common Market. By the 1970s, foreign investment had become a major issue of domestic politics.

For these reasons—the effect of domestic political factors on the capacity and propensity to export capital and the tendency, over time, for foreign investment to become politicized—the analysis of foreign investment cannot be restricted to the operation of economic and market forces. Domestic (and, as we shall see, international) politics are an important determinant of the decision of the core to emphasize a foreign investment strategy both during its rise and subsequent decline. Let us now consider the strategies available to a relatively declining core.

## INDUSTRIAL DECLINE AND DOMESTIC RESPONSE

From this perspective, a crisis arises when these major technological innovations have run their course and the industries they have created have ceased to be the critical areas of innovation and growth. For Schumpeter, the trough between the decline of a dominant industrial sector and the emergence of new leading sectors explained the long-waves in the business cycle. One need not accept this aspect of his model, however, to appreciate that the exploitation and subsequent exhaustion of major technological breakthroughs are primary determinants of the rise of the core, its investment activity, and the subsequent rise of peripheral economies.

On the basis of this conception of the nature and importance of technological innovation, let us return to the primary issue with which we have been concerned: the strategies available to a declining core economy. Specifically, if the United States has largely exhausted the potential inherent in existing technology, much as Great Britain did in the latter part of the nineteenth century, what are the prospects that it will pursue a rejuvenation rather than a protectionist strategy? The reasons for concern in this regard are very real.

Industrial economies tend to be highly conservative and to resist change. Schumpeter's process of creative destruction is an expensive one for industrial firms with heavy investment in existing plants; labor can be equally resistant. The propensity of corporations is to invest in particular industrial sectors or product lines even though these areas may be declining. That is to say, the sectors are declining as theaters of innovation; they are no longer the leading sectors of industrial society. In response to rising foreign competition and relative decline, the tendency of corporations is to seek protection of their home market or new markets abroad for old products. Behind this structural rigidity is the fact that for any firm, its experience, existing real assets, and know-how dictate a relatively limited range of investment opportunities. Its instinctive reaction, therefore, is to protect what it has. As a result, there may be no powerful interests in the economy favoring a major shift of energy and resources into new industries and economic activities. In short, an economy's capacity to transform itself is increasingly limited as it advances in age.

The rejuvenation of an economy and the shift of resources to new leading sectors would appear to result only from catastrophe, such as defeat in war, political revolution, or other major economic dislocation, such as shortages in energy and raw materials. It took near-defeat in World War I for Great Britain to begin to restructure her economy, though even then she did not go far enough. Russia's collapse and the Bolshevik Revolution accelerated her industrialization. It is not surprising today that the three most dynamic industrial powers—Japan, West Germany, and East Germany—were the defeated nations in the last world war. Nor is it surprising that outside the military realm, the two victors—the United States and the Soviet Union—are falling behind industrially. . . .

In conclusion, the only time when there are sufficient forces in a declining economy to regenerate it may be when it is too late. If so, then the only two realistic strategies may be those of foreign investment (direct or portfolio) and some form of economic autarky. In both the cases of Great Britain and the United States, the holders of capital preferred to send it abroad. In the short run, this capital export made good sense. In the long run, however, it decreased the probability that the home economy would be reinvigorated; furthermore, it generated protectionist and autarkic attitudes in labor and other sectors of the society. For these reasons, the long-term benefit to the core of a foreign investment strategy is open to question.

## THE SPREAD OF INDUSTRY AND INTERNATIONAL CONFLICT

The object of economic nationalism or mercantilism is to accelerate the industrialization of the periphery and to reduce its dependence on the core. Through commercial and other public policies, mercantilism seeks to channel the forces of economic growth to the advantage of the periphery. For the peripheral nation, this means the acquisition or strengthening of an independent industrial and technological base if it is to escape its role as raw material supplier, branch-plant economy, and dependent importer of technology.

In effect, economic nationalism arises in the periphery as a protective measure against market forces which first concentrate wealth and then divide the international economy into advanced core and dependent periphery. It reflects the desire of the periphery to possess and control an industrial core wherein wealth, attractive careers, and power are located. Its objective is to transform the division of labor through industrialization and to transform the peripheral nation into a relatively independent industrial core.

Because of the initial industrial superiority and competitive advantages of the core, the later the industrialization of the periphery, the greater the effort must be to develop viable industries and to break into world markets, and, as a result, the greater the need for a strong national authority to offset market forces, which tend to concentrate wealth, economic activity, and power in the core. For this reason, while the spread of growth, like the concentration of wealth, is to be explained in large part by market forces, a seemingly necessary condition for spread to take place at the rate desired by the periphery is the existence of some centralized political power which can counteract the economic power of existing centers and the centralizing tendency of market forces. This authority was provided in Germany (in the nineteenth century) largely by the banking institutions, in the United States by industrial corporations protected by high tariffs, and in Japan and Russia by the national government.

Once set upon the course of industrialization, however, these late industrializers have enjoyed the "advantages of backwardness," which have eventually enabled them to surpass the rate of growth of the industrial leader. Utilizing the most advanced, efficient industries and the lessons learned by the more advanced economies, these late starters eventually caught up with or overtook the first industrial center—Great Britain—in the latter part of the century, in time shifting the center of world industrial power and, of course, the international balance of power.

The process being described here may be characterized as follows. During the earlier phase of an interdependent world economy, such as that created by Great Britain in the nineteenth century or by the United States after World War II, polarization effects tend to predominate over spread effects. Over time, however, owing to diseconomies in the core and to the growth of the periphery, spread begins to and finally does overtake polarization. The periphery begins to grow and industrialize faster than the core. As this happens, the cost to the periphery of asserting its independence from the core begins to decrease, and the benefits of dependence on the core decline. As the economic strength of the periphery increases, more and more groups in the periphery perceive that their interests lie with a greater assertion of economic independence from the core. Then rising expectations and the appreciation of growing strength relative to the core cause these groups to swing over to disengagement from the core. Thus, as the periphery grows in strength the tendency is for it to break away from the core.

In the modern world, perhaps the first example of this phenomenon was the American Revolution. Once American colonies had reached a certain level of development, the restrictions placed on their development by Great Britain grew intolerable. With the French defeat in Canada and the colonies' decreased dependance on Great Britain for their security, the colonies had an alternative to dependence on Great Britain. Today, the rapid industrial development of Canada has whetted the desire of Canadians to break with what they consider to be the drawbacks of economic dependence on and economic integration with the United States. And in Europe, Latin America, Japan, and elsewhere, the growing strength of these peripheral economies relative to the American core is leading to efforts to lessen dependence on the latter. In each case, economic nationalism is an expression of growing strength and rising expectations.

Underlying the growth of nationalism in the periphery today is the increasing ability of the peripheral economy to assert its independence from the core economy. In the first place, the development of the peripheral economy and particularly of its industrial sector decreases its need for foreign investment. It is increasingly able to generate its own investment capital, develop technology, and provide managerial expertise, or at least to acquire these factors of production on more favorable terms. In the area of natural resources, once the investment is in place, the advantage shifts from the supplier to the recipient of the investment. Second, as the peripheral economy advances and its attractiveness to investors increases, the resulting greater competition among foreign investors decreases the dependence of the peripheral economy on the core's investors. This is especially true in the contemporary world, where

European and Japanese investors are challenging the dominant position of American multinational corporations. Finally, the relative decline of the core economy further weakens the bargaining position of the core's multinational corporations. They become increasingly dependent on foreign markets, while the peripheral economy in itself is less dependent on the core's market for its own exports. As a result of these changes the costs of a more nationalistic policy on the part of the periphery are reduced; that is, its ability to assert its independence of the core is increased. The periphery is thus both more willing and more able to change the terms on which foreign investment takes place.

The eventual consequence of the redistribution of wealth and power, then, is the undermining of the economic and political order which first benefited the core and particularly its foreign investors more than the periphery. As the peripheral nations gain industrially and their power increases, they seek to reorganize the world economy in order to advance their own economic and political interests. In time, therefore, the redistribution of wealth and power leads to a reorganization of international economic relations in a manner which reflects the power and interests of the rising states in the system. The corollary, of course, is that to the extent that the rising peripheral economics are successful and make foreign investors serve their particular interests, they cause a reassessment in the core with respect to the benefits to the core of foreign investment. Important groups in the core begin to question whether foreign investment and, in the American case, the continued overseas expansion of its corporations are in the economic and political interest of the core. Thus, the issue of foreign investment becomes increasingly politicized in both core and periphery.

As the original core declines and as new cores in the periphery "catch up" industrially, the old core and the new cores increasingly come into conflict over markets, raw materials, and investment outlets. The rising industrial powers cut into the profit margins that the original core has enjoyed. The outbreak of economic conflicts at the end of the nineteenth century (and again in the 1970s) would appear to be correlated with the core's loss of industrial leadership.

In this situation, there are three possibilities. The first is that the original core somehow manages to retain or reassert its dominant position relative to the emergent cores; it continues to set the rules. Great Britain was able to do this at least with respect to the international monetary system and foreign investment long after she ceased to be the dominant industrial power, though eventually the system collapsed with the Great Depression. The second possibility is a shift from a hierarchically organized international economic system to one composed of relatively equal cores; the several cores together negotiate the rules governing trade, money, and investment. In the mid-1970s, this is essentially what the industrial powers are seeking to accomplish.

Finally, the system can break down and fragment into conflicting imperial systems or regional blocs. This tendency was a major aspect of the latter part of the nineteenth century and became the dominant feature of the world economy during the period between the two world wars. With the relative decline of American power, it has reasserted itself in the 1970s.

Although none of these three possibilities is inevitable, the argument of this study is that the third possibility is most likely. At least, the tendency toward breakdown or fragmentation of the system greatly increases with the relative decline of the original core. As the core declines, there is likely to be an outbreak of economic and mercantilistic conflict. This conflict is endemic in the system until one nation establishes itself as the new dominant core. To prevent this, one can only hope that the strongest economic powers will exercise self-restraint and negotiate a new set of effective rules reflecting the new international balance of economic and military power.

# TRADE

The study of international trade lies at the very core of international economic relations. The concept of comparative advantage, first articulated by David Ricardo, is its very soul. In fact, until the dawn of the twentieth century the study of the International Political Economy (IPE) focused almost exclusively on refining and adapting this concept. Many theories have been developed since then to explain the causes and consequences of trade.

The first selection illustrating the economic approach surveys these theories with particular emphasis on why countries adopt protectionist measures even though they stand to gain from free trade. In the second selection, Paul Krugman, a renowned economist at MIT, takes the idea one step further. He argues that contemporary obsession with the competitiveness of nations—roughly defined as the ability of a country's exports to command a large market share of the world's exports—is misleading at best and even dangerous. It is misleading because the concept of competitiveness erroneously focuses exclusive attention on trade as the key to national development and growth. He argues that since trade still continues to account for only a low percentage of a major country's gross national product, a change in its trade position cannot have significant effects on its output. Moreover, the concept may be dangerous because it has led some economists to argue for more state involvement in the allocation of resources, something that could potentially have very negative consequences.

The third selection, by Bruno Frey, illustrates the logic and application of public choice to IPE. Public choice is a theory that applies economic logic to political phenomena, in this case, international relations. It assumes that individuals are self-interested. Government decisions on trade are the result of the balance of pressures by individuals or groups and the various interests they represent.

Political approaches give somewhat different answers. In his seminal contribution, Stephen Krasner argues that world trade is the result of the interests of the dominant power, or hegemon, in the international system. He argues in a similar vein as Gilpin that the presence of a hegemon leads to a more open trading system. In contrast to the economic approach, Krasner emphasizes the point that the relative power of hegemons determines their trading patterns rather than the other way around. This idea, known as the hegemonic stability theory, has generated considerable attention and subsequent refinement.

Gowa and Mansfield examine a related but different question: Do security alliances affect trade patterns? They find that indeed they do. A country is more likely to trade with its allies than its opponents. Finally, Zahariadis examines the question of subsidies, which are similar to trade restrictions except for the fact that they operate in the domestic economy. He finds that: (1) trade deficits lead to the disbursement of more subsidies through the government's budget, and (2) that left-leaning parties in government are the principal initiators of subsidies.

All in all, the selections illustrate the plethora of approaches to the causes and consequences of trade. They also illuminate the similarities as well as the differences between economic and political studies.

# PROTECTIONIST TRADE POLICIES: A SURVEY OF THEORY, EVIDENCE AND RATIONALE

Cletus C. Coughlin, K. Alec Chrystal, and Geoffrey E. Wood

This article surveys the theory, evidence and rationale concerning protectionist trade policies. The first section illustrates the gains from free trade using the concept of comparative advantage. Recent developments in international trade theory that emphasize other reasons for gains from trade are also reviewed. The theoretical discussion is followed by an examination of recent empirical studies that demonstrate the large costs of protectionist trade policies. Then, the rationale for restricting trade is presented. The concluding section summarizes the paper's main arguments.

## THE GAINS FROM FREE TRADE

The most famous demonstration of the gains from trade appeared in 1817 in David Ricardo's *Principles of Political Economy and Taxation.* We use his example involving trade between England and Portugal to demonstrate how both countries can gain from trade. The two countries produce the same two goods, wine and cloth, and the only production costs are labor costs. The figures below list the amount of labor (e.g., worker-days) required in each country to produce one bottle of wine or one bolt of cloth.

|          | Wine | Cloth |
|----------|------|-------|
| England  | 3    | 7     |
| Portugal | 1    | 5     |

Since both goods are more costly to produce in England than in Portugal, England is absolutely less efficient at producing both goods than its prospective trading partner. Portugal has an absolute advantage in both wine and cloth. At first glance, this appears to rule out mutual gains from trade; however, as we demonstrate below, absolute advantage is irrelevant in discerning whether trade can benefit both countries.

The ratio of the production costs for the two goods is different in the two countries. In England, a bottle of wine will exchange for 3/7 of a bolt of cloth because the labor content of the wine is 3/7 of that for cloth. In Portugal, a bottle of wine will exchange for 1/5 of a bolt of cloth. Thus, wine is relatively cheaper in Portugal than in England and, conversely, cloth is relatively cheaper in England than in Portugal. The example indicates that Portugal has a comparative advantage in wine production and England has a comparative advantage in cloth production.

The different relative prices provide the basis for both countries to gain from international trade. The gains arise from both exchange and specialization.

The gains from *exchange* can be highlighted in the following manner. If a Portuguese wine producer sells five bottles of wine at home, he receives one bolt of cloth. If he trades in England, he receives more than two bolts of cloth. Hence, he can gain by exporting his wine to England. English cloth-producers are willing to trade in Portugal; for every 3/7 of a bolt of cloth they sell there, they get just over two bottles of wine. The English gain from exporting cloth to (and importing wine from) Portugal, and the Portuguese gain from exporting wine to (and importing cloth from) England. Each country gains by exporting the good in which it has a comparative advantage and by importing the good in which it has a comparative disadvantage.

Gains from *specialization* can be demonstrated in the following manner. Initially, each country is producing some of both goods. Suppose that, as a result of trade, 21 units of labor are shifted from wine to cloth production in England, while, in Portugal, 10 units of labor are shifted from cloth to wine production. This reallocation of labor does not alter the total amount of labor used in the two countries; however, it causes the production changes listed below.

|  | Bottles of Wine | Bolts of Cloth |
|---|---|---|
| England | − 7 | +3 |
| Portugal | +10 | −2 |
| Net | + 3 | +1 |

The shift of 21 units of labor to the English cloth industry raises cloth production by three bolts, while reducing wine production by seven bottles. In Portugal, the shift of 10 units of labor from cloth to wine raises wine production by 10 bottles, while reducing cloth production by two bolts. This reallocation of labor increases the total production of both goods: wine by three bottles and cloth by one bolt. This increased output will be shared by the two countries. Thus, the consumption of both goods and the wealth of both countries are increased by the specialization brought about by trade based on comparative advantage.

## TRADE THEORY SINCE RICARDO

Since 1817, numerous analyses have generated insights concerning the gains from trade. They chiefly examine the consequences of relaxing the assumptions used in the preceding example. For example, labor was the only resource used to produce the two goods in the example above; yet, labor is really only one of many resources used to produce goods. The example also assumed that the costs of producing additional units of the goods are constant. For example, in England, three units of labor are used to produce one bottle of wine regardless of the level of wine production. In reality, unit production costs could either increase or decrease as more is produced. A third assumption was that the goods are produced in perfectly competitive markets. In other words, an individual firm has no effect on the price of the good that it produces. Some industries, however, are dominated by a small number of firms, each of which can affect the market price of the good by altering its production decision. Some of these extensions are discussed in the appendix.

These theoretical developments generally have strengthened the case for an open trading system. They suggest three sources of gains from trade. First, as the market potentially served by firms expands from a national to a world market, there are gains associated with declining per unit production costs. A second source of gains results from the reduction in the monopoly power of domestic firms. Domestic firms, facing more pressure from foreign competitors, are forced to produce the output demanded by consumers at the lowest possible cost. Third is the gain to consumers from increased product variety and lower prices. Generally speaking, the gains from trade result from the increase in competitive pressures as the domestic economy becomes less insulated from the world economy.

## COSTS OF TRADE PROTECTIONISM

All forms of protection are intended to improve the position of domestic relative to foreign producers. This can be done through policies that increase the home market price of the foreign product, decrease the production costs of domestic firms, or somehow restrict the access of foreign producers to the domestic market.

The specific goal of protectionist trade policies is to expand domestic production in the protected industries, benefiting the owners, workers and suppliers of resources to the protected industry. The government imposing protectionist trade policies may also benefit, for example, in the form of tariff revenue.

The expansion of domestic production in protected industries is not cost-less; it requires additional resources from other industries. Consequently, output in other domestic industries is reduced. These industries also might be made less competitive because of higher prices for imported inputs. Since protectionist trade policies frequently increase the price of the protected good, domestic consumers are harmed. They lose in two ways. First, their consumption of the protected good is reduced because of the associated rise in its price. Second, they consume less of other goods, as their output declines and prices rise.

The preceding discussion highlights the domestic winners and losers due to protectionist trade policies. Domestic producers of the protected good and the government (if tariffs are imposed) gain: domestic consumers and other domestic producers lose. Foreign interests are also affected by trade restrictions. The protection of domestic producers will harm some foreign producers; oddly enough, other foreign producers may benefit. For example, if quotas are placed on imports, some foreign producers may receive higher prices for their exports to the protected market.

## FORMS OF PROTECTIONISM

Protection may be implemented in numerous ways. All forms of protection are intended to improve the position of a domestic relative to foreign producer. This can be done by policies that increase the home market price of the foreign product, decrease the costs of domestic producers or restrict the access of foreign producers to the home market in some other way.

**TARIFFS.** Tariffs, which are simply taxes imposed on goods entering a country from abroad, result in higher prices and have been the most common form of protection for domestic producers. Tariffs have been popular with governments because it appears that the tax is being paid by the foreigner who wishes to sell his goods in the home economy and because the tariff revenue can be used to finance government services or reduce other taxes.

In the 20th century, U.S. tariff rates peaked as a result of the Smoot-Hawley Tariff of 1930. For example, in 1932, tariff revenue as a percentage of total imports was 19.6 percent. An identical calculation for 1985 yields a figure of 3.8 percent. The decline was due primarily to two reasons. First, since many of the tariffs under Smoot-Hawley were set as specific dollar amounts, the rising price level in the United States eroded the effective tariff rate. Second, since World War II, numerous tariff reductions have been negotiated under the General Agreement on Tariffs and Trade.

On the other hand, various other forms of protection, frequently termed non-tariff barriers, have become increasingly important. A few of the more frequently used devices are discussed below.

**QUOTAS.** A quota seems like a sensible alternative to a tariff when the intention is to restrict foreign producers' access to the domestic market.

Importers typically are limited to a maximum number of products that they can sell in the home market over specific periods. A quota, similar to a tariff, causes prices to increase in the home market. This induces domestic producers to increase production and consumers to reduce consumption. One difference between a tariff and a quota is that the tariff generates revenue for the government, while the quota generates a revenue gain to the owner of import licenses. Consequently, foreign producers might capture some of this revenue.

In recent years, a slightly different version of quotas, called either orderly marketing agreements or voluntary export restraints, has been used. In an orderly marketing agreement, the domestic government asks the foreign government to restrict the quantity of exports of a good to the domestic country. The request can be viewed as a demand, like the U.S.–Japan automobile agreement in the 1980s, because the domestic country makes it clear that more restrictive actions are likely unless the foreign government "voluntarily" complies. In effect, the orderly marketing agreement is a mutually agreed-upon quota.

**REGULATORY BARRIERS.** There are many other ways of restricting foreigners' access to domestic markets. Munger has noted that the tariff code itself tends to limit trade. The 1983 *Tariff Schedules of the United States Annotated* consists of 792 pages, plus a 78-page appendix. Over 200 tariff rates pertain to watches and clocks. Simply ascertaining the appropriate tariff classification, which requires legal assistance and can be subject to differences of opinion, is a deterrent.

Product standards are another common regulatory barrier. These standards appear in various forms and are used for many purposes. The standards can be used to serve the public interest by ensuring that imported food products are processed according to acceptable sanitary standards and that drugs have been screened before their introduction in the United States. In other cases, the standards, sometimes intentionally, protect domestic producers. An example of unintended restrictions may be the imposition of safety or pollution standards that were not previously being met by foreign cars.

**SUBSIDIES.** An alternative to restricting the terms under which foreigners can compete in the home market is to subsidize domestic producers. Subsidies may be focused upon an industry in general or upon the export activities of the industry. An example of the former, discussed by Morici and Megna (1983), is the combination of credit programs, special tax incentives and direct subsidy payments that benefit the U.S. shipbuilding industry. An example of the latter is the financial assistance to increase exports provided by the U.S. Export-Import Bank through direct loans, loan guarantees and insurance, and discount loans. In either case, production will expand.

An important difference between subsidies and tariffs involves the revenue implications for government. The former involves the government in paying out money, whereas tariffs generate income for the government. The effect on domestic production and welfare, however, can be the same under subsidies as under tariffs and quotas. In all cases, the protected industry is being subsidized by the rest of the economy.

EXCHANGE CONTROLS. All of the above relate directly to the flow of goods. A final class of restrictions works by restricting access to the foreign money required to buy foreign goods. For example, a government that wished to protect its exporting and import-competing industries may try to hold its exchange rate artificially low. As a result, foreign goods would appear expensive in the home market while home goods would be cheap overseas. Home producers implicitly are subsidized and home consumers implicitly are taxed. This policy is normally hard to sustain. The central bank, in holding the exchange rate down has to buy foreign exchange with domestic currency. This newly issued domestic currency increases the domestic money stock and eventually causes inflation. Inflationary policies are not normally regarded as a sensible way of protecting domestic industry.

There is another aspect to exchange controls. The justification is that preventing home residents from investing overseas benefits domestic growth as it leads to greater domestic real investment. In reality, it could do exactly the opposite. Restricting access to foreign assets may raise the variance and lower the return to owners of domestic wealth. In the short run, it also may appreciate the domestic exchange rate and, thereby, make domestic producers less competitive.

COSTS OF PROTECTIONISM THROUGHOUT THE WORLD. In 1982, the Organization for Economic Cooperation and Development (OECD) began a project to analyze the costs and benefits of protectionist policies in manufacturing in OECD countries. The OECD (1985) highlighted a number of ways that protectionist policies have generated costs far in excess of benefits. Since protectionist policies increase prices, the report concludes that the attainment of sustained non-inflationary growth is hindered by such price-increasing effects. Moreover, economic growth is potentially reduced if the uncertainty created by varying trade policies depresses investment.

Wood and Mudd and many others, have shown that imports do not cause higher unemployment. Conversely, the OECD study stresses the fact that a reduction in imports via trade restrictions does not cause greater employment. A reduction in the value of imports results in a similar reduction in the value of exports. One rationale for this finding is that a reduction in the purchases of foreign goods reduces foreign incomes and, in turn, causes reduced foreign purchases of domestic goods.

While the reduction in imports increases employment in industries that produce products similar to the previously imported goods, the reduction in exports decreases employment in the export industries. In other words, while some jobs are saved, others are lost; however, this economic reality may not be obvious to businessmen, labor union leaders, politicians and others.

Luttrell has stressed that the jobs saved by protectionist legislation are more readily observed than the jobs lost due to protectionist legislation. In other words, the jobs that are protected in, say, the textiles industry by U.S. import restrictions on foreign textiles are more readily apparent (and publicized) than the jobs in agriculture and high technology industries that do not materialize because of the import restrictions. These employment effects will net to approximately zero.

The OECD study also stresses that developing countries need exports to offset their debts. Thus, protectionist trade policies by developed countries affect not only the economic activity of the developing countries, but the stability of the international financial system as debtor nations find it increasingly difficult to service their debts.

Not only does a free trade policy by developed countries benefit developing countries, but a free trade policy by developing countries benefits developing countries. A given amount of new investment generated more additional output in countries following a free trade policy than a restricted trade policy. The reason is that a free trade environment allows capital to flow to its most highly valued uses, while a restricted trade environment distorts economic incentives.

## ARGUMENTS FOR RESTRICTING TRADE

If protectionism is so costly, why is protectionism so pervasive? This section reviews the major arguments for restricting trade and provides explanations for the existence of protectionist trade policies.

**NATIONAL DEFENSE.**  The national defense argument says that import barriers are necessary to ensure the capacity to produce crucial goods in a national emergency. While this argument is especially appealing for weapons during a war, there will likely be demands from other industries that deem themselves essential. For example, the footwear industry will demand protection because military personnel need combat boots.

The national defense argument ignores the possibility of purchases from friendly countries during the emergency. The possibilities of storage and depletion raise additional doubts about the general applicability of the argument. If crucial goods can be stored, for example, the least costly way to prepare for an emergency might be to buy the goods from foreigners at the low world price before an emergency and store them. If the crucial goods are depletable mineral resources, such as oil, then the restriction of oil imports before an emergency will cause a more rapid depletion of domestic reserves. Once again, stockpiling might be a far less costly alternative.

**INCOME REDISTRIBUTION.**  Since protectionist trade policies affect the distribution of income, a trade restriction might be defended on the grounds that it favors some disadvantaged group. It is unlikely, however, that trade policy is the best tool for dealing with the perceived evils of income inequality, because of its bluntness and adverse effects on the efficient allocation of resources. Attempting to equalize incomes directly by tax and transfer payments is likely less costly than using trade policy. In addition, as Hickok's study indicates, trade restrictions on many items increase rather than decrease income inequality.

OPTIMUM TARIFF ARGUMENT. The optimum tariff argument applies to situations in which a country has the economic power to alter world prices. This power exists because the country (or a group of countries acting in consort like the Organization of Petroleum Exporting Countries) is such a large producer or consumer of a good that a change in its production or consumption patterns influences world prices. For example, by imposing a tariff, the country can make foreign goods cheaper. Since a tariff reduces the demand for foreign goods, if the tariff-imposing country has some market power, the world price for the good will fall. The tariff-imposing country will gain because the price per unit of its imports will have decreased.

There are a number of obstacles that preclude the widespread application of this argument. Few countries possess the necessary market power and, when they do, only a small number of goods is covered. Secondly, in a world of shifting supply and demand, calculating the optimum tariff and adjusting the rate to changing situations is difficult. Finally, the possibility of foreign retaliation to an act of economic warfare is likely. Such retaliation could leave both countries worse off than they would have been in a free trade environment.

BALANCING THE BALANCE OF TRADE. Many countries enact protectionist trade policies in the hope of eliminating a balance of trade deficit or increasing a balance of trade surplus. The desire to increase a balance of trade surplus follows from the mercantilist view that larger trade surpluses are beneficial from a national perspective.

This argument is suspect on a number of grounds. First, there is nothing inherently undesirable about a trade deficit or desirable about a surplus. For example, faster economic growth in the United States than in the rest of the world would tend to cause a trade deficit. In this case, the trade deficit is a sign of a healthy economy. Second, protectionist policies that reduce imports will cause exports to decrease by a comparable amount. Hence, an attempt to increase exports permanently relative to imports will fail. It is doubtful that the trade deficit will be reduced even temporarily because import quantities do not decline quickly in response to the higher import prices and the revenues of foreign producers might rise.

PROTECTION OF JOBS. The protection of jobs argument is closely related to the balance of trade argument. Since a reduction in imports via trade restrictions will result in a similar reduction in exports, the overall employment effects, as found in the OECD (1985) study and many others, are negligible. While the *overall* effects are negligible, workers (and resource owners) in specific industries are affected differently.

A domestic industry faced with increased imports from its foreign competition is under pressure to reduce production and lower costs. Productive resources must move from this industry to other domestic industries. Workers must change jobs and, in some cases, relocate to other cities. Since this change is forced upon these workers, these workers bear real costs that they are likely to resist. A similar statement can be made about the owners of capital in the affected industry.

Workers and other resource owners will likely resist these changes by lobbying for trade restrictions. The previously cited studies on the costs of protectionism demonstrated that trade restrictions entail substantial real costs as well. These costs likely exceed the adjustment costs because the adjustment costs are one-time costs, while the costs of protectionism continue as long as trade restrictions are maintained.

**INFANT INDUSTRIES.** The preceding argument is couched in terms of protecting a domestic industry. A slightly different argument, the so-called infant industry case, is couched in terms of *promoting* a domestic industry. Suppose an industry, already established in other countries, is being established in a specific country. The country might not be able to realize its comparative advantage in this industry because of the existing cost and other advantages of foreign firms. Initially, owners of the fledgling firm must be willing to suffer losses until the firm develops its market and lowers its production costs to the level of its foreign rivals. In order to assist this entrant, tariff protection can be used to shield the firm from some foreign competition.

After this temporary period of protection, free trade should be restored; however, the removal of tariff protection frequently is resisted. As the industry develops, its political power to thwart opposing legislation also increases.

Another problem with the infant industry argument is that a tariff is not the best way to intervene. A production subsidy is superior to a tariff if the goal is to expand production. A subsidy will do this directly, while a tariff has the undesirable side effect of reducing consumption.

In many cases, intervention might not be appropriate at all. If the infant industry is a good candidate for being competitive internationally, borrowing from the private capital markets can finance the expansion. Investors are willing to absorb losses *temporarily* if the prospects for future profits are sufficiently good.

**SPILLOVER EFFECTS.** The justification for protecting an industry, infant or otherwise, frequently entails a suggestion that the industry generates spillover benefits for other industries or individuals for which the industry is not compensated. Despite patent laws, one common suggestion is that certain industries are not fully compensated for their research and development expenditures. This argument is frequently directed toward technologically progressive industries where some firms can capture the results of other firms' research and development simply by dismantling a product to see how it works.

The application of this argument, however, engenders a number of problems. Spillovers of knowledge are difficult to measure. Since spillovers are not market transactions, they do not leave an obvious trail to identify their beneficiaries. The lack of market transactions also complicates an assessment of the value of these spillovers. To determine the appropriate subsidy, one must be able to place a dollar value on the spillovers generated by a given research and development expenditure. Actually, the calculation requires much more than the already difficult task of reconstructing the past, it requires complex estimates of the spillovers' future worth as well. Since resources are moved from other industries to the targeted industry, the government must understand the functioning of the entire economy.

Finally, there are political problems. An aggressive application of this argument might lead to retaliation and a mutually destructive trade war. In addition, as interest groups compete for the governmental assistance, there is no guarantee that the right groups will be assisted or that they will use the assistance efficiently.

**STRATEGIC TRADE POLICY.** Recent theoretical developments have identified cases in which so-called strategic trade policy is superior to free trade. As we discussed earlier, decreasing unit production costs and market structures that contain monopoly elements are common in industries involved in international trade. Market imperfections immediately suggest the potential benefits of governmental intervention. In the strategic trade policy argument, government policy can alter the terms of competition to favor domestic over foreign firms and shift the excess returns in monopolistic markets from foreign to domestic firms.

Krugman illustrates an example of the argument. Assume that there is only one firm in the United States, Boeing, and one multinational firm in Europe, Airbus, capable of producing a 150-seat passenger aircraft. Assume also that the aircraft is produced only for export, so that the returns to the firm can be identified with the national interest. This export market is profitable for either firm if it is the only producer; however, it is unprofitable for both firms to produce the plane. Finally, assume the following payoffs are associated with the four combinations of production: 1) if both Boeing and Airbus produce the aircraft, each firm loses $5 million; 2) if neither Boeing nor Airbus produces the aircraft, profits are zero; 3) if Boeing produces the aircraft and Airbus does not, Boeing profits by $100 million and Airbus has zero profits; and 4) if Airbus produces the aircraft and Boeing does not, Airbus profits by $100 million and Boeing has zero profits.

Which firm(s) will produce the aircraft? The example does not yield a unique outcome. A unique outcome can be generated if one firm, say Boeing, has a head start and begins production before Airbus. In this case, Boeing will reap profits of $100 million and will have deterred Airbus from entering the market because Airbus will lose $5 million if it enters after Boeing.

Strategic trade policy, however, suggests that judicious governmental intervention can alter the outcome. If the European governments agree to subsidize Airbus' production with $10 million no matter what Boeing does, then Airbus will produce the plane. Production by Airbus will yield more profits than not producing, no matter what Boeing does. At the same time, Boeing will be deterred from producing because it would lose money. Thus, Airbus will capture the entire market and reap profits of $110 million, $100 million of which can be viewed as a transfer of profits from the United States.

The criticisms of a strategic trade policy are similar to the criticisms against protecting a technologically progressive industry that generates spillover benefits. There are major informational problems in applying a strategic trade policy. The government must estimate the potential payoff of each course of action. Economic knowledge about the behavior of industries that have monopoly elements is limited. Firms may behave competitively or cooperatively and may compete by setting prices or output. The behavior of rival governments also must be anticipated. Foreign retaliation must be viewed as likely where substantial profits are at stake. In addition, many interest groups will compete for the governmental assistance. Though only a small number of sectors can be considered potentially strategic, many industries will make a case for assistance.

**RECIPROCITY AND THE "LEVEL PLAYING FIELD."** Bhagwati and Irwin note that U.S. trade policy discussions in recent years have frequently stressed the importance of "fair trade." The concept of fair trade, which is technically referred to as reciprocity, means different things to different people.

Under the General Agreement on Tariffs and Trade, negotiations to reduce trade barriers focus upon matching concessions. This form of reciprocity, known as first-difference reciprocity, attempts to reduce trade barriers by requiring a country to provide a tariff reduction of value comparable to one provided by the other country. In this case, reciprocity is defined in terms of matching changes.

Recent U.S. demands, exemplified by the Gephardt amendment to the current trade legislation, reveal an approach that is called full reciprocity. This approach seeks reciprocity in terms of the level of protection bilaterally and over a specific range of goods. Reciprocity requires equal access and this access can be determined by bilateral trade balances. A trade deficit with a trading partner is claimed to be *prima facie* evidence of unequal access. Examples abound. For example, U.S. construction firms have not had a major contract in Japan since 1965, while Japanese construction firms did $1.8 billion worth of business in the United States in 1985 alone. Recent legislation bars Japanese participation in U.S. public works projects until the Japanese offer reciprocal privileges.

As the name suggests, the fundamental argument for fair trade is one of equity. Domestic producers in a free trade country argue that foreign trade barriers are unfair because it places them at a competitive disadvantage. In an extreme version, it is asserted that this unfair competition will virtually eliminate U.S. manufacturing, leaving only jobs that consist primarily of flipping hamburgers at fast-food restaurants or, as Bhagwati and Irwin have said, rolling rice cakes at Japanese-owned sushi bars. While domestic producers *are* relatively disadvantaged, the wisdom of a protectionist response is doubtful. Again, the costs of protectionism exceed substantially the benefits from a national perspective.

In an attempt to reinforce the argument for fair trade, proponents also argue that retaliatory threats, combined with changes in tariffs and non-tariff barriers, allow for the simultaneous protection of domestic industries against unequal competition and induce more open foreign markets. This more flexible approach is viewed as superior to a "one-sided" free trade policy. The suggestion that a fair trade policy produces a trading environment with fewer trade restrictions allows proponents to assert that such a policy serves to promote both equity and efficiency. In other words, not only will domestic and foreign producers in the same industry be treated equally, but the gains associated with a freer trading environment will be realized.

On the other hand, critics of a fair trade policy argue that such a policy is simply disguised protectionism—it simply achieves the goals of specific interest groups at the expense of the nation at large. In many cases, fair traders focus on a specific practice that can be portrayed as protectionist while ignoring the entire package of policies that are affecting a nation's competitive position. In these cases, the foreign country is more likely either not to respond or retaliate by increasing rather than reducing their trade barriers. In the latter case, the escalation of trade barriers causes losses for both nations, which is exactly opposite to the alleged effects of an activist fair trade policy.

Critics of fair trade proposals are especially bothered by the use of bilateral trade deficits as evidence of unfair trade. In a world of many trading countries, the trade between two countries need not be balanced for the trade of each to be in global balance. Differing demands and productive capabilities across countries will cause a specific country to have trade deficits with some countries and surpluses with other countries. These bilateral imbalances are a normal result of countries trading on the basis of comparative advantage. Thus, the focus on the bilateral trade deficit can produce inappropriate conclusions about fairness and, more importantly, policies attempting to eliminate bilateral trade deficits are likely to be very costly because they eliminate the gains from a multilateral trading system.

## CONCLUSION

The proliferation of protectionist trade policies in recent years provides an impetus to reconsider their worth. In the world of traditional trade theory, characterized by perfect competition, a definitive recommendation in favor of free trade can be made. The gains from international trade result from a re-allocation of productive resources toward goods that can be produced less costly at home than abroad and the exchange of some of these goods for goods that can be produced at less cost abroad than at home.

Recent developments in international trade theory have examined the consequences of international trade in markets where there are market imperfections, such as monopoly and technological spillovers. Do these imperfections justify protectionist trade policies? The answer continues to be no. While protectionist trade policies may offset monopoly power overseas or advantageously use domestic monopoly power, trade restrictions tend to reduce the competition faced by domestic producers, protecting domestic producers at the expense of domestic consumers.

The empirical evidence is clear-cut. The costs of protectionist trade policies far exceed the benefits. The losses suffered by consumers exceed the gains reaped by domestic producers and government. Low-income consumers are relatively more adversely affected than high-income consumers. Not only are there inefficiencies associated with excessive domestic production and restricted consumption, but there are costs associated with the enforcement of the protectionist legislation and attempts to influence trade policy.

The primary reason for these costly protectionist policies relies on a public choice argument. The desire to influence trade policy arises from the fact that trade policy changes benefit some groups, while harming others. Consumers are harmed by protectionist legislation; however, ignorance, small individual costs, and the high costs of organizing consumers prevent the consumers from being an effective force. On the other hand, workers and other resource owners in an industry are more likely to be effective politically because of their relative ease of organizing and their individually large and easy-to-identify benefits. Politicians interested in re-election will most likely respond to the demands for protectionist legislation of such an interest group.

The empirical evidence also suggests that the adverse consumer effects of protectionist trade policies are not short-lived. These policies generate lower economic growth rates than the rates associated with free trade policies. In turn, slow growth contributes to additional protectionist pressures.

Interest group pressures from industries experiencing difficulty and the general appeal of a "level playing field" combine to make the reduction of trade barriers especially difficult at the present time in the United States. Nonetheless, national interests will be served best by such an admittedly difficult political course.

# COMPETITIVENESS: A DANGEROUS OBSESSION

Paul Krugman

... The idea that a country's economic fortunes are largely determined by its success on world markets is a hypothesis, not a necessary truth; and as a practical, empirical matter, that hypothesis is flatly wrong. That is, it is simply not the case that the world's leading nations are to any important degree in economic competition with each other, or that any of their major economic problems can be attributed to failures to compete on world markets. The growing obsession in most advanced nations with international competitiveness should be seen, not as a well-founded concern, but as a view held in the face of overwhelming contrary evidence. And yet it is clearly a view that people very much want to hold—a desire to believe that is reflected in a remarkable tendency of those who preach the doctrine of competitiveness to support their case with careless, flawed arithmetic.

This article makes three points. First, it argues that concerns about competitiveness are, as an empirical matter, almost completely unfounded. Second, it tries to explain why defining the economic problem as one of international competition is nonetheless so attractive to so many people. Finally, it argues that the obsession with competitiveness is not only wrong but dangerous, skewing domestic policies and threatening the international economic system. This last issue is, of course, the most consequential from the standpoint of public policy. Thinking in terms of competitiveness leads, directly and indirectly, to bad economic policies on a wide range of issues, domestic and foreign, whether it be in health care or trade.

## MINDLESS COMPETITION

Most people who use the term "competitiveness" do so without a second thought. It seems obvious to them that the analogy between a country and a corporation is reasonable and that to ask whether the United States is competitive in the world market is no different in principle from asking whether General Motors is competitive in the North American minivan market.

In fact, however, trying to define the competitiveness of a nation is much more problematic than defining that of a corporation. The bottom line for a corporation is literally its bottom line: if a corporation cannot afford to pay its workers, suppliers, and bondholders, it will go out of business. So when we say that a corporation is uncompetitive, we mean that its market position is unsustainable—that unless it improves its performance, it will cease to exist. Countries, on the other hand, do not go out of business. They may be happy or unhappy with their economic performance, but they have no well-defined bottom line. As a result, the concept of national competitiveness is elusive.

One might suppose, naively, that the bottom line of a national economy is simply its trade balance, that competitiveness can be measured by the ability of a country to sell more abroad than it buys. But in both theory and practice a trade surplus may be a sign of national weakness, a deficit a sign of strength. For example, Mexico was forced to run huge trade surpluses in the 1980s in order to pay the interest on its foreign debt since international investors refused to lend it any more money; it began to run large trade deficits after 1990 as foreign investors recovered confidence and began to pour in new funds. Would anyone want to describe Mexico as a highly competitive nation during the debt crisis era or describe what has happened since 1990 as a loss in competitiveness?

Most writers who worry about the issue at all have therefore tried to define competitiveness as the combination of favorable trade performance and something else. In particular, the most popular definition of competitiveness nowadays runs along the lines of the one given in Council of Economic Advisors Chairman Laura D'Andrea Tyson's *Who's Bashing Whom?*: competitiveness is "our ability to produce goods and services that meet the test of international competition while our citizens enjoy a standard of living that is both rising and sustainable." This sounds reasonable. If you think about it, however, and test your thoughts against the facts, you will find out that there is much less to this definition than meets the eye.

Consider, for a moment, what the definition would mean for an economy that conducted very little international trade, like the United States in the 1950s. For such an economy, the ability to balance its trade is mostly a matter of getting the exchange rate right. But because trade is such a small factor in the economy, the level of the exchange rate is a minor influence on the standard of living. So in an economy with very little international trade, the growth in living standards—and thus "competitiveness" according to

Tyson's definition—would be determined almost entirely by domestic factors, primarily the rate of productivity growth. That's domestic productivity growth, period—not productivity growth relative to other countries. In other words, for an economy with very little international trade, "competitiveness" would turn out to be a funny way of saying "productivity" and would have nothing to do with international competition.

But surely this changes when trade becomes more important, as indeed it has for all major economies? It certainly could change. Suppose that a country finds that although its productivity is steadily rising, it can succeed in exporting only if it repeatedly devalues its currency, selling its exports ever more cheaply on world markets. Then its standard of living, which depends on its purchasing power over imports as well as domestically produced goods, might actually decline. In the jargon of economists, domestic growth might be outweighed by deteriorating terms of trade. So "competitiveness" could turn out really to be about international competition after all.

There is no reason, however, to leave this as a pure speculation; it can easily be checked against the data. Have deteriorating terms of trade in fact been a major drag on the U.S. standard of living? Or has the rate of growth of U.S. real income continued essentially to equal the rate of domestic productivity growth, even though trade is a larger share of income than it used to be?

To answer this question, one need only look at the national income accounts data the Commerce Department publishes regularly in the *Survey of Current Business*. The standard measure of economic growth in the United States is, of course, real GNP—a measure that divides the value of goods and services produced in the United States by appropriate price indexes to come up with an estimate of real national output. The Commerce Department also, however, publishes something called "command GNP." This is similar to real GNP except that it divides U.S. exports not by the export price index, but by the price index for U.S. imports. That is, exports are valued by what Americans can buy with the money exports bring. Command GNP therefore measures the volume of goods and services the U.S. economy can "command"—the nation's purchasing power—rather than the volume it produces. And as we have just seen, "competitiveness" means something different from "productivity" if and only if purchasing power grows significantly more slowly than output.

Well, here are the numbers. Over the period 1959–73, a period of vigorous growth in U.S. living standards and few concerns about international competition, real GNP per worker-hour grew 1.85 percent annually, while command GNP per hour grew a bit faster, 1.87 percent. From 1973 to 1990, a period of stagnating living standards, command GNP growth per hour slowed to 0.65 percent. Almost all (91 percent) of that slowdown, however, was explained by a decline in domestic productivity growth: real GNP per hour grew only 0.73 percent.

Similar calculations for the European Community and Japan yield similar results. In each case, the growth rate of living standards essentially equals the growth rate of domestic productivity—not productivity relative to competitors, but simply domestic productivity. Even though world trade is larger than ever before, national living standards are overwhelmingly determined by domestic factors rather than by some competition for world markets.

How can this be in our interdependent world? Part of the answer is that the world is not as interdependent as you might think: countries are nothing at all like corporations. Even today, U.S. exports are only 10 percent of the value-added in the economy (which is equal to GNP). That is, the United States is still almost 90 percent an economy that produces goods and services for its own use. By contrast, even the largest corporation sells hardly any of its output to its own workers; the "exports" of General Motors—its sales to people who do not work there—are virtually all of its sales, which are more than 2.5 times the corporation's value-added.

Moreover, countries do not compete with each other the way corporations do. Coke and Pepsi are almost purely rivals: only a negligible fraction of Coca-Cola's sales go to Pepsi workers, only a negligible fraction of the goods Coca-Cola workers buy are Pepsi products. So if Pepsi is successful, it tends to be at Coke's expense. But the major industrial countries, while they sell products that compete with each other, are also each other's main export markets and each other's main suppliers of useful imports. If the European economy does well, it need not be at U.S. expense; indeed, if anything a successful European economy is likely to help the U.S. economy by providing it with larger markets and selling it goods of superior quality at lower prices.

International trade, then, is not a zero-sum game. When productivity rises in Japan, the main result is a rise in Japanese real wages; American or European wages are in principle at least as likely to rise as to fall, and in practice seem to be virtually unaffected.

It would be possible to belabor the point, but the moral is clear: while competitive problems could arise in principle, as a practical, empirical matter the major nations of the world are not to any significant degree in economic competition with each other. Of course, there is always a rivalry for status and power—countries that grow faster will see their political rank rise. So it is always interesting to *compare* countries. But asserting that Japanese growth diminishes U.S. status is very different from saying that it reduces the U.S. standard of living—and it is the latter that the rhetoric of competitiveness asserts.

One can, of course, take the position that words mean what we want them to mean, that all are free, if they wish, to use the term "competitiveness" as a poetic way of saying productivity, without actually implying that international competition has anything to do with it. But few writers on competitiveness would accept this view. They believe that the facts tell a very different story, that we live, as Lester Thurow put it in his best-selling book, *Head to Head,* in a world of "win-lose" competition between the leading economies. How is this belief possible?

## CARELESS ARITHMETIC

One of the remarkable, startling features of the vast literature on competitiveness is the repeated tendency of highly intelligent authors to engage in what may perhaps most tactfully be described as "careless arithmetic." Assertions are made that sound like quantifiable pronouncements about measurable magnitudes, but the writers do not actually present any data on these magnitudes and thus fail to notice that the actual numbers contradict their assertions. Or data are presented that are supposed to support an assertion, but the writer fails to notice that his own numbers imply that what he is saying cannot be true. Over and over again one finds books and articles on competitiveness that seem to the unwary reader to be full of convincing evidence but that strike anyone familiar with the data as strangely, almost eerily inept in their handling of the numbers. Some examples can best illustrate this point. . . .

TRADE DEFICITS AND THE LOSS OF GOOD JOBS.   In a recent article published in Japan, Lester Thurow explained to his audience the importance of reducing the Japanese trade surplus with the United States. U.S. real wages, he pointed out, had fallen six percent during the Reagan and Bush years, and the reason was that trade deficits in manufactured goods had forced workers out of high-paying manufacturing jobs into much lower-paying service jobs.

This is not an original view; it is very widely held. But Thurow was more concrete than most people, giving actual numbers for the job and wage loss. A million manufacturing jobs have been lost because of the deficit, he asserted, and manufacturing jobs pay 30 percent more than service jobs.

Both numbers are dubious. The million-job number is too high, and the 30 percent wage differential between manufacturing and services is primarily due to a difference in the length of the workweek, not a difference in the hourly wage rate. But let's grant Thurow his numbers. Do they tell the story he suggests?

The key point is that total U.S. employment is well over 100 million workers. Suppose that a million workers were forced from manufacturing into services and as a result lost the 30 percent manufacturing wage premium. Since these workers are less than 1 percent of the U.S. labor force, this would reduce the average U.S. wage rate by less than 1/100 of 30 percent—that is, by less than 0.3 percent.

This is too small to explain the 6 percent real wage decline *by a factor of 20.* Or to look at it another way, the annual wage loss from deficit-induced deindustrialization, which Thurow clearly implies is at the heart of U.S. economic difficulties, is on the basis of his own numbers roughly equal to what the U.S. spends on health care every week.

Something puzzling is going on here. How could someone as intelligent as Thurow, in writing an article that purports to offer hard quantitative evidence of the importance of international competition to the U.S. economy, fail to re-alize that the evidence he offers clearly shows that the channel of harm that he identifies was *not* the culprit?

## THE THRILL OF COMPETITION

The competitive metaphor—the image of countries competing with each other in world markets in the same way that corporations do—derives much of its attractiveness from its seeming comprehensibility. Tell a group of busi-nessmen that a country is like a corporation writ large, and you give them the comfort of feeling that they already understand the basics. Try to tell them about economic concepts like comparative advantage, and you are asking them to learn something new. It should not be surprising if many prefer a doctrine that offers the gain of apparent sophistication without the pain of hard thinking. The rhetoric of competitiveness has become so widespread, however, for three deeper reasons.

First, competitive images are exciting, and thrills sell tickets. The subtitle of Lester Thurow's huge best-seller, *Head to Head,* is "The Coming Economic Battle among Japan, Europe, and America"; the jacket proclaims that "the decisive war of the century had begun . . . and America may already have decided to lose." Suppose that the subtitle had described the real situation: "The coming struggle in which each big economy will succeed or fail based on its own efforts, pretty much independently of how well the others do." Would Thurow have sold a tenth as many books?

Second, the idea that U.S. economic difficulties hinge crucially on our fail-ures in international competition somewhat paradoxically makes those dif-ficulties seem easier to solve. The productivity of the average American worker is determined by a complex array of factors, most of them unreach-able by any likely government policy. So if you accept the reality that our "competitive" problem is really a domestic productivity problem pure and simple, you are unlikely to be optimistic about any dramatic turnaround. But if you can convince yourself that the problem is really one of failures in in-ternational competition—that imports are pushing workers out of high-wage jobs, or subsidized foreign competition is driving the United States out of the high value-added sectors—then the answers to economic malaise may seem to you to involve simple things like subsidizing high technology and being tough on Japan.

Finally, many of the world's leaders have found the competitive metaphor extremely useful as a political device. The rhetoric of competitiveness turns out to provide a good way either to justify hard choices or to avoid them. The example of Delors in Copenhagen shows the usefulness of competitive meta-phors as an evasion. Delors had to say something at the EC summit; yet to say anything that addressed the real roots of European unemployment would have involved huge political risks. By turning the discussion to essentially irrelevant but plausible-sounding questions of competitiveness, he bought himself some time to come up with a better answer (which to some extent he provided in December's white paper on the European economy—a paper that still, however, retained "competitiveness" in its title).

By contrast, the well-received presentation of Bill Clinton's initial economic program in February 1993 showed the usefulness of competitive rhetoric as a motivation for tough policies. Clinton proposed a set of painful spending cuts and tax increases to reduce the Federal deficit. Why? The real reasons for cutting the deficit are disappointingly undramatic: the deficit siphons off funds that might otherwise have been productively invested, and thereby exerts a steady if small drag on U.S. economic growth. But Clinton was able to offer a stirring patriotic appeal, calling on the nation to act now in order to make the economy competitive in the global market—with the implication that dire economic consequences would follow if the United States does not.

Many people who know that "competitiveness" is a largely meaningless concept have been willing to indulge competitive rhetoric precisely because they believe they can harness it in the service of good policies. An overblown fear of the Soviet Union was used in the 1950s to justify the building of the interstate highway system and the expansion of math and science education. Cannot the unjustified fears about foreign competition similarly be turned to good, used to justify serious efforts to reduce the budget deficit, rebuild infrastructure, and so on?

A few years ago this was a reasonable hope. At this point, however, the obsession with competitiveness has reached the point where it has already begun dangerously to distort economic policies.

## THE DANGERS OF OBSESSION

Thinking and speaking in terms of competitiveness poses three real dangers. First, it could result in the wasteful spending of government money supposedly to enhance U.S. competitiveness. Second, it could lead to protectionism and trade wars. Finally, and most important, it could result in bad public policy on a spectrum of important issues.

During the 1950s, fear of the Soviet Union induced the U.S. government to spend money on useful things like highways and science education. It also, however, led to considerable spending on more doubtful items like bomb shelters. The most obvious if least worrisome danger of the growing obsession with competitiveness is that it might lead to a similar misallocation of resources. To take an example, recent guidelines for government research funding have stressed the importance of supporting research that can improve U.S. international competitiveness. This exerts at least some bias toward inventions that can help manufacturing firms, which generally compete on international markets, rather than service producers, which generally do not. Yet most of our employment and value-added is now in services, and lagging productivity in services rather than manufactures has been the single most important factor in the stagnation of U.S. living standards.

A much more serious risk is that the obsession with competitiveness will lead to trade conflict, perhaps even to a world trade war. Most of those who have preached the doctrine of competitiveness have not been old-fashioned protectionists. They want their countries to win the global trade game, not drop out. But what if, despite its best efforts, a country does not seem to be winning, or lacks confidence that it can? Then the competitive diagnosis inevitably suggests that to close the borders is better than to risk having foreigners take away high-wage jobs and high-value sectors. At the very least, the focus on the supposedly competitive nature of international economic relations greases the rails for those who want confrontational if not frankly protectionist policies.

We can already see this process at work, in both the United States and Europe. In the United States, it was remarkable how quickly the sophisticated interventionist arguments advanced by Laura Tyson in her published work gave way to the simple-minded claim by U.S. Trade Representative Mickey Kantor that Japan's bilateral trade surplus was costing the United States millions of jobs. And the trade rhetoric of President Clinton, who stresses the supposed creation of high-wage jobs rather than the gains from specialization, left his administration in a weak position when it tried to argue with the claims of NAFTA foes that competition from cheap Mexican labor will destroy the U.S. manufacturing base.

Perhaps, the most serious risk from the obsession with competitiveness, however, is its subtle indirect effect on the quality of economic discussion and policymaking. If top government officials are strongly committed to a particular economic doctrine, their commitment inevitably sets the tone for policy-making on all issues, even those which may seem to have nothing to do with that doctrine. And if an economic doctrine is flatly, completely and demonstrably wrong, the insistence that discussion adhere to that doctrine inevitably blurs the focus and diminishes the quality of policy discussion across a broad range of issues, including some that are very far from trade policy per se. . . .

So let's start telling the truth: competitiveness is a meaningless word when applied to national economies. And the obsession with competitiveness is both wrong and dangerous.

# The Public Choice
# View of International
# Political Economy

Bruno S. Frey

In this article I endeavor to show that, first, public choice has been applied specifically to international political economy, and that there is a large and rapidly growing literature on the subject. Second, public choice offers an interesting and worthwhile approach to the area, an approach that complements the political science-based views of international political economy in a useful way. Consequently, the claim for exclusivity made by some writers based in political science should be replaced by the realization of the need for mutual cross-fertilization of the two (partly competing) approaches. Section I provides a short survey of those parts of the public choice approach most relevant for international political economy.

## 1. The Public Choice Approach

**A. GENERAL CHARACTERISTICS.** Public choice, sometimes called the "economic theory of politics" or "(new) political economy," seeks to analyze political processes and the interaction between the economy and the polity by using the tools of modern (neoclassical) analysis. It provides, on the one hand, an explicit positive approach to the workings of political institutions and to the behavior of governments, parties, voters, interest groups, and (public) bureaucracies; and it seeks, on the other, normatively to establish the most desirable and effective political institutions. Public choice is part of a movement that endeavors to apply the "rational behavior" approach to areas beyond traditional economics. In recent years, an increasing number of political scientists, sociologists, and social psychologists have taken up this approach. It thus constitutes one of the rare successful examples of interdisciplinary research.

Both the rational behavior approach to social problems and public choice theory are characterized by three major features. First, the individual is the basic unit of analysis. The individual is assumed to be "rational" in the sense of responding in a systematic and hence predictable way to incentives: courses of action are chosen that yield the highest net benefits according to the individual's own utility function. Contrary to what nonspecialists often believe, it is not assumed that individuals are fully informed. Rather, the amount of information sought is the result of an (often implicit) cost-benefit calculus. Indeed, in the political arena it often does not pay the individual to be well-informed—this is known as "rational ignorance."

Second, the individual's behavior is explained by concentrating on the changes in the constraints to which he or she is exposed; that is, the preferences are assumed to be constant. Individuals are assumed to be capable of comparing alternatives, of seeing substitution possibilities, and of making marginal adjustments.

The third characteristic is that the analysis stresses rigor (and is sometimes formal). The results must yield a proposition that (at least in principle) can be subjected to econometric or politicometric testing.

There is no need to go into general public choice theory here; only its applications to problems of international political economy are relevant to this discussion.

**B. THE CONCEPTS APPLIED IN INTERNATIONAL POLITICAL ECONOMY.** In the international field, some theoretical concepts developed in public choice are used particularly often. Public goods theory and politico-economic modeling will be briefly mentioned here in order to illuminate the public choice approach to international political economy.

PUBLIC GOODS THEORY. Public goods is the concept most frequently used within economics-based international political economy. Its usefulness is well illustrated in a contribution by Charles Kindleberger, in which he looks at various aspects of the international economy from the point of view of public goods, and at the tendency for free riding, in which a public good is available to all irrespective of whether they have contributed to its supply. Thus, law and order can be considered a public good forming an important complement to foreign trade. Its absence can lead to a serious disruption in international exchange. The institution of the state may also be regarded as a public good. The high costs arising when it does not exist are illustrated by the example of Germany in 1790. At that time there were 1,700 tariff boundaries with three hundred rulers levying tolls as they pleased. Under such circumstances it was no wonder that the advantages of trade exchange could not be exploited to any great degree. The existence of national monetary institutions may also be looked upon as a public good.

There are a great many other applications of the public goods concept and the concomitant free-rider problem, such as trade liberalization, nationalism, alliances, and burden sharing. A further application is the preservation of nature beyond natural frontiers, such as the campaign against whaling or the protection of the atmosphere.

The public goods concept is extremely useful and intuitively plausible. The ease of application may, however, sometimes hide underlying problems. The exact conditions under which free riding occurs are still unknown; often it is simply assumed that actors do not contribute to the common cause. Laboratory experiments on public goods situations suggest that free riding does not occur as often as pure economic theory would have us think. Moreover, institutional conditions are often such that free riding is discouraged.

Even when national actors fully perceive that it is advantageous for them to cooperate in the provision of a public good, it is difficult and sometimes even impossible to coordinate joint action. In view of the general impossibility of forcing independent national actors to cooperate, the free-rider problem can be overcome by finding *rules* or *constitutional agreements* that lay down the conditions for cooperation.

In order to find a set of rules that the participants are willing to accept in a state of (partial) uncertainty about the future (i.e., beyond the veil of ignorance), the actors must believe that obeying the rules will be advantageous to them. The agreement must lead to a beneficial change according to the expectations of all actors (Pareto-superiority), because only these conditions will there be voluntary cooperation—that is, unanimity among the participants. These conditions are not easily set up and maintained in the international system. Once a set of rules or a constitution has been agreed upon, the problem is to ensure that the rules are observed and that individual nations have no incentive to back out of or attempt to alter the agreement. The "constitutional" approach has been applied to various problems in international political economy, among them environmental and fisheries pacts, international public health accords, cooperation about forecasting (and in the future possibly influencing) the weather, the use of outer space, and the international judicial system.

The establishment and enforcement of rules has occupied a central position in two areas. First, *international monetary arrangements* may be considered to be, if well designed, advantageous to all, but the incentives for deviation are also marked. It is therefore necessary to consider not only the Pareto-superiority of an international monetary scheme but also the benefits and costs to the individual participating nations. This aspect has been overlooked in the many proposals made in this area; they usually assume (implicitly) that there is a "benevolent international dictator" who will put them into effect.

An important related question is why certain rules have not influenced behavior as much as one might have expected. One example is provided by the Bretton Woods system, in which changes in exchange rates have been made too infrequently, and generally too late. The reason is that forces militate against both devaluation and revaluation. Voters, it is believed, interpret devaluation as an admission of financial failure, with negative consequences for the government in power. Revaluation is good for the voters (as consumers) but very bad for well-organized groups of exporters and import competitors; so the government may again run into trouble. In view of this unwillingness to adjust exchange rates, an agreement allowing freely flexible exchange rates may be preferable because the issue is then taken out of government (and central bank) politics.

The second international area in which rules play an important role is that of *international common property resources.* The need for international conventions and rules is obvious in view of the pollution of the atmosphere and the overfishing and overexploitation of the oceans. The difficulty in reaching agreement on what these rules should be is equally well known. It is hard to obtain consensus because no country can be forced to accept rules. The only acceptable rules are those that produce such high aggregate net benefits that they can be distributed among the participating countries in such a way that everyone finds it advantageous to agree and to stick to the rules. Such rules do not usually exist; it is quite possible that agreement on some of the current proposals concerning international common property resources would be worse for participating countries than no agreement at all.

POLITICO-ECONOMIC MODELING.  Politico-economic models or, as they are often called, political business-cycle models, study the interdependence between the economy and the polity by explicitly analyzing the behavior of actors. They test the resulting propositions using econometric, or rather politicometric, techniques. The simplest such model analyzes a circular system: the state of the economy influences the voters' evaluation of the government's performance, which is reflected by a vote of government popularity function. If the government considers its chances of re-election to be poor, it uses economic policy instruments to influence the state of the economy and thus the voters' decisions. (The government's actions may depend on its ideology if it considers its re-election chances to be good.) The model is, of course, a great simplification of reality, but it has already been shown that the framework can be extended to incorporate additional actors and relationships.

A politico-economic model for a closed country can be extended in two ways to include international politico-economic relationships. The first approach concentrates on the *internal* connections between the economy and the polity but also introduces international influences. In this case the politico-economic model outlined above is amended by factors emerging from the international sphere. One such factor is the state of the balance of payments, which may influence the voters' evaluation of the government's performance. A survey of over one hundred empirical studies of vote and popularity functions finds, however, that only six included the balance of payments among the indicators of economic conditions. Only in the case of the United Kingdom did it influence voters' decisions in a statistically significant way. In the other cases, Denmark and Australia, the coefficients were small and insignificant. Thus, it has to be concluded that even in countries with seemingly permanent and serious balance-of-payments troubles the voters either do not perceive them, or do not directly punish the government for them to any significant extent.

International political events may also affect votes and government popularity. Empirical studies of the United States show that, when the country is subjected to an international political crisis, the population tends to "rally round the flag." Another influence that may be introduced into politico-economic models is the foreign intervention in a country's internal polity that may occur if a foreign nation considers the results of a particular election undesirable. Government politicians may also have specific international political preferences and influence the internal economy accordingly, provided that their re-election chances are not thereby seriously diminished.

Finally, the use of economic policy instruments is influenced by international economic conditions. The possibility of creating a political business cycle aimed at improving re-election chances depends on institutional conditions within the international economy. Thomas Willett has argued that an expansionary economic policy yields more favorable short-run inflation-unemployment (or real income) trade-offs with a system of adjustable pegs than with a depreciating exchange rate. A system of adjustable pegs may thus be expected to increase the government's incentive to attempt to gain votes by introducing an expansionary policy before elections and devaluing thereafter.

The second approach goes one step further, by considering the *mutual interdependence* of domestic and foreign economies and polities. This research strategy is particularly well-developed with regard to arms race models. . . .

## 2. TARIFFS AND TRADE RESTRICTIONS

Most economists approach the analysis of tariffs and other restrictions on trade from the same standpoint. They start from the basic proposition of international trade theory: that free trade leads to higher real income and is desirable not only for the world as a whole but also for individual countries. The problem for political economists of the neoclassical public choice orientation, therefore, is to explain why tariffs nonetheless exist, and why governments so rarely seem to take the welfare-increasing (Pareto-optimal) step of abolishing tariffs. A government might be expected to win votes by abolishing tariffs, either because a majority of the electorate would directly benefit or because the government could redistribute the gains so that a majority of the electorate would be better off than in a situation with tariffs. If citizens were to determine tariffs by a single direct majority vote in an assembly, the *median voter* would vote in favor of free trade.

The simplistic assumptions of the median-voter model must, however, be modified in a number of important respects if it is to represent reality. This provides an explanation for the continuing existence and possibly even growth of tariffs. At least five modifications must be considered.

The first is that the losers in any tariff reduction, the people engaged in the domestic production of the goods concerned, are not compensated. If they form a majority, they will obstruct the reduction or the elimination of tariffs.

The second necessary modification is to consider the fact that prospective gainers have less incentive than prospective voters to participate in the vote, to inform themselves, and to organize and support a pressure group. Tariff reductions are a public good whose benefits are received by everybody, including those not taking the trouble and incurring the cost to bring about the reduction. The prospective cost of tariff reduction to the losers is, however, much more direct and concentrated, so that it is worth their while to engage in a political fight against tariff reduction. In addition, the well-defined short-term losses to be experienced by the losers are much more visible, and therefore better perceived, than uncertain gains to be made in the distant future by the winners. The fight over trade restrictions benefits those sectors protected from competition but otherwise serves no socially useful purpose, because it wastes scarce resources. This aspect is the subject of the *theory of rent seeking*. It is useful to differentiate between two activities, both of which, from society's point of view, waste resources. "Rent seeking" is the activity by which trade restrictions (tariffs, quotas) generate rents to one's advantage; "revenue seeking" is the fight over the distribution of revenues, and is thus a general distributional phenomenon.

A third modification of the simple median-voter model considers the possibility that the prospective losers in a free-trade regime may be better represented in parliament and in the government than the prospective winners, depending on the system of voting.

A fourth modification reflects the fact that logrolling or vote trading can make it possible for two measures, each of which would increase the country's use of labor in an attempt to increase tariffs. The political struggle between pro- and anti-free-trade interests is described by the so-called Cournot-Nash process. Each group assumes the resources used by the other group to influence the tariff will be constant and then calculates its own optimal input of lobbying resources on this basis. Assuming that the process is stable, an equilibrium level and distribution of lobbying expenditures is reached. This equilibrium also determines the level of the tariff resulting from the political struggle.

This model elegantly analyzes the endogenous determination of tariffs from a theoretical and highly aggregated point of view. One of its main weaknesses (and one of which its authors are well aware) is that the public-goods character of tariffs and free trade, and the concomitant free-rider effect, are not taken into account.

The factors influencing tariff policy discussed in the preceding paragraphs have also been the subject of econometric analysis. R. E. Baldwin seeks to explain the probability of a Congressman voting for (indicated by a dummy variable taking the value 0) or against (the dummy variable takes the value of 1) the trade-liberalizing bill introduced in Congress by a Republican president in 1973. The explanatory variables are, first, the party affiliation (if the

Congressman is a Republican the dummy variable takes the value 1, in the case of a Democrat it takes the value 0—a negative sign is expected because the bill is introduced by a Republican president); second, the proportion of import-sensitive industries in the Congressman's constituency (with an expected positive sign); third, the proportion of export-oriented industries in the constituency (with an expected negative sign); and finally, the contribution to the Congressman's campaign made by the three major unions opposing the bill (expected positive sign). The probit estimate yields the following equation.

| | Probability of supporting the 1973 trade bill |
|---|---|
| $= -0.40$ | (constant) |
| $-1.20**$ (6.79) | (party affiliation) |
| $+3.49**$ (2.62) | (import-sensitive industries) |
| $+1.16$ (1.28) | (export-oriented industries) |
| $+0.0004**$ (3.22) | (union campaign contribution) |

(The values in parentheses are the approximate t values, i.e., the ratio of the maximum likelihood estimate of the coefficient divided by the standard error. The presence of two asterisks indicates statistical significance at the 99% level.)

According to the $x^2$ test, the equation is significant at the 99 percent level. The variables relating to party affiliation, import sensitivity, and union contributions all have the expected sign and are statistically significant. The proportion of export-oriented industries in a constituency has no statistically significant influence on its Congressman's voting behavior (and even has the wrong sign). This suggests—as some earlier approaches hypothesized—that export interests are less intensive and less organized than import-competing interests, which are well aware of the losses they will incur from a lower tariff barrier. . . .

Another actor plays an important role in tariff formation: the *public administration*. This body has considerable influence on the "supply side" of tariff setting because it prepares, formulates, and implements trade bills once government and parliament have made a decision.

The activity of public bureaucrats with respect to tariffs may be analyzed with the help of the "rational" model of behavior, for example, by maximizing utility subject to constraints. The main elements in the bureaucrats' utility function may be assumed to be the prestige, power, and influence that they enjoy relative to the group of people they are officially designed to "serve," their clientele. In most cases this clientele will be located in a specific economic sector; in the case of public officials in the ministry of agriculture, for example, the clientele would be those groups with agricultural interests.

They are, moreover, proud of being able to show that they are competent to perform their job ("performance excellence"). Public bureaucrats will therefore tend to fight for the interests of "their" economic sector, and will work for tariffs and other import restrictions in order to protect it from outside competition. They will prefer to use instruments under their own control rather than to follow general rules imposed by formal laws. They will thus prefer various kinds of nontariff protection and support (subsidies) to general tariffs.

The public bureaucracy faces constraints imposed by parliament and government. However, both of these actors have little incentive to control public administration more tightly, because they depend on it to attain their own goals. In addition, political actors have much less information available to them than the public bureaucracy does, in particular with respect to the sometimes very complex issues of protection. The limited incentive of politicians to control the public administration gives bureaucrats considerable discretionary power, which they use to their own advantage. . . .

## 4. CONCLUDING REMARKS

The public choice approach to international political economy has both strengths and weaknesses, a proposition, of course, true for any approach, including that adopted by political scientists. Five points merit amplification.

First, the public choice view provides *fresh insights* into the area, in the same way that the economics-based approach illuminated general politics. This is not to claim that the approach is superior to any other; rather, that it is able to illuminate particular aspects of international political economy (while being unable to contribute much in other areas). As will become clear from these concluding remarks, the specific strengths of the public choice view are also responsible for its specific weaknesses. This is true whenever one considers the advantages of applying a new method to an already established field, such as international political economy. There is a tendency to use theoretical and empirical methods without paying sufficient attention to the particular historical and institutional conditions existing in the field of study. A quick application is tempting, because it is seemingly easy to undertake, and the shortcomings of the analysis may not be obvious. It is necessary, however, to investigate thoroughly whether particular theoretical concepts such as public goods and free riding really capture the essential features of reality.

Second, an advantage of the public choice approach to international political economy is that the analysis is based on an explicit and unified *theory of human behavior,* and on a *technical apparatus* capable of producing theoretical solutions and empirically testable propositions. This technical elegance leads, however, to a tendency to sacrifice relevance for rigor. There are already some areas of this type of international political economy where the heavily formalistic apparatus used is out of all proportion to the resulting advances in knowledge.

Third, the public choice approach concentrates on specific aspects of international political economy, making it possible to isolate and analyze relatively simple relationships. The *high degree of abstraction* allows public choice scholars to gain major insights into complex problem areas. But it also involves the danger of leaving out relevant aspects or of keeping constant (by the "ceteris paribus" assumption) variables that are so closely and importantly connected with the problem being studied that they should be considered an endogenous part of the model. While this survey has concentrated on microanalytical and partial analyses, there are approaches within public choice that attempt to provide an overall view (in particular the politico-economic models).

Fourth, the emphasis on deriving propositions that are at least in principle amenable to *empirical testing* is healthy, because it forces reality on the researcher. Econometric, or rather politicometric, analyses also provide factual knowledge about the relationships among the variables being studied. The disadvantage of this empirical orientation is that aspects difficult or impossible to measure quantatitively are easily excluded. Thus, the relationships for which data are easily available are those that tend to be studied. A common shortcoming of empirical economic research is that the operationalization of individual theories is often done in a rather cavalier way. In that respect economists could certainly learn from quantitative political scientists, as well as from other social scientists.

Empirical research has so far been predominantly concerned with the United States. This makes it more difficult to evaluate the contribution of public choice to international political economy, because it is difficult to know what part of the results is due to the public choice view, what part to the particular conditions obtaining in the United States. It is therefore important that empirical tests of the theories should be undertaken for other nations.

Fifth and finally, the public choice view is *interdisciplinary,* in a specific sense of the word: it combines the economic and political aspects of international political economy but uses a single theoretical approach. (Usually, interdisciplinarity is understood to mean that theoretical approaches have to be combined.) This has the advantage that the two areas can be fused together, but it carries the already mentioned danger that only selected aspects of their interrelationship will be treated. There can be little doubt, however, that economists engaged in research on international political economy can gain from the work done by political scientists, especially from their experience of the institutions and political processes encountered in the international sphere. Up to now, there has been relatively little contact between public choice researchers and other scholars in the field. This survey will have achieved its goal if it has convinced the reader that the opposite proposition is also true: political scientists would benefit from considering and studying the public choice approach to international political economy.

# State Power
# and the Structure
# of International Trade

Stephen D. Krasner

## Introduction

In recent years, students of international relations have multinationalized, transnationalized, bureaucratized, and transgovernmentalized the state until it has virtually ceased to exist as an analytic construct. Nowhere is that trend more apparent than in the study of the politics of international economic relations. The basic conventional assumptions have been undermined by assertions that the state is trapped by a transnational society created not by sovereigns, but by nonstate factors. Interdependence is not seen as a reflection of state policies and state choices (the perspective of balance-of-power theory), but as the result of elements beyond the control of any state or a system created by states.

This perspective is at best profoundly misleading. It may explain developments within a particular international economic structure, but cannot explain the structure itself. That structure has many institutional and behavioral manifestations. The central continuum along which it can be described is openness. International economic structures may range from complete autarky (if all states prevent movements across their borders), to complete openness (if no restrictions exist). In this paper I will present an analysis of one aspect of the international economy—the structure of international trade; that is, the degree of openness for the movement of goods as opposed to capital, labor, technology, or other factors of production.

Since the beginning of the nineteenth century, this structure has gone through several changes. These can be explained, albeit imperfectly, by state-power theory: an approach that begins with the assumption that the structure of international trade is determined by the interests and power of states acting to maximize national goals. The first step in the argument is to relate four basic state interests—aggregate national income, social stability, political power, and economic growth—to the degree of openness for the movement of goods. The relationship between these interests and openness depends upon the potential economic power of any given state. Potential economic power is operationalized in terms of the relative size and level of economic development of the state. The second step in the argument is to relate different distributions of potential power, such as multipolar and hegemonic, to different international trading structures. The most important conclusion of this theoretical analysis is that a hegemonic distribution of potential economic power is likely to result in an open trading structure. That argument is largely, although not completely, substantiated by empirical data. For a fully adequate analysis it is necessary to amend a state-power argument to take account of the impact of past state decisions on domestic social structures as well as on international economic ones. The two major organizers of the structure of trade since the beginning of the nineteenth century, Great Britain and the United States, have both been prevented from making policy amendments in line with state interests by particular societal groups whose power had been enhanced by earlier state policies.

## THE CAUSAL ARGUMENT: STATE INTERESTS, STATE POWER, AND INTERNATIONAL TRADING STRUCTURES

Neoclassical trade theory is based upon the assumption that states act to maximize their aggregate economic utility. This leads to the conclusion that maximum global welfare and Pareto optimality are achieved under free trade. While particular countries might better their situations through protectionism, economic theory has generally looked askance at such policies. In his seminal article on the optimal tariff, Harry Johnson was at pains to point out that the imposition of successive optimal tariffs could lead both trading partners to a situation in which they were worse off than under competitive conditions. Neoclassical theory recognizes that trade regulations can also be used to correct domestic distortions and to promote infant industries, but these are exceptions or temporary departures from policy conclusions that lead logically to the support of free trade.

Historical experience suggests that policy makers are dense, or that the assumptions of the conventional argument are wrong. Free trade has hardly been the norm. Stupidity is not a very interesting analytic category. An alternative approach to explaining international trading structures is to assume that states seek a broad range of goals. At least four major state interests affected by the structure of international trade can be identified. They are: political power, aggregate national income, economic growth, and social stability. The way in which each of these goals is affected by the degree of openness depends upon the potential economic power of the state as defined by its relative size and level of development.

Let us begin with aggregate national income because it is most straightforward. Given the exceptions noted above, conventional neoclassical theory demonstrates that the greater the degree of openness in the international trading system, the greater the level of aggregate economic income. This conclusion applies to all states regardless of their size or relative level of development. The static economic benefits of openness are, however, generally inversely related to size. Trade gives small states relatively more welfare benefits than it gives large ones. Empirically, small states have higher ratios of trade to national product. They do not have the generous factor endowments or potential for national economies of scale that are enjoyed by larger—particularly continental—states.

The impact of openness on social stability runs in the opposite direction. Greater openness exposes the domestic economy to the exigencies of the world market. That implies a higher level of factor movements than in a closed economy, because domestic production patterns must adjust to changes in international prices. Social instability is thereby increased, since there is friction in moving factors, particularly labor, from one sector to another. The impact will be stronger in small states than in large, and in relatively less developed than in more developed ones. Large states are less involved in the international economy: a smaller percentage of their total factor endowment is affected by the international market at any given level of openness. More developed states are better able to adjust factors: skilled workers can more easily be moved from one kind of production to another than can unskilled laborers or peasants. Hence social stability is, *ceteris paribus*, inversely related to openness, but the deleterious consequences of exposure to the international trading system are mitigated by larger size and greater economic development.

The relationship between political power and the international trading structure can be analyzed in terms of the relative opportunity costs of closure for trading partners. The higher the relative cost of closure, the weaker the political position of the state. Hirschman has argued that this cost can be measured in terms of direct income losses and the adjustment costs of reallocating factors. These will be smaller for large states and for relatively more developed states. Other things being equal, utility costs will be less for large states because they generally have a smaller proportion of their economy engaged in the international economic system. Reallocation costs will be less for more advanced states because their factors are more mobile. Hence a state that is relatively large and more developed will find its political power enhanced by an open system because its opportunity costs of closure are less. The large state can use the threat to alter the system to secure economic or noneconomic objectives. Historically, there is one important exception to this generalization—the oil-exporting states. The level of reserves for some of these states, particularly Saudi Arabia, has reduced the economic opportunity costs of closure to a very low level despite their lack of development.

The relationship between international economic structure and economic growth is elusive. For small states, economic growth has generally been empirically associated with openness. Exposure to the international system makes possible a much more efficient allocation of resources. Openness also probably furthers the rate of growth of large countries with relatively advanced technologies because they do not need to protect infant industries and can take advantage of expanded world markets. In the long term, however, openness for capital and technology, as well as goods, may hamper the growth of large, developed countries by diverting resources from the domestic economy, and by providing potential competitors with the knowledge needed to develop their own industries. Only by maintaining its technological lead and continually developing new industries can even a very large state escape the undesired consequences of an entirely open economic system. For medium-size states, the relationship between international trading structure and growth is impossible to specify definitively, either theoretically or empirically. On the one hand, writers from the mercantilists through the American protectionists and the German historical school, and more recently analysts of *dependencia,* have argued that an entirely open system can undermine a state's effort to develop, and even lead to underdevelopment. On the other hand, adherents of more conventional neoclassical positions have maintained that exposure to international competition spurs economic transformation. The evidence is not yet in. All that can confidently be said is that openness furthers the economic growth of small states and of large ones so long as they maintain their technological edge.

**FROM STATE PREFERENCES TO INTERNATIONAL TRADING STRUCTURES.** The next step in this argument is to relate particular distributions of potential economic power, defined by the size and level of development of individual states, to the structure of the international trading system, defined in terms of openness.

Let us consider a system composed of a large number of small, highly developed states. Such a system is likely to lead to an open international trading structure. The aggregate income and economic growth of each state are increased by an open system. The social instability produced by exposure to international competition is mitigated by the factor mobility made possible by higher levels of development. There is no loss of political power from openness because the costs of closure are symmetrical for all members of the system.

Now let us consider a system composed of a few very large, but unequally developed states. Such a distribution of potential economic power is likely to lead to a closed structure. Each state could increase its income through a more open system, but the gains would be modest. Openness would create more social instability in the less developed countries. The rate of growth for more backward areas might be frustrated, while that of the more advanced ones would be enhanced. A more open structure would leave the less developed states in a politically more vulnerable position, because their greater factor rigidity would mean a higher relative cost of closure. Because of these disadvantages, large but relatively less developed states are unlikely to accept an open trading structure. More advanced states cannot, unless they are militarily much more powerful, force large backward countries to accept openness.

Finally, let us consider a hegemonic system—one in which there is a single state that is much larger and relatively more advanced than its trading partners. The costs and benefits of openness are not symmetrical for all members of the system. The hegemonic state will have a preference for an open structure. Such a structure increases its aggregate national income. It also increases its rate of growth during its ascendancy—that is, when its relative size and technological lead are increasing. Further, an open structure increases its political power, since the opportunity costs of closure are least for a large and developed state. The social instability resulting from exposure to the international system is mitigated by the hegemonic power's relatively low level of involvement in the international economy, and the mobility of its factors.

What of the other members of a hegemonic system? Small states are likely to opt for openness because the advantages in terms of aggregate income and growth are so great, and their political power is bound to be restricted regardless of what they do. The reaction of medium-size states is hard to predict; it depends at least in part on the way in which the hegemonic power utilizes its resources. The potentially dominant state has symbolic, economic, and military capabilities that can be used to entice or compel others to accept an open trading structure.

At the symbolic level, the hegemonic state stands as an example of how economic development can be achieved. Its policies may be emulated, even if they are inappropriate for other states. Where there are very dramatic asymmetries, military power can be used to coerce weaker states into an open structure. Force is not, however, a very efficient means for changing economic policies, and it is unlikely to be employed against medium-size states.

Most importantly, the hegemonic state can use its economic resources to create an open structure. In terms of positive incentives, it can offer access to its large domestic market and to its relatively cheap exports. In terms of negative ones, it can withhold foreign grants and engage in competition, potentially ruinous for the weaker state, in third-country markets. The size and economic robustness of the hegemonic state also enable it to provide the confidence necessary for a stable international monetary system, and its currency can offer the liquidity needed for an increasingly open system.

In sum, openness is most likely to occur during periods when a hegemonic state is in its ascendancy. Such a state has the interest and the resources to create a structure characterized by lower tariffs, rising trade proportions, and less regionalism. There are other distributions of potential power where openness is likely, such as a system composed of many small, highly developed states. But even here, that potential might not be realized because of the problems of creating confidence in a monetary system where adequate liquidity would have to be provided by a negotiated international reserve asset or a group of national currencies. Finally, it is unlikely that very large states, particularly at unequal levels of development, would accept open trading relations.

## THE DEPENDENT VARIABLE:
## DESCRIBING THE STRUCTURE OF
## THE INTERNATIONAL TRADING SYSTEM

The structure of international trade has both behavioral and institutional attributes. The degree of openness can be described both by the *flow* of goods and by the *policies* that are followed by states with respect to trade barriers and international payments. The two are not unrelated, but they do not coincide perfectly.

In common usage, the focus of attention has been upon institutions. Openness is associated with those historical periods in which tariffs were substantially lowered: the third quarter of the nineteenth century and the period since the Second World War.

Tariffs alone, however, are not an adequate indicator of structure. They are hard to operationalize quantitatively. Tariffs do not have to be high to be effective. If cost functions are nearly identical, even low tariffs can prevent trade. Effective tariff rates may be much higher than nominal ones. Nontariff barriers to trade, which are not easily compared across states, can substitute for duties. An undervalued exchange rate can protect domestic markets from foreign competition. Tariff levels alone cannot describe the structure of international trade.

A second indicator, and one which is behavioral rather than institutional, is trade proportions—the ratios of trade to national income for different states. Like tariff levels, these involve describing the system in terms of an agglomeration of national tendencies. A period in which these ratios are increasing across time for most states can be described as one of increasing openness.

A third indicator is the concentration of trade within regions composed of states at different levels of development. The degree of such regional encapsulation is determined not so much by comparative advantage (because relative factor endowments would allow almost any backward area to trade with almost any developed one), but by political choices or dictates. Large states, attempting to protect themselves from the vagaries of a global system, seek to maximize their interests by creating regional blocs. Openness in the global economic system has in effect meant greater trade among the leading industrial states. Periods of closure are associated with the encapsulation of certain advanced states within regional systems shard with certain less developed areas.

A description of the international trading system involves, then, an exercise that is comparative rather than absolute. A period when tariffs are falling, trade proportions are rising, and regional trading patterns are becoming less extreme will be defined as one in which the structure is becoming more open.

**TARIFF LEVELS.** In sum, after 1820 there was a general trend toward lower tariffs (with the notable exception of the United States), which culminated between 1860 and 1879; higher tariffs from 1879 through the interwar years, with dramatic increases in the 1930's; and less protectionism from 1945 through the conclusion of the Kennedy Round in 1967.

**TRADE PROPORTIONS.** With the exception of one period, ratios of trade to aggregate economic activity followed the same general pattern as tariff levels. Trade proportions increased from the early part of the nineteenth century to about 1880. Between 1880 and 1900 there was a decrease, sharper if measured in current prices than constant ones, but apparent in both statistical series for most countries. Between 1900 and 1913—and here is the exception from the tariff pattern—there was a marked increase in the ratio of trade to aggregate economic activity. This trend brought trade proportions to levels that have generally not been reattained. During the 1920's and 1930's the importance of trade in national economic activity declined. After the Second World War it increased.

**REGIONAL TRADING PATTERNS.** The final indicator of the degree of openness of the global trading system is regional bloc concentration. There is a natural affinity for some states to trade with others because of geographical propinquity or comparative advantage. In general, however, a system in which there are fewer manifestations of trading within given blocs, particularly among specific groups of more and less developed states, is a more open one. Over time there have been extensive changes in trading patterns between particular areas of the world whose relative factor endowments have remained largely the same.

## The Independent Variable:
## Describing the Distribution of
## Potential Economic Power among States

Analysts of international relations have an almost pro forma set of variables designed to show the distribution of potential power in the international *political* system. It includes such factors as gross national product, per capita income, geographical position, and size of armed forces. A similar set of indicators can be presented for the international *economic* system.

Statistics are available over a long time period for per capita income, aggregate size, share of world trade, and share of world investment. They demonstrate that, since the beginning of the nineteenth century, there have been two first-rank economic powers in the world economy—Britain and the

United States. The United States passed Britain in aggregate size sometime in the middle of the nineteenth century and, in the 1880's, became the largest producer of manufactures. America's lead was particularly marked in technologically advanced industries turning out sewing machines, harvesters, cash registers, locomotives, steam pumps, telephones, and petroleum. Until the First World War, however, Great Britain had a higher per capita income, a greater share of world trade, and a greater share of world investment than any other state. The peak of British ascendance occurred around 1880, when Britain's relative per capita income, share of world trade, and share of investment flows reached their highest levels. Britain's potential dominance in 1880 and 1900 was particularly striking in the international economic system, where her share of trade and foreign investment was about twice as large as that of any other state.

It was only after the First World War that the United States became relatively larger and more developed in terms of all four indicators. This potential dominance reached new and dramatic heights between 1945 and 1960. Since then, the relative position of the United States has declined, bringing it quite close to West Germany, its nearest rival, in terms of per capita income and share of world trade. The devaluations of the dollar that have taken place since 1972 are reflected in a continuation of this downward trend for income and aggregate size.

In sum, Britain was the world's most important trading state from the period after the Napoleonic Wars until 1913. Her relative position rose until about 1880 and fell thereafter. The United States became the largest and most advanced state in economic terms after the First World War, but did not equal the relative share of world trade and investment achieved by Britain in the 1880's until after the Second World War.

## TESTING THE ARGUMENT

The continuation that hegemony leads to a more open trading structure is fairly well, but not perfectly, confirmed by the empirical evidence presented in the preceding sections. The argument explains the periods 1820 to 1879, 1880 to 1900, and 1945 to 1960. It does not fully explain those from 1900 to 1913, 1919 to 1939, or 1960 to the present.

In sum, although the general pattern of the structure of international trade conforms with the predictions of a state-power argument—two periods of openness separated by one of closure—corresponding to periods of rising British and American hegemony and an interregnum, the whole pattern is out of phase. British commitment to openness continued long after Britain's position had declined. American commitment to openness did not begin until well after the United States had become the world's leading economic power and has continued during a period of relative American decline. The state-power argument needs to be amended to take these delayed reactions into account.

## Amending the Argument

The structure of the international trading system does not move in lockstep with changes in the distribution of potential power among states. Systems are initiated and ended, not as a state-power theory would predict, but close assessments of the interests of the state at every given moment, but by external events—usually cataclysmic ones. The closure that began in 1879 coincided with the Great Depression of the last part of the nineteenth century. The final dismantling of the nineteenth-century international economic system was not precipitated by a change in British trade or monetary policy, but by the First World War and the Depression. The potato famine of the 1840's prompted abolition of the Corn Laws; and the United States did not assume the mantle of world leadership until the world had been laid bare by six years of total war. Some catalytic external event seems necessary to move states to dramatic policy initiatives in line with state interests.

Once the policies have been adopted, they are pursued until a new crisis demonstrates that they are no longer feasible. States become locked in by the impact of prior choices on their domestic political structures. The British decision to opt for openness in 1846 corresponded with state interests. It also strengthened the position of industrial and financial groups over time, because they had the opportunity to operate in an international system that furthered their objectives. That system eventually undermined the position of British farmers, a group that would have supported protectionism if it had survived. Once entrenched, Britain's export industries, and more importantly the City of London, resisted policies of closure. In the interwar years, the British rentier class insisted on restoring the prewar parity of the pound—a decision that placed enormous deflationary pressures on the domestic economy—because they wanted to protect the value of their investments.

Institutions created during periods of rising ascendancy remained in operation when they were no longer appropriate. For instance, the organization of British banking in the nineteenth century separated domestic and foreign operations. The Court of Directors of the Bank of England was dominated by international banking houses. Their decisions about British monetary policy were geared toward the international economy. Under a different institutional arrangement more attention might have been given after 1900 to the need to revitalize the domestic economy. The British state was unable to free itself from the domestic structures that its earlier policy decisions had created, and continued to follow policies appropriate for a rising hegemony long after Britain's star had begun to fall.

Similarly, earlier policies in the United States begat social structures and institutional arrangements that trammeled state policy. After protecting import-competing industries for a century, the United States was unable in the 1920's to opt for more open policies, even though state interests would have been furthered thereby. Institutionally, decisions about tariff reductions were taken primarily in congressional committees, giving virtually any group seeking protection easy access to the decision-making process. When there were conflicts among groups, they were resolved by raising the levels of protection for everyone. It was only after the cataclysm of the depression that the decision-making processes for trade policy were changed. The Presidency, far more insulated from the entreaties of particular societal groups than congressional committees, was then given more power. Furthermore, the American commercial banking system was unable to assume the burden of regulating the international economy during the 1920's. American institutions were geared toward the domestic economy. Only after the Second World War, and in fact not until the late 1950's, did American banks fully develop the complex institutional structures commensurate with the dollar's role in the international monetary system.

Having taken the critical decisions that created an open system after 1945, the American Government is unlikely to change its policy until it confronts some external event that it cannot control, such as a worldwide deflation, drought in the great plains, or the malicious use of petrodollars. . . .

The structure of international trade changes in fits and starts; it does not flow smoothly with the redistribution of potential state power. Nevertheless, it is the power and the policies of states that create order where there would otherwise be chaos or at best a Lockian state of nature. The existence of various transnational, multinational, transgovernmental, and other nonstate actors that have riveted scholarly attention in recent years can only be understood within the context of a broader structure that ultimately rests upon the power and interests of states, shackled though they may be by the societal consequences of their own past decisions.

# POWER POLITICS AND INTERNATIONAL TRADE

Joanne Gowa and Edward D. Mansfield

Here, we argue that what has become the standard prisoner's dilemma representation neglects the most critical aspect of free-trade agreements in the anarchic international system, namely, their security externalities. We consider these external effects explicitly. In order to do so, we construct and analyze a simple game-theoretic model. The results of this analysis demonstrate that tariff games between allies differ systematically from those played between actual or potential adversaries.

These differences imply that free trade is more likely within, rather than across, political-military alliances. However, our analysis also suggests that the evolutionary prospects of alliances vary: those that are the products of bipolar systems are more likely to evolve into free-trade coalitions than are their multipolar counterparts. Less credible exit threats and clearer responsibilities for alliance stability explain the advantage of a bipolar system.

We test this argument using data drawn from an 80-year period beginning in 1905. The empirical analysis supports our argument. It demonstrates that alliances have a direct, statistically significant, and large effect upon bilateral trade. Moreover, it shows that on average, alliances have a much stronger effect on trade in a bipolar than in a multipolar world.

## POWER, TRADE, AND TARIFFS

Unlike many arguments about the use of economic statecraft, ours is cast at the macroeconomic rather than at the microeconomic level. In other words, the argument we advance here is *not* about, for example, attempts to use economic statecraft to embargo exports of particular products or to inhibit the development of technologically advanced industries in other countries. Instead, it is an argument that is based upon the effect of free trade on the real income and power potential of states.

We argue that the play of power politics is an inexorable element of any agreement to open international markets because trade produces security externalities. These externalities arise because the source of gains from trade is the increased efficiency with which domestic resources can be employed. This increased efficiency itself frees economic resources for military uses. As a consequence, trade enhances the potential military power of any country that engages in it.

The anarchic structure of the international system, in turn, compels its constituent states to attend closely to the potential military power of both allies and potential or actual adversaries. It does so because the absence of any supranational authority in the international system enables a state to resort to force at any time to achieve its goals. The probability that a state will do so depends in part upon its power, which, in turn, depends partly upon its real income.

As a consequence, the real income gains that motivate free trade are also the source of the security externalities that can either impede or facilitate it: trade with an adversary produces a security diseconomy; trade with an ally produces a positive externality. In either case, agreements to open international markets create a divergence between the private and social costs of trade. A socially suboptimal level of trade results, suggesting that government intervention in trade can be welfare-enhancing for the nation as a whole.

## OPTIMAL TARIFF GAMES

Successful intervention in trade to correct the security externalities associated with it depends upon the ability of a country to affect the real income of the state which is its target. Although any tariff will distort resource allocation in the target country and therefore decrease its real income, it will do so without imposing net costs on the home country only if the latter can affect its terms of trade.

Thus, in the absence of the requisite market power, a tariff will impose costs primarily upon the state that levies it. In its presence, a tariff will allow a state to increase its own real income at its adversary's expense. If a state can affect world prices, then, it can use a tariff to narrow the gap between the private and social costs of trade. Thus, a tariff can be welfare-superior to a policy of free trade for a state in an anarchic international political system.

This argument is, of course, a variant of the traditional optimal tariff argument. Its novelty inheres in the two conclusions . . . (1) tariff games between allies differ systematically from those played between adversaries;

and (2) intraalliance free trade is more likely in a bipolar than in a multipolar system.

**THE INFLUENCE OF POLARITY.** While this model suggests that all alliances will influence trade barriers, it seems clear that alliances have exerted a stronger effect after, than before, World War II. Inspection of the incentive compatibility constraint that applies to the intraallied tariff game suggests one explanation of this difference. All other things being equal, the extent to which allies trade freely with each other depends upon the discount factor, $\delta$. The discount factor is a function of the risk of exit, which, in turn, is a function of systematic polarity.

The risk of exit is the threat that an ally will abandon an existing alliance to join an alternative one. For several reasons, this risk is higher in multipolar than in bipolar systems. First, while bipolar coalitions are the products largely of system structure, alliances in a multipolar system are the results of choice among several possible alternatives.

Second, in a bipolar system, realignment is impossible for either pole. By default, alliance stability is also the exclusive responsibility of each. Neither can expect any other state to prevent the defection of an ally from within its bloc. In a multipolar system, however, the interest in preserving alliance stability can be distributed across more than one pole. As a consequence, alliance stability can become problematic, as each pole seeks to transfer the burden of maintaining the alliance to another.

The implications of different exit risks for trade are clear. Any great-power member of a coalition in a multipolar world has strong incentives to discriminate among its allies in terms of its investment in them, because its allies confront divergent opportunity costs of exit. In contrast, the incentive to discriminate in a bipolar world is much weaker, since allies are much more uniformly and securely locked into coalitions. In a bipolar world, in other words, the gains from trade can be more easily privatized. As a consequence, investments in allies in a multipolar system are likely to be expressed in the form of discriminatory trade preferences; in a bipolar system, free trade is the more likely outcome.

In short, because the risk of exit is lower in a bipolar than in a multipolar system, the security externalities of any free-trade agreement are more likely to remain internalized within the alliances of the former than in those of the latter. As a result, allies in a multipolar system will tend to discount the future benefits accruing from open markets among them more heavily than will their bipolar counterparts. The greater stability of bipolar coalitions allows the value of future benefits to approximate present benefits more closely.

For any given structure of payoffs, then, free trade is more likely to emerge within the alliances of a bipolar than in those of a multipolar system. It is not surprising, therefore, that the effect of alliances on trade seems to have been greater after rather than before World War II. We shall now subject this and our more general hypothesis about the impact of alliances on trade to a systematic empirical test.

## THE RESEARCH DESIGN

Ideally, we would include in our sample all major powers and their allies. However, data limitations led us to focus on trade relations among the United States, Great Britain, France, Italy, Germany, the Soviet Union, and Japan during the period from 1905 to 1985. Though this is clearly a limited sample, these states include most of the major powers in the international system during this period. Moreover, since we expect the impact of alliances on trade to be most pronounced in cases of alliances involving major powers, this analysis will offer an important, though preliminary, test of our model.

We also expect that bilateral alliances will affect trade flows more strongly than will multilateral alliances. While the *aggregate* flow of trade across a group of more than two states may be higher when these states are engaged in an alliance than when they are not, this need not imply that *all* bilateral trade flows among these states will be higher under these circumstances. For example, the existence of an alliance among states A, B, C, and D would be expected to produce an increase in the total trade among these states. This, however, would not necessarily lead to an increase in bilateral trade between A and B. Indeed, A and B may engage in less commerce during the course of this alliance than in the absence of the alliance (although they would be expected to offset this by trading more with C and/or D). But if our argument holds, bilateral alliances should be directly related to bilateral trade. Under these circumstances, the effects of alliances on aggregate intraalliance trade can be assessed directly by examining trade flows between the two partners.

## THE MODEL

In this section, we develop a simple model of the relationship between alliances and bilateral trade. It is clear that any analysis of this sort should incorporate economic, as well as political, determinants of trade. Among economists, gravity models of bilateral trade flows have been widely used.

In order to analyze the economic determinants of bilateral trade, we use a well-known variant of this model, which includes the gross national product (GNP) and the population of both the importer and the exporter, as well as the geographic distance between the two states. Consistent with previous research based on this model, we expect that the nominal value of bilateral trade will be directly related to the nominal GNP of both the importer and the exporter and inversely related to the population of both the importer and exporter and to the geographic distance between them.

In addition to GNP, population, and distance, we include two variables related to alliances in our model: one indicating whether a bilateral alliance exists between the trading partners and one indicating whether a multilateral alliance exists between these states. Finally, because we expect interstate wars to reduce trade among the belligerents, we also include a variable that indicates whether or not the importer and exporter are at war.

Hence, our model is

$$\log X_{ij(t)} = \log A + B_1 \log Y_{i(t-1)} + B_2 \log Y_{j(t-1)}$$
$$+ B_3 \log P_{i(t-1)} + B_4 \log P_{j(t-1)}$$
$$+ B_5 \log D_{ij(t-1)} + B_6 \log BA_{ij(t-1)}$$
$$+ B_7 \log MA_{ij(t-1)} + B_8 \log War_{ij(t-1)} + \log z_{ij}, \qquad (1)$$

where $\log X_{ij(t)}$ is the natural logarithm of the nominal value of exports (expressed in U.S. dollars) by state i to state j in year t, $\log Y_{i(t-1)}$ is the natural logarithm of the nominal GNP (expressed in U.S. dollars) of state i in year $t - 1$, $\log Y_{j(t-1)}$ is the natural logarithm of the nominal GNP (expressed in U.S. dollars) of state j in year $t - 1$, $\log P_{i(t-1)}$ is the natural logarithm of the population of state i in year $t - 1$, $\log P_{j(t-1)}$ is the natural logarithm of the population of state j in year $t - 1$, $\log D_{ij(t-1)}$ is the natural logarithm of the geographic distance between states i and j in year t, $\log BA_{ij(t-1)}$ is a dummy variable that equals 1 if an alliance exists between states i and j in year $t - 1$ that is comprised of no members except i and j (and 0 otherwise), $\log MA_{ij(t-1)}$ is a dummy variable that equals 1 if an alliance exists between states i and j in year $t - 1$ that includes at least one additional member (and 0 otherwise), $\log War_{ij(t-1)}$ is a dummy variable that equals 1 if states i and j are engaged in a war in year $t - 1$ (and 0 otherwise), and $\log z_{ij}$ is an error term. Note that in antilogarithmic form all dummy variables in this model take on values of e (the base of the natural logarithms) and one; the natural logarithms of these variables, therefore, take on values of one and zero. Since it is generally assumed that these variables exert a lagged effect on the value of exports and in order to avoid problems of simultaneity, we assume a lag of one year in equation 1 for each variable. The log-linear specification of this model is used because it is consistent with many previous studies of trade that have used gravity models and because it has number of advantages relative to a linear specification.

Since we are interested in the relationship between alliances and trade at given points in time, as well as over time, equation 1 is estimated for a series of cross sections, beginning in 1905. Our analysis begins with 1905 (year t) because complete data for all of the independent variables in equation 1 are not available prior to 1904 (year $t - 1$). After 1905, the parameters in equation 1 are estimated for the first year of each subsequent ten-year interval. However, we do not estimate the model during World Wars I and II, since trade data are often not available for these years. Further, equation 1 is not estimated during the late 1940s because the occupation of Germany and Japan precluded both states from making autonomous decisions about trade policies or alliance partners. As a result, there are some cases in which the intervals are not ten years in length.

## TABLE 1 — REGRESSION OF EXPORTS ON GNP, POPULATION, DISTANCE AND WAR, 1905–85

| Parameter | Period of Multipolarity | | | | | Period of Bipolarity | | | |
|---|---|---|---|---|---|---|---|---|---|
| | 1905 | 1913 | 1920 | 1930 | 1938 | 1955 | 1965 | 1975 | 1985 |
| Intercept | -4.57 (7.88) | -8.79 (9.99) | 57.21*** (14.74) | 7.39 (5.06) | 12.44* (6.19) | 34.81*** (8.19) | 5.69 (5.17) | 6.29 (4.25) | 12.14** (4.88) |
| log GNP$_i$ | .95*** (.17) | 1.68*** (.23) | 2.78*** (.34) | 1.53*** (.14) | 1.67*** (.20) | 1.12*** (.26) | .28 (.26) | .83*** (.20) | .96*** (.32) |
| log GNP$_j$ | 1.10*** (.18) | .90*** (.25) | 2.17*** (.27) | 1.25*** (.14) | 1.57*** (.22) | .93*** (.25) | .44** (.26) | .55*** (.21) | 1.19*** (.32) |
| log Population$_i$ | -.02 (.33) | -.95*** (.35) | -4.10*** (.83) | -1.21*** (.23) | -1.68*** (.34) | -1.88*** (.49) | .14 (.39) | -.68*** (.26) | -1.13*** (.42) |
| log Population$_j$ | -1.21*** (.27) | -.92*** (.31) | -4.83*** (.59) | -1.74*** (.23) | -2.27*** (.32) | -1.82*** (.49) | -.38 (.39) | -.45** (.25) | -1.42*** (.40) |
| log Distance$_{ij}$ | -.33*** (.09) | -.06 (.10) | .27 (.13) | -.35*** (.06) | -.06 (.09) | -.01 (.09) | -.12* (.06) | -.23*** (.05) | -.28*** (.07) |
| log Bilat. alliance$_{ij}$ | -.37 (.31) | -.57 (.36) | .20 (.77) | 1.04*** (.42) | -.30 (.40) | 3.02*** (.55) | 2.58*** (.39) | 2.07*** (.32) | 2.10*** (.43) |
| log Multilat. alliance$_{ij}$ | -.61 (.55) | -.31 (.72) | .96*** (.39) | —[a] | .48* (.35) | .86*** (.46) | 1.65*** (.33) | .99*** (.18) | .84*** (.26) |
| log War$_{ij}$ | -7.12*** (.61) | —[b] | 1.55 (.72) | —[b] | —[b] | —[b] | —[b] | —[b] | —[b] |
| Adjusted R² | .92 | .71 | .83 | .86 | .80 | .78 | .82 | .82 | .80 |
| N | 39 | 39 | 37[c] | 40 | 37[d] | 41 | 40 | 41 | 41 |

*Note:* Entries are unstandardized regression coefficients with standard errors in parentheses. Years shown are year t in equation 1. For each year, there are 42 observations minus the number of outliers.

[a] No multilateral alliances existed among the major powers in 1929.

[b] No wars between major powers were conducted during these years.

[c] No data on the Soviet Union's exports to Germany are available for 1920.

[d] No data on Italian exports to the Soviet Union are available for 1938.

*p ≤ .10 (one-tailed test); intercept p ≤ .10 (two-tailed test).

**p ≤ .05 (one-tailed test); intercept p ≤ .05 (two-tailed test).

ESTIMATES OF THE PARAMETERS. Ordinary least squares estimates of the parameters in equation 1 are presented in Table 1. In each regression, at least one outlier was identified. The results in Table 1 are estimated without these observations. However, it should be noted that very little difference exists between the results with these observations included and the results presented in Table 1.

These findings indicate that on average, our model explains over 80% of the variation in the value of exports and that the overall fit of the model differs little across the nine years that are analyzed. Our results also indicate that the regression coefficients of GNP, population, geographic distance, and war usually point in the expected directions and are statistically significant. First, the regression coefficient of log $Y_i$ is positive in nine cases and statistically significant in eight instances; and the regression coefficient of log $Y_j$ is positive and statistically significant in all nine cases. Second, the regression coefficient of log $P_i$ is negative in eight cases and statistically significant in seven instances; and the regression coefficient of log $P_j$ is negative in nine cases and statistically significant in eight instances. Third, the regression coefficient of log $D_{ij}$ is negative in eight cases and statistically significant in five instances. Finally, the regression coefficient of log $War_{ij}$ is negative and statistically significant in one out of two cases.

These results also confirm the hypothesis that alliances are directly related to the value of exports. The regression coefficient of log $BA_{ij}$ is positive in six out of nine cases and statistically significant in five instances; and the regression coefficient of log $MA_{ij}$ is positive and statistically significant in six out of eight cases. Further, the mean of the nine regression coefficients of log $BA_{ij}$ is about 1.09 and (assuming that these regression coefficients are statistically independent) the standard error of the mean is about .15. The mean of the eight regression coefficients of log $MA_{ij}$ is about .61, and the standard error of the mean is about .16. On average, therefore, the relationships between bilateral alliances and multilateral alliances, on the one hand, and bilateral trade on the other seem to be direct and statistically significant.

Moreover, the quantitative impacts of both bilateral and multilateral alliances on the predicted value of bilateral trade are substantial. Even if the mean of the regression coefficients of log $BA_{ij}$ was two standard errors less than 1.09, a change from the absence of a bilateral alliance to the existence of such an alliance would more than double the predicted value of exports. And even if the mean of the regression coefficients of log $MA_{ij}$ was two standard errors less than .61, a change from the absence of a multilateral alliance to the existence of such an alliance would increase the predicted value of exports by more than one-third.

As expected, the system's structure influences the strength and the magnitude of the effect of alliances on trade. The means of the regression coefficients of log $BA_{ij}$ and log $MA_{ij}$ have been substantially larger during periods of bipolarity than during periods of multipolarity; and the differences between these means are statistically significant (for log $BA_{ij}$, t = 6.26, $p < .005$; for log $MA_{ij}$, t = 2.34, $p < .05$). Thus, our results indicate that on average, the magnitude of the effects of alliances on trade has been considerably more pronounced during bipolar periods than during multipolar periods.

There is also some support for our hypothesis that bilateral alliances exert larger effects on trade than multilateral alliances, although the evidence is weaker than expected. When all years in Table 1 are considered, the mean of the regression coefficients of log $BA_{ij}$ is almost twice as large as the mean of the regression coefficients of log $MA_{ij}$, but the difference between these means is not statistically significant. When only bipolar periods are examined, the mean of the regression coefficients of log $BA_{ij}$ is substantially larger than the mean of the regression coefficients of log $MA_{ij}$, and the difference between these means is statistically significant ($t = 4.50$, $p < .005$). But when only multipolar periods are analyzed, the mean of the regression coefficients of log $MA_{ij}$ is somewhat larger than the mean of the regression coefficients of log $BA_{ij}$; and, although the difference between these means is not statistically significant, this result is clearly at odds with our hypothesis. Hence, the extent to which our hypothesis concerning the effects of different types of alliances on trade is supported seems to depend in large measure on system structure.

## THE ROBUSTNESS OF THE RESULTS

It is possible that including the Soviet Union in our sample may have exaggerated the impact of alliances on trade (in Table 1). The Soviet Union had both a command and a relatively autarkic economy during most of the twentieth century. It also concluded few alliances with other major powers in our sample after World War I. Thus, the strength of the observed relationship between alliances and trade might be due to the composition of our sample. In order to determine whether this is the case, ordinary least squares estimates of the parameters in equation 1 were obtained for those dyads that did not involve the Soviet Union.

On average, therefore, the relationships between both bilateral and multilateral alliances and bilateral trade continue to be direct and statistically significant. It should also be noted that on average, the magnitude of the effects of bilateral alliances on trade continues to be larger than that of multilateral alliances and that on average, the magnitude of the effects of both bilateral and multilateral alliances on bilateral trade continues to be significantly larger during periods of bipolarity than during periods of multipolarity.

## CONCLUSION

We have argued that a free-trade policy can be suboptimal for states in an anarchic international system. Under some conditions, an effort to induce trade to follow the flag can be welfare-enhancing. The results of our empirical analysis support the implications of our argument about the relationship between alliances and trade. They show that alliances exert a direct, statistically significant, and large effect on bilateral trade flows. They also show that the effects of alliances vary. Bilateral alliances sometimes influence trade flows more strongly than do multilateral alliances; and alliances embedded in bipolar systems have stronger effects upon trade than do their counterparts in multipolar systems.

The argument we develop here also suggests that there may be other sources of cross-alliance variation that our empirical analysis could not detect. One plausible source is differences across alliances with respect to the gains that would accrue from free trade and its associated externalities. According to the tenets of the Heckscher-Ohlin-Samuelson model of international trade, for example, gains from trade and differences in relative factor endowments are directly related. Thus, this model implies that allies with very different factor endowments will confront stronger incentives to trade freely with each other than will allies with more similar endowments.

The weight a state assigns to its ally will also affect the magnitude of the security externality that free trade generates. Cross-alliance variations in $w_{ij}$ might occur, for example, because of differences in the probability of war, the technology of weapons production, or the need (if any) for an ex ante coordination of forces. In addition, the magnitude of the external effects of trade depends upon the transaction costs of opening borders to trade. These costs might vary as a consequence, for example, of whether an alliance has been given formal institutional expression.

Because of these and other possible sources of cross-alliance variation, it is clear that we have not offered an exhaustive analysis of the impact of alliances on trade. Nonetheless, we have established the conditions under which it makes sense for states to attempt to tie trade to the flag. In addition, we show that alliances have influenced bilateral trade flows not only after, but also before, 1945. In doing so, we suggest that the end of the Cold War will precipitate changes in the play of power politics both in the political–military sphere and in the pattern of international trade.

# Why State Subsidies? Evidence from European Community Countries, 1981–1986

Nikolaos Zahariadis

State subsidies have long been the subject of international controversy. The issue is particularly contentious in Europe where steps toward regional integration and the single European market have pitted national governments against each other and against supranational authorities. What elevates the significance of the European case is that under European Community (EC) guidelines most subsidies are not permitted. Yet national governments do not always follow EC rules. British steel makers, for example, bitterly complained to EC authorities about heavy state subsidies paid by the Spanish, French, and German governments to their steel and coal producers. Indeed, the issue of subsidies is so important that controlling them has become "one of the Community's policy priorities."

Why, then, do national governments continue with varying zeal to subsidize substantial portions of their economies? It is important to understand why policies are adopted because until we do so, claims Nobel laureate George Stigler, "we will be poorly equipped to give useful advice on how to change those policies." In this article I try to explain why EC members disburse state subsidies. Beyond exploring policy concerns over the objectives of state subsidies, I am also interested in enhancing the theoretical understanding of economic policy making and its implications for European integration.

## CONTENDING PERSPECTIVES ON STATE SUBSIDIES

Part of the lack of empirical focus on the subject of state subsidies stems from the paucity of comparable cross-national data. For reasons ranging from commercial to national security, governments have refused to publish such information with any consistency or transparency.

Nevertheless, recent work by the EC Commission has partially remedied this situation. Hence, this study is an exploratory attempt to map out the theoretical terrain by empirically testing several competing explanations of why European governments allocate state subsidies.

One argument for subsidies focuses on socioeconomic conditions. National governments, according to this explanation, provide state subsidies to fight unemployment because they fear the social upheavals and political repercussions likely to result from high unemployment (Metcalf, 1984). Indeed, studies have routinely corroborated the strong impact of unemployment rates on the popularity of governments. Governments can obviously ill-afford not to pay attention to unemployment since it affects their electoral chances. A common strategy, therefore, is to use subsidies as a stimulus to aid those industries or regions where job losses are feared to be the highest in an effort to alleviate social adversity, provide a minimal level of income, and cash in on the potential political dividends at election time. As Denton forcefully argues, "without doubt the one problem above all of these in provoking the growth of financial aid to industry has been unemployment." Blais finds that in OECD countries where unemployment is high, subsidies are also high.

### H1: HIGHER UNEMPLOYMENT LEADS TO HIGHER SUBSIDIES. Another stream of research offers a party political explanation. Starting from the view that policy involves government choice, scholars have sought to examine the role of party government in public spending. Two questions must be answered in order to fully address the question of partisanship. First, why should parties matter, and if they do, which policies are they likely to pursue?

There are three electoral/institutional reasons why partisanship should influence the mix of policies to be pursued. First, governments that rely on party activists for electoral campaigns tend to pursue policies that reflect the more intensely partisan preferences of these activists. Second, potential entry by third parties deters the policy convergence toward the median voter. If the two major parties converge around the middle, third parties are likely to enter the race, assuming few or no barriers to entry. In that case, parties will differentiate themselves by taking positions that allow them to maximize their own votes but also deter the entry of third parties into the race. This movement in policy positions will be away from the middle signaling policy divergence. Finally, coalitional politics in multiparty-proportional representation systems tend to produce a few large parties that differ along a left-right dimension and several small parties that converge around the middle or at the fringes. Governments will be formed with the largest party as the senior partner and several smaller ones, but they are not likely to include the second-largest party. As a result, the policies to be pursued by the government will reflect the largest party's preferences relative to its strength in government and Parliament.

Since parties differ, which policies are likely to be pursued? The ideological affinity of parties of the left and the right to certain economic policies is the key. Although the sectoral distribution of subsidies may vary with each party, parties of the left generally exhibit a proclivity toward more state intervention in the economy. Such governments would therefore be more likely to favor subsidies for their own sake as a means of controlling and socializing more industries and to a greater degree. The ideological affinity of the British Labour Party to subsidize industry is indeed legendary. Conversely, parties of the right do not favor subsidies in principle because they believe in the unhampered working of the free market, which subsidies might distort, and because they are ideologically averse to higher public spending.

**H2: GOVERNMENTS THAT LEAN TOWARD THE LEFT ARE LIKELY TO DISBURSE MORE SUBSIDIES.** Explanations have so far centered on examining the impact of factors internal to an economy. It is highly probable, however, that external factors exert considerable influence on the level of state aid. There is a voluminous literature that argues that world markets condition domestic policies in different ways across countries. Cameron finds that exposure to international competition affects the growth of the public economy. Katzenstein further observes that smaller countries that tend to be more dependent upon trade have registered greater growth in government expenditures and that this "growth is primarily due to a substantial increase in transfer payments, primarily from government to households but also to producers" (quoted in Blais, 1986:86). Demands by interest groups for this sort of protection can take two forms. First, the decision may be motivated by a desire to continue subsidizing certain industries in order to reduce dependence on external sources for reasons of national security. Continued support for the aerospace and other defense-related industries is a good example. Second, some industries are considered to be vital to the economy's long-term growth. Consequently, governments are anxious to insulate these industries from global competition in an effort to, at worst, maintain a presence and, at best, create a national champion. For example, because of heavy losses partly attributable to operating in one of the most globally competitive industries, the French government has recently decided, with EC approval, to pump close to FFr 6.6 billion into Bull, the ailing computer giant. This is not surprising given the implicit understanding that the push for multilateral trade liberalization in the post–World War II years was to be predicated upon domestic intervention. Overall, Blais (1986) finds that, ceteris paribus, a 4 percent reduction in the average tariff is accompanied by a corresponding increase in state subsidies of 1 percent. It would appear, he concludes, that "industrial assistance is the aspect of intervention most closely tied to the openness of the economy" (p. 92).

### H3: MORE INTENSE COMPETITION FROM ABROAD LEADS TO HIGHER SUBSIDIES.

### A CLOSER LOOK AT SUBSIDY INSTRUMENTS

Subsidies have been treated so far as a monolithic program. However, a complete understanding of the workings of government necessitates that we disaggregate public action into distinct subsidy instruments or tools. A tool approach is significant because each instrument has its own distinct procedures, rationale, and network of organizational relationships.

The key assumption of this approach is that the multitude of programs that modern government uses can be analytically captured by reference to a few dimensions that describe how they work. Salamon and Lund distinguish between instruments along two key dimensions: the nature of the activity and the structure of the delivery system. The nature of the activity refers to the basic type of stimulus that government uses to achieve a result. On the one hand, money payments, such as grants, have more strings attached as government essentially gives money away, but it naturally wants to control where the money goes and how it is spent. Because grants are more target specific, they are more likely to be disbursed when unemployment in certain industries is high or when specific firms or sectors are threatened by foreign competition. On the other hand, loans have more discretionary aims because the principal and perhaps part of the interest will be paid back. Because disbursement of loans usually involves private intermediaries, that is, banks, the likelihood of fungibility by the recipients to other uses is greater. Loans are more likely to be subject to partisan manipulation because of their diffuse nature and because they do not appear in the budget. Governments can use them to satisfy a wide range of recipients with less visibility, and by consequence, less potential political cost. Since leftist governments generally prefer state intervention, and given that loans are more amenable to partisan manipulation, it follows that leftist governments are more likely to disburse loans.

### H4: GOVERNMENTS THAT LEAN TO THE LEFT DISBURSE HIGHER AMOUNTS OF LOANS. The structure of the delivery system refers to institutional arrangements needed to carry out the government's objectives. Here I am interested in one key aspect of the delivery mechanism, financing. It makes a difference as to who funds subsidy mechanisms. If funds appear directly as budgetary outlays, they are more subject to those who control the government at any one time. Budgets, so the argument goes, are likely to be used at least partially for partisan purposes to reward friends and to punish foes. Tax incentives are far less subject to partisan control, but they

may be preferred by right-wing governments whose market ideology normally calls for providing incentives, not handouts. In contrast to outlays, tax incentives do not call for the creation of new administrative agencies since tax authorities can easily take over this task. Unemployment is a good reason behind granting subsidies in the form of direct budgetary outlays because it is the quickest and most effective, but not necessarily the most efficient way to jump-start growth in depressed regions or industries. The relationship between trade and these two instruments is similar to that between trade and total aid. When competition from abroad makes substantial inroads into the domestic market, voices for protection from affected industries will increase. Under these conditions, governments of all political persuasions will find it difficult to resist subsidizing their industries.

### H5: HIGHER UNEMPLOYMENT LEADS TO HIGHER DIRECT BUDGET OUTLAYS.

### H6: GOVERNMENTS THAT LEAN TO THE RIGHT DISBURSE HIGHER AMOUNTS OF SUBSIDIES IN THE FORM OF TAX INCENTIVES.

### H7: HIGHER TRADE DEFICITS LEAD TO HIGHER DISBURSEMENTS OF BUDGET OUTLAYS AND TAX INCENTIVES. It has been argued that subsidies are disbursed in the form of four tools, each with its own rationale. The task in the next few pages is to test the impact of each explanation on total subsidies as well as on each subsidy instrument.

## MODELING THE ALLOCATION OF STATE SUBSIDIES

For purposes of this study the definition of subsidy conforms to that of the EC, that is, it includes all undertakings that fall within the scope of Articles 92 and 93 of the Treaty of Rome. Hence, it is defined as any aid "granted by a Member State or through State resources in any form whatsoever which distorts or threatens to distort competition by favouring certain undertakings or the production of certain goods" (Article 92). The "discriminatory" nature of subsidies thus defined qualitatively distinguishes them from general measures, such as Social Security contributions, that apply uniformly across the entire economy.

### MODEL SPECIFICATION AND MEASUREMENT. The time period under investigation is 1981–1986 (6 years), and the countries to be examined include nine EC members. Despite a modest sample and time period, the investigation contains fifty-four observations, which yields enough degrees of freedom for regression to produce reliable results.

The dependent variable is subsidies, which is approached from a macroeconomic point of view. It is important to consider the aggregate figures, at least initially, because we should know where countries stand on the issue before examining industry-specific trends. In this way, I am following the advice of Sir Leon Brittan, who, in his capacity as Commissioner on Competition, suggested examining the overall volume of aid first. Besides, a strictly sectoral approach would not be sensitive to regional aid that has less to do with the peculiarities of a given sector and more with adverse conditions in the region. Data for the dependent variable, state subsidies, are taken from the EC Commission. They include all aid that falls under Articles 92 and 93 of the Treaty of Rome as well as aid provided under EC agreements, such as steel, coal, shipbuilding, railroads, fisheries, and agriculture. According to the survey, the data are the most complete and reliable figures that exist to date on state subsidies by EC members. Subsidies are measured as disbursed aid as a percent of GDP.

I am using percentages rather than absolute figures because I want to take into account differences in size of the economy. In addition, I look at four subsidy instruments: budgetary outlays, tax incentives, loans, and grants. They are all similarly divided by GDP and expressed in percentages.

The three explanations to be tested are operationalized as follows. The socioeconomic explanation is straightforward: it is measured by unemployment as a percentage of civilian labor force. The expectation is that when unemployment is high, governments seek to stimulate demand by increasing public spending and therefore subsidies. The operationalization of the party control explanation is similarly straightforward. I adopt the indicator of ministry portfolios and seats in Parliament held by the governing party or coalition of parties.

The political complexion of the government is measured on a five-point scale (1 = right domination of more than 66.6 percent; 2 = center-right complexion with right and center having between 33.3 and 66.6 percent; 3 = balanced situation where center has more than 50 percent or left and right form government not dominated by either; 4 = center-left complexion where left and center have between 33.3 and 66.6 percent; 5 = left domination where left has more than 66.6 percent). The expectation is that governments that lean more toward the left are more prone to intervene in the economy and are therefore likely to disburse higher amounts of subsidies.

I operationalize the world markets explanation as the percent of merchandise trade deficit or surplus over GDP. Because I am interested in the effects of factors external to a nation's economy, I expect state subsidies to increase as the trade deficit widens. It is quite obvious that under such adverse conditions, governments will be pressured by various producer groups to provide relief in order either to reduce dependence on external sources or to cushion the blow from international competition and promote restructuring and greater efficiency.[1] I did not use the indicator utilized in some studies,

---

[1] If there is a relationship between unemployment and trade, it ought to manifest itself in the form of multicollinearity. To test for that, I followed Lewis-Beck's advice and regressed each independent variable on the other independent variables, but in every equation the adjusted

openness (total trade over GDP), because the aggregate nature of total trade data does not adequately reflect adverse external disturbances. For example, the value of total trade will not show variation when imports increase and exports shrink by the same amount, although the pressure by foreign competition has obviously intensified.

To capture the budgetary logic of granting subsidies, I lagged each independent variable by one year so that party control or trade deficit at time $t-1$ are used to predict subsidies at time t. To aid in further capturing a more accurate picture of the subsidy question, I included two control variables. The first stems from the time period under investigation. Because all EC countries were in economic recession during most of the years examined here, it is possible that the explanations would be systematically biased. It could be argued that in times of economic contraction, subsidies are more likely to be disbursed because the need for them is greater. To take account for such bias, I included real GDP growth lagged by one year.

The other control variable aims to take into account the efforts of elections. It is possible that more subsidies are likely to be allocated near election time by vote-maximizing politicians seeking reelection. This argument is related to the political party explanation, but the key dimension here is not ideology, which varies by party, but the likelihood of electoral success, which varies by incumbent regardless of ideology. The point is inspired by the political business cycle literature which is both voluminous and comparative, but concern here is only with the argument that links elections to the manipulation of budgetary instruments. The formulation follows Alt's conceptualization of significant changes in policies occurring in bursts around the time of elections. The easiest and most straightforward way to capture the relationship is to incorporate a dummy variable. In order to be as accurate as possible in as many cases as possible, I measure election or previous-to-election year as 1 and 0 at all other times.

All in all, I am using three independent and two control variables to explain why EC governments subsidize their economies. All predictor variables are lagged by one year except for the variable measuring the effects of elections.

## DISCUSSION OF FINDINGS

I regressed state subsidies on three predictor variables—unemployment, party, and trade—while controlling for economic growth and elections. The results are mixed (Table 1). The $R^2$s are high in all models, which means that the models have a good fit, although the presence of dummies accounts for some of the variance. Because the hypotheses advanced earlier are directional, one-tailed tests of significance were used. In those LSDV models

---

$R^2$ was below 0.207. This means that multicollinearity is not a problem in my model. In a separate bivariate regression of unemployment on trade the coefficient was even lower ($R^2 = 0.056$).

where low Durbin-Watson tests indicated the presence of autocorrelation and where error terms did not decay rapidly over time, GLS-LSDV models were run. This was the case when examining total subsidies and budgetary outlays. In addition, because Denmark and Greece did not give any aid in the form of tax incentives and Greece did not disburse loan aid in 1981–1983, they were dropped from the relevant equations.

Partisan control of government has a positive effect on subsidies. A gain of 33 percent of influence in the government and Parliament in favor of the left results in a 0.06 percent increase in subsidies relative to GDP. Although this point holds for total subsidies, an analysis of the various subsidy instruments reveals interesting variations. As hypothesized, loans are also influenced by partisan control, but the effects are more moderate. The coefficient is statistically significant at the 0.10 confidence interval, but the t-statistic is closer to the 0.05 level. This suggests a weak effect; an increase of one-third influence in favor of the left produces a 0.02 percent rise in loans. Parties do not appear to exercise a significant influence on direct budgetary outlays, confirming Jankowski and Wlezien's findings about total budget outlays. Some analysts expect parties to make a difference only in the long run because of bureaucratic inertia and structural constraints in politics. The findings here suggest a more refined conclusion. The argument appears to be the case in regard to budgetary outlays, tax incentives, and grants, but not in the case of total subsidies or loans. The hypothesis regarding right-wing preference for tax incentives is therefore disconfirmed. Although rightist governments may prefer tax incentives to budgetary outlays, they do not disburse either in deference to their ideological proclivities.

Trade effects are highly significant in the two policy tools regarding financing. The sign of the relationship is in the hypothesized direction in budgetary outlays and highly significant. When the trade deficit widens by 1 percent, governments spend an additional 0.08 percent on subsidies as a percent of GDP. A higher trade deficit usually signals intensified pressures from foreign competition. As import-competing industries are feeling the pinch and depending on their degree of export dependence and multinationalization, they will seek relief from the government of the day. Faced with mounting political pressure, governments, regardless of ideological proclivity, respond by raising the level of subsidies in the hope of buying time to encourage restructuring and promote economic efficiency. Concurrently, interest groups representing these industries may coalesce with others in exporting sectors to form a powerful subsidy-seeking lobby. They charge that the deficit has widened not because of a loss in comparative advantage, but because foreign competitors are being unfairly subsidized by their home governments either monetarily or in terms of barriers to market entry. The end result will likely center on domestic subsidies in order to "level the playing field."

Trade also affects the adoption of tax incentives. The coefficient is significant but the relationship is the inverse from that hypothesized; lower trade deficits correlate with more tax breaks. One percent decrease in trade deficit

| TABLE 1 | EXPLANATION OF SUBSIDIES IN NINE EC COUNTRIES | | | | |
|---|---|---|---|---|---|

| Variable | Total aid[a] GLS-LSDV | Budget[a] GLS-LSDV | Taxes[b] LSDV | Grants[a] LSDV | Loans[c] LSDV |
|---|---|---|---|---|---|
| Unemployment | 0.01 (0.03) | 0.03 (0.02) | −0.01 (0.03) | 0.04 (0.03) | 0.01 (0.01) |
| Party | 0.06** (0.03) | 0.02 (0.02) | 0.03 (0.04) | 0.04 (0.04) | 0.02* (0.01) |
| Trade | −0.01 (0.04) | −0.08*** (0.02) | 0.09*** (0.03) | 0.02 (0.03) | −0.01 (0.01) |
| Growth | −0.01 (0.02) | −0.03* (0.02) | 0.03 (0.03) | 0.01 (0.03) | −0.01 (0.01) |
| Election | 0.06 (0.07) | 0.03 (0.05) | 0.07 (0.08) | 0.01 (0.01) | 0.05** (0.03) |
| *Country intercepts* | | | | | |
| Belgium | 0.38 | 0.21 | 0.21 | 0.01 | 0.02 |
| Denmark | −0.48 | −0.39 | | −0.20 | 0.20 |
| France | 0.03 | −0.00 | 0.11 | −0.39 | 0.39 |
| Germany | −0.11 | −0.16 | 0.06 | 0.20 | 0.05 |
| Greece | 0.98 | 0.50 | | 1.60 | |
| Italy | 2.66 | 2.26 | 0.45 | 2.28 | 0.03 |
| Ireland | 2.30 | 0.49 | 1.83 | 2.14 | −0.03 |
| Holland | −0.18 | −0.15 | −0.10 | −0.10 | 0.03 |
| Adjusted $R^2$ | .855 | .824 | .853 | .912 | .783 |
| $p$ | .188 | .358 | | | |

Standard errors reported in parentheses.

[a]N = 54

[b]N = 42; excludes Denmark and Greece

[c]N = 48; excludes Greece

*p < .10; **p < .05; ***p < .001

leads to 0.09 percent increase in aid over GDP. The reason for this relationship rests with the substitutability between the two instruments. Governments decide to look for alternative instruments to accomplish the same task, for three reasons. First, problems may prove too stubborn to attack with one set of tools, so the government switches to another set it believes to be more effective. Second, when environmental conditions change, such as budgetary famines, governments seek to employ less costly tools. Finally, governments may switch to alternative tools when they want to give the impression that they are not directly involved in some area. Hood calls this process "deliberate serendipity," referring to the idea of government using tools for unacknowledged reasons and for purposes other than the ones for which the instrument was designed. In the case of subsidies, the second and third rationales seem appropriate. When government does not wish to be seen as being involved, it may choose to subsidize industries indirectly. Under contracting deficits, competition from abroad is no longer a viable rationale for extending subsidies. However, clientelistic politics tells us that the powerful coalitions that were formed to demand subsidies will still want to be aided, arguing that they need more time to adjust, for example, steel, or that foreigners must adjust first, for example, agriculture. Under these conditions, governments may decide to switch to less costly and indirect instruments that permit the same kind of behavior but are less visible. Tax incentives, or tax expenditures as they are sometimes called, still make it cheaper to produce the same goods and services, but they don't show up in the government's budget. The issue can, of course, be politicized by advocates of deficit reduction, but the fact remains that no money is being spent while individual recipients have discretionary power over how to spend the money "saved." As such, governments can still engage in the same behavior as before while being less vulnerable to unfair subsidization charges from abroad.

The two control variables were significant in a few instances. Economic growth was statistically significant in only one case. Quite naturally, during hard economic times governments disburse more subsidies relative to GDP, but the relationship holds only for direct budget outlays. The magnitude of change is weak because a 1 percent decrease in real economic growth produces a rise of only 0.03 percent in subsidies. The manipulation of other forms of subsidy seems impervious to such broad macroeconomic conditions. Elections did not have an impact in any but the loan decision. The coefficients were in the hypothesized direction in all instances, but significant in only one. In a review of the comparative literature on the manipulation of budgets, Alesina concludes that the effects are not large in magnitude, and policy instruments are not systematically manipulated before every election. The findings here confirm his conclusion. In most cases, it does appear that elections and subsidies are not related, although when incumbents pass the budget prior to their reelection campaign, they will increase the amount of loans they disburse by 0.05 percent. This is a minor increase given that loans are the least funded of all four types of subsidies examined here; the mean is only 0.15 percent relative to GDP.

Looking at the results in terms of model goodness-of-fit, most do relatively well except for grants. Two of the five variables in the grant equation, trade and economic growth, do not have the predicted signs, but none is statistically significant despite a high $R^2$. This is not evidence of multicollinearity but rather the consequence of dummy variables. It should be remembered that dummy intercepts tell us how different countries are from the reference country, in this case, the United Kingdom. Needless to say, a different reference country would have produced different signs, sizes, and strengths of dummy relationships. Ideally, one would like to see how units deviate from some meaningful norm, but, unfortunately, these reference categories are often arbitrary. Looking at country intercepts, we find that, relative to the United Kingdom, the model underestimates Italy, Ireland, and Greece, and, somewhat, Germany and Belgium, while it overestimates Holland a bit, France, and Denmark.

Two explanations can be advanced to account for the results. One may be that the time horizon of this study is too short to capture the essence of the motivating principles behind grants. Policy objectives do not necessarily remain constant over time, and in many instances grants continue to be disbursed long after they have successfully completed their objectives or long after they have been found to be totally ineffective. In fact, Rose and Davies argue that governments normally inherit programs started by previous governments for reasons that no longer make sense or perhaps never did, but because they serve powerful clients these programs are continued. It could very well be that the decision to subsidize certain industries was taken before the 1980s and programs did not adjust to changing economic circumstances. So the study as a whole, but especially the question of grants, could benefit from a longer time horizon. Another reason may be that because grants have significant redistributive consequences, their use is too firm-specific to be picked up by the macroeconomic variables employed here. On the positive side, this strengthens the point that the use of different instruments is motivated by different rationales, but we still don't know which ones motivate grants.

Apart from what they show, the results are also quite revealing in what they don't show. In contrast to Blais (1986), unemployment was found not to have a systematic effect on any of the five subsidy indicators. Although there are specific instances of explicitly using subsidies as countercycle stimuli to fight unemployment, such as the French Socialist nationalizations of 1981–82, the explanation does not hold systematically across EC countries. One reason for the difference may be that Blais examined the larger sample of OECD countries whereas the study here limits itself to EC states. Another reason relates to research design. Blais employed a cross-sectional design whereas the analysis here pools both spatial and time effects. The point is that subsidies in the EC are not disbursed in response to higher unemployment despite political rhetoric to the contrary.

## CONCLUSION

In this study I have sought to explain why EC governments subsidize their economies. I assessed the impact of three explanations—socioeconomic, party control, and world markets—on state subsidies. No explanation receives unqualified support because none was consistently significant in each model, but some explained subsidies better than others. Keeping in mind the temporal limitation of the study, the results have implications for the theoretical study of policy as well as European integration.

Two theoretical points need to be made. First, explanations for subsidy allocations differ by policy instrument. Although parties make a difference in the general allocation decision, they are not equally significant when subsidies are disaggregated into various components. Leftist governments do give more aid and loans than their rightist counterparts, but competition from abroad also makes a difference when choosing between direct budgetary outlays or indirect tax incentives. All this suggests a far more nuanced and cautious approach to the reasons behind disbursing state subsidies than is usually advocated. EC governments do not do it for any one reason used consistently across subsidy instruments.

Second, the analysis here provides a partial glimpse of the calculus of choice between subsidy tools. The findings confirm and circumscribe linkages and trade-offs between policies and instruments. External factors, such as trade considerations, are linked to the manipulation of certain policy instruments, although they do not appear important in the overall subsidy decision. Countries that experience trade deficits are more likely to link trade with budget subsidies and to insist on substituting reductions in the former with increases in the latter. Protectionism, in other words, can manifest itself not just at the border but also in the domestic economy. Reductions in tariffs do not necessarily lead to more open markets. This finding amends Blais's (1986) argument of linkages between trade and subsidies by showing that it holds true only in the case of budget outlays. It also qualifies endogenous models of trade-subsidy linkages. Rodrik, for example, conceptualizes a pressure group model with politicians faced with a choice between tariffs and production subsidies. In theory, this model argues that politicians are faced with a rational choice between two alternative instruments. The study here amends such conceptualizations by showing that linkages are possible only under adverse trade conditions and only in the case of budgetary outlays. Trade deficits, rather than endogenous factors, trigger such linkages.

Extending the issue of linkages, the analysis has also revealed substitutions, or trade-offs, between instruments. Some scholars in the policy instrument literature argue that choice between tools is often made by default in government. Tools are rarely consciously chosen in full realization of all existing alternative instruments. While there may be merit to this argument when examining many diverse instruments, trade-offs do exist between related tools. When trade deficits are widening, the instrument of choice is direct budgetary outlays. In the face of smaller deficits, however, governments are eager to switch to tax incentives, trading off the visibility and negative budgetary repercussions of direct aid with the relatively invisible but equally politically rewarding tax incentives. The point made here also extends Salamon and Lund's argument over visibility and enactment. They maintain that less visible tools are easier to adopt. While this is true, less visible tools are not always preferable. The choice between outlays and tax incentives depends upon trade conditions and the consequent need for government to adopt a higher or lower profile.

The findings have implications for future European integration as well. The overall levels of subsidies seem hostage to the ideological proclivities of governing parties. Consequently, decisions to assist industry are difficult to reconcile at the European level because member-governments are of different political persuasions. The only way they can reach consensus is when all or at least most governments are occupied by parties of the center-right. But that is likely to be ephemeral since parties of many ideological persuasions come in and out of government over time. Trade concerns regarding direct and indirect subsidies are even more difficult to resolve because of the emergence of two competing blocs: those member-states seeking more subsidies because of trade effects and those that are not. Under adverse trade conditions, EC countries appear willing to circumvent trade liberalization measures by creating a "fortress Europe," but one whose barriers are not at the border but inside the domestic economy of each country. As integration proceeds, calls for the harmonization of policies among member-states will come into conflict with an increasing inability or unwillingness on the part of certain national governments to reduce the amount of their subsidies. Further demands to "level the playing field" will provide a fertile ground for a strong anti-integration backlash among EC countries over the issue of state subsidies. Unwillingness is likely to disappear when all EC members sustain trade surpluses, but then non-EC countries are likely to complain of discriminatory practices. The cases of Japan's or China's trade surpluses and the consequent complaints by outsiders are instructive. In this context, Stigler's advice becomes even more relevant: we need to learn more about the motivations behind state subsidies before the bickering intensifies.

## REFERENCES

Blais, A. (1986) *A Political Sociology of Public Aid to Industry.* Toronto: University of Toronto Press.

# MONETARY RELATIONS

Money is very important not only for the conduct of commercial transactions but also for the stability and welfare of society. The selections offered here illustrate the different ways that economists and political scientists use to study finance and tease out the political and economic implications of these transactions. What is interesting about the two approaches are the different aspects of money that are of interest to each analyst. While economists tend to be more interested in the efficiency of the exchange rate system and its impact on social welfare, political scientists are more interested in exchange rates as state tools of stabilization and control of the economy.

The first selection written by Nobel laureate Milton Friedman over forty years ago makes the case for flexible, or free-floating, exchange rates. He criticizes the fixed exchange rate system established at Bretton Woods in 1944 for its inability to enhance society's welfare and for the inherent risks it entails. Suppose we are faced with a situation, argues Friedman, where the amount of goods and services people want to buy with a particular currency is higher than the amount people want to sell at the exchange rate price. What can we do? In a system of free-floating rates—that is, a system where rates are determined in the open market—the rate will increase to meet the demand. Consequently, no action is necessary. Under a fixed system, however, more direct intervention is required. There will have to be changes in internal prices or income, the imposition of direct controls prohibiting the purchase of these goods, or the use of monetary reserves to offset the imbalance. All these cases are accompanied by potentially serious problems such as the creation of unemployment, the potential for maladjustment, or the quick depletion of reserves. Therefore, flexible exchange rates are the better solution.

But this system is not without its critics. Friedman addresses several criticisms of the flexible system. The uncertainty that is inherent in this system can be countered by a futures market where buyers and sellers can hedge against future fluctuations. Furthermore, the system does not lead to instability either through speculators or some other internal mechanism because differences in economic conditions help determine prices. When imbalances are corrected, the system returns to equilibrium. It is interesting to note Friedman's argument concerning the role of speculators in light of the attack on several European currencies in the early 1990s, the push for European monetary integration, and the complaints against speculators in the Asian crisis of 1997.

Goodman and Pauly examine a different aspect of the system. They analyze the reasons behind capital decontrols in recent years in different countries. Their main point is that changes in finance and production reduced the usefulness of national capital controls. Economists argued that the movement toward flexible exchange rates facilitated the growth of international funds. However, Goodman and Pauly maintain that the actual decision to decontrol capital flows in major countries depended on the ability of privileged groups, namely big business and financial institutions, to pressure the state to act in their favor. These groups could exercise their clout because increases in the pool of money available, technological advances which reduced the time needed to transfer funds across borders, and the multinationalization of production made it easier for companies to leave undesirable sites of production. As a result, big business and financial institutions became privileged segments of society at the expense of state and labor. As evidenced in the other sections of this book, political analysis does not necessarily negate economic thought, but rather complements and enriches it by shedding new light on old questions.

# The Case for
# Flexible Exchange Rates

Milton Friedman

... Promotion of rearmament, liberalization of trade, avoidance of allocations and other direct controls both internal and external, harmonization of internal monetary and fiscal policies—all these problems take on a different cast and become far easier to solve in a world of flexible exchange rates and its corollary, free convertibility of currencies. The sooner a system of flexible exchange rates is established, the sooner unrestricted multilateral trade will become a real possibility. And it will become one without in any way interfering with the pursuit by each nation of domestic economic stability according to its own lights. . . .

Suppose the aggregate effect of changes in the conditions affecting international payments has been to increase the amount of a country's currency people want to buy with foreign currency relatively to the amount other people want to sell for foreign currency at the pre-existing exchange rate—to create an incipient surplus in the balance of payments. How can these inconsistent desires be reconciled? (1) The country's currency may be bid up, or put up, in price. This increase in the exchange rate will tend to make the currency less desirable relative to the currency of other countries and so eliminate the excess demand at the pre-existing rate. (2) Prices within the country may rise, thus making its goods less desirable relative to goods in other countries, or incomes within the country may rise, thus increasing the demand for foreign currencies. (3) Direct controls over transactions involving foreign exchange may prevent holders of foreign balances from acquiring as much domestic exchange as they would otherwise like to; for example, they may be prevented from buying domestic goods by the inability to get a required export license. (4) The excess amount of domestic currency desired may be provided out of monetary reserves, the foreign currency acquired being added to re-serves of foreign currencies—the monetary authorities (or exchange equal-ization fund or the like) may step in with a "desire" to buy or sell the difference between the amounts demanded and supplied by others.

## A. CHANGES IN EXCHANGE RATES

FLEXIBLE EXCHANGE RATES.    Under flexible exchange rates freely de-termined in open markets, the first impact of any tendency toward a surplus or deficit in the balance of payments is on the exchange rate. If a country has an incipient surplus of receipts over payments—an excess demand for its currency—the exchange rate will tend to rise. If it has an incipient deficit, the exchange rate will tend to fall. If the conditions responsible for the rise or the fall in the exchange rate are generally regarded as temporary, actual or poten-tial holders of the country's currency will tend to change their holdings in such a way as to moderate the movement in the exchange rate. If a rise in the exchange rate, for example, is expected to be temporary, there is an incentive for holders of the country's currency to sell some of their holdings for foreign currency in order to buy the currency back later on at a lower price. By doing so, they provide the additional domestic currency to meet part of the excess demand responsible for the initial rise in the exchange rate; that is, they ab-sorb some of what would have been surplus receipts of foreign currency at the former exchange rate. Conversely, if a decline is expected to be temporary, there is an incentive to buy domestic currency for resale at a higher price. Such purchases of domestic currency provide the foreign currency to meet some of what would have been a deficit of foreign currency at the former ex-change rate. In this way, such "speculative" transactions in effect provide the country with reserves to absorb temporary surpluses or to meet temporary deficits. On the other hand, if the change in the exchange rate is generally re-garded as produced by fundamental factors that are likely to be permanent, the incentives are the reverse of those listed above, and speculative transac-tions will speed up the rise or decline in the exchange rate and thus hasten its approach to its final position.

This final position depends on the effect that changes in exchange rates have on the demand for and supply of a country's currency, not to hold as bal-ances, but for other purposes. A rise in the exchange rate produced by a ten-dency toward a surplus makes foreign goods cheaper in terms of domestic currency, even though their prices are unchanged in terms of their own cur-rency, and domestic goods more expensive in terms of foreign currency, even though their prices are unchanged in terms of domestic currency. This tends to increase imports, reduce exports, and so offset the incipient surplus. Con-versely, a decline in the exchange rate produced by a tendency toward a deficit makes imports more expensive to home consumers, and exports less expensive to foreigners, and so tends to offset the incipient deficit.

## B. CHANGES IN INTERNAL PRICES OR INCOME

In principle, changes in internal prices could produce the same effects on trade as changes in the exchange rate. For example, a decline of 10 per cent in every internal price in Germany (including wages, rents, etc.) with an unchanged dollar price of the mark would clearly have identically the same effects on the relative costs of domestic and foreign goods as a decline of 10 per cent in the dollar price of the mark, with all internal prices unchanged. Similarly, such price changes could have the same effects on speculative transactions. If expected to be temporary, a decline in prices would stimulate speculative purchases of goods to avoid future higher prices, thus moderating the price movement.

If internal prices were as flexible as exchange rates, it would make little economic difference whether adjustments were brought about by changes in exchange rates or by equivalent changes in internal prices. But this condition is clearly not fulfilled. The exchange rate is potentially flexible in the absence of administrative action to freeze it. At least in the modern world, internal prices are highly inflexible. They are more flexible upward than downward, but even on the upswing all prices are not equally flexible. The inflexibility of prices, or different degrees of flexibility, means a distortion of adjustments in response to changes in external conditions. The adjustment takes the form primarily of price changes in some sectors, primarily of output changes in others.

Wage rates tend to be among the less flexible prices. In consequence, an incipient deficit that is countered by a policy of permitting or forcing prices to decline is likely to produce unemployment rather than, or in addition to, wage decreases. The consequent decline in real income reduces the domestic demand for foreign goods and thus the demand for foreign currency with which to purchase these goods. In this way, it offsets the incipient deficit. . . .

Changes in interest rates are perhaps best classified under this heading of changes in internal prices. Interest-rate changes have in the past played a particularly important role in adjustment to external changes, partly because they have been susceptible to direct influence by the monetary authorities, and partly because, under a gold standard, the initial impact of a tendency toward a deficit or surplus was a loss or gain of gold and a consequent tightening or ease in the money market. The rise in the interest rate produced in this way by an incipient deficit increased the demand for the currency for capital purposes and so offset part or all of the deficit. This reduced the rate at which the deficit had to be met by a decline in internal prices, which was itself set in motion by the loss of gold and associated decrease in the stock of money responsible for the rise in interest rates. Conversely, an incipient surplus increased the stock of gold and eased the money market. The resulting decline in the interest rate reduced the demand for the currency for capital purposes and so offset part or all of the surplus, reducing the rate at which the surplus had to be met by the rise in internal prices set in motion by the gain of gold and associated rise in the stock of money. . . .

## C. DIRECT CONTROLS

In principle, direct controls on imports, exports, and capital movements could bring about the same effects on trade and the balance of payments as changes in exchange rates or in internal prices and incomes. The final adjustment will, after all, involve a change in the composition of imports and exports, along with specifiable capital transactions. If these could be predicted in advance, and if it were technically possible to control selectively each category of imports, exports, and capital transactions, direct controls could be used to produce the required adjustment.

It is clear, however, that the changes in imports and exports and the required capital transactions cannot be predicted; the fact that each new foreign-exchange crisis in a country like Britain is officially regarded as a bolt from the blue is ample evidence for this proposition.

Aside from the many unfortunate results of such a process which are by now abundantly clear, it has a perverse effect on the foreign-payments problem itself, particularly when direct controls are used, as they have been primarily, to counter an actual or incipient deficit. The apparent deficit that has to be closed by direct controls is larger than the deficit that would emerge at the same exchange rate without the direct controls and, indeed, might be eliminated entirely or converted into a surplus if the direct controls on imports and exports and their inevitable domestic accompaniments were removed. The mere existence of the direct controls makes the currency less desirable for many purposes because of the limitations it places on what holders of the currency may do with it, and this is likely to reduce the demand for the currency more than it would be reduced by the fluctuations in exchange rates or other adaptive mechanisms substituted for the direct controls. . . .

## D. USE OF MONETARY RESERVES

Given adequate reserves, tendencies toward a surplus or a deficit can be allowed to produce an actual surplus or deficit in transactions other than those of the monetary authority (or exchange equalization fund, or whatever the name may be) without a change in exchange rates, internal prices or incomes, or direct controls, the additional domestic or foreign currency demanded being supplied by the monetary authority. This device is feasible and not undesirable for movements that are small and temporary, though, if it is clear that the movements are small and temporary, it is largely unnecessary, since, with flexible exchange rates, private speculative transactions will provide the additional domestic or foreign currency demanded with only minor movements in exchange rates. . . .

## OBJECTIONS TO FLEXIBLE EXCHANGE RATES

### 1. FLEXIBLE EXCHANGE RATES MEAN INSTABILITY RATHER THAN STABILITY.

On the naïve level on which this objection is frequently made, it involves the already-mentioned mistake of confusing the symptom of difficulties with the difficulties themselves. A flexible exchange rate need not be an unstable exchange rate. If it is, it is primarily because there is underlying instability in the economic conditions governing international trade. And a rigid exchange rate may, while itself nominally stable, perpetuate and accentuate other elements of instability in the economy. The mere fact that a rigid official exchange rate does not change while a flexible rate does is no evidence that the former means greater stability in any more fundamental sense. If it does, it is for one or more of the reasons considered in the points that follow.

### 2. FLEXIBLE EXCHANGE RATES MAKE IT IMPOSSIBLE FOR EXPORTERS AND IMPORTERS TO BE CERTAIN ABOUT THE PRICE THEY WILL HAVE TO PAY OR RECEIVE FOR FOREIGN EXCHANGE.

Under flexible exchange rates traders can almost always protect themselves against changes in the rate by hedging in a futures market. Such futures markets in foreign currency readily develop when exchange rates are flexible. Any uncertainty about returns will then be borne by speculators. The most that can be said for this argument, therefore, is that flexible exchange rates impose a cost of hedging on traders, namely, the price that must be paid to speculators for assuming the risk of future changes in exchange rates. But this is saying too much. The substitution of flexible for rigid exchange rates changes the form in which uncertainty in the foreign-exchange market is manifested; it may not change the extent of uncertainty at all and, indeed, may even decrease uncertainty. For example, conditions that would tend to produce a decline in a flexible exchange rate will produce a shortage of exchange with a rigid exchange rate. This in turn will produce either internal adjustments of uncertain character or administrative allocation of exchange. Traders will then be certain about the rate but uncertain about either internal conditions or the availability of exchange. The uncertainty can be removed for some transactions by advance commitments by the authorities dispensing exchange; it clearly cannot be removed for all transactions in view of the uncertainty about the total amount of exchange available; the reduction in uncertainty for some transactions therefore involves increased uncertainty for others, since all the risk is now concentrated on them. Further, such administrative allocation of exchange is always surrounded by uncertainty about the policy that will be followed. It is by no means clear whether the uncertainty associated with a flexible rate or the uncertainty associated with a rigid rate is likely to be more disruptive to trade.

3. SPECULATION IN FOREIGN-EXCHANGE MARKETS TENDS TO BE
DESTABILIZING. This point is, of course, closely related to the preceding
one. It is said that speculators will take a decline in the exchange rate as a signal for a further decline and will thus tend to make the movements in the exchange rate sharper than they would be in the absence of speculation. The
special fear in this connection is of capital flight in response to political uncertainty or simply to movements in the exchange rate. Despite the prevailing opinion to the contrary, I am very dubious that in fact speculation in
foreign exchange would be destabilizing. Evidence from some earlier experiences and from current free markets in currency in Switzerland, Tangiers,
and elsewhere seems to me to suggest that, in general, speculation is stabilizing rather than the reverse, though the evidence has not yet been analyzed
in sufficient detail to establish this conclusion with any confidence. People
who argue that speculation is generally destabilizing seldom realize that this
is largely equivalent to saying that speculators lose money, since speculation
can be destabilizing in general only if speculators on the average sell when
the currency is low in price and buy when it is high. It does not, of course, follow that speculation is not destabilizing; professional speculators might on
the average make money while a changing body of amateurs regularly lost
larger sums. But, while this may happen, it is hard to see why there is any
presumption that it will; the presumption is rather the opposite. To put the
same point differently, if speculation were persistently destabilizing, a government body like the Exchange Equalization Fund in England in the 1930's
could make a good deal of money by speculating in exchange and in the process almost certainly eliminate the destabilizing speculation. But to suppose
that speculation by governments would generally be profitable is in most
cases equivalent to supposing that government officials risking funds that
they do not themselves own are better judges of the likely movements in
foreign-exchange markets than private individuals risking their own funds.

The widespread belief that speculation is likely to be destabilizing is
doubtless a major factor accounting for the cavalier rejection of a system of
flexible exchange rates in the immediate postwar period. Yet this belief does
not seem to be founded on any systematic analysis of the available empirical
evidence. It rests rather, I believe, primarily on an oversimplified interpretation of the movements of so-called "hot" money during the 1930's. At the
time, any speculative movements which threatened a depreciation of a currency (i.e., which threatened a *change* in an exchange rate) were regarded as
destabilizing, and hence these movements were so considered. In retrospect,
it is clear that the speculators were "right"; that forces were at work making
for depreciation in the value of most European currencies relative to the dollar independently of speculative activity; that the speculative movements
were anticipating this change; and, hence, that there is at least as much reason to call them "stabilizing" as to call them "destabilizing."

In addition, the interpretation of this evidence has been marred by a failure to distinguish between a system of exchange rates held temporarily rigid
but subject to change from time to time by government action and a system

of flexible exchange rates. Many of the capital movements regarded as demonstrating that foreign-exchange speculation is destabilizing were stimulated by the existence of rigid rates subject to change by government action and are to be attributed primarily to the absence of flexibility of rates and hence of any incentive to avoid the capital movements. This is equally true of post–World War II experience with wide swings in foreign-payments positions. For reasons noted earlier, this experience has little direct bearing on the character of the speculative movements to be expected under a regime of genuinely flexible exchange rates.

4. FLEXIBLE EXCHANGE RATES INVOLVE INCREASED UNCERTAINTY IN THE INTERNAL ECONOMY. It is argued that in many countries there is a great fear of inflation and that people have come to regard the exchange rate as an indicator of inflation and are highly sensitive to variations in it. Exchange crises, such as would tend to occur under rigid exchange rates, will pass unnoticed, it is argued, except by people directly connected with international trade, whereas a decline in the exchange rate would attract much attention, be taken as a signal of a future inflation, and produce anticipatory movements by the public at large. In this way a flexible exchange rate might produce additional uncertainty rather than merely change the form in which uncertainty is manifested. There is some merit to this argument, but it does not seem to me to be a substantial reason for avoiding a flexible exchange rate. Its implication is rather that it would be desirable, if possible, to make the transition to a flexible rate at a time when exchange rates of European countries relative to the dollar would be likely to move moderately and some to rise. It further would be desirable to accompany the transition by willingness to take prompt monetary action to counter any internal reactions. A fear of inflation has little or no chance of producing inflation, except in a favorable monetary environment. A demonstration that fears of inflation are groundless, and some experience with the absence of any direct and immediate connection between the day-to-day movements in the exchange rate and internal prices would very shortly reduce to negligible proportions any increase in uncertainty on purely domestic markets, as a result of flexible yet not highly unstable exchange rates. Further, public recognition that a substantial decline in the exchange rate is a symptom of or portends internal inflation is by no means an unmixed evil. It means that a flexible exchange rate would provide something of a barrier to a highly inflationary domestic policy.

Very nearly the opposite of this argument is also sometimes made against flexible exchange rates. It is said that, with a flexible exchange rate, governments will have less incentive and be in a less strong position to take firm internal action to prevent inflation. A rigid exchange rate, it is said, gives the government a symbol to fight for—it can nail its flag to the mast of a specified exchange rate and resist political pressure to take action that would be inflationary in the name of defending the exchange rate. Dramatic foreign-exchange crises establish an atmosphere in which drastic if unpopular action is possible. On the other hand, it is said, with a flexible exchange rate, there is no definite sticking point; inflationary action will simply mean a decline in the exchange rate but no dramatic crisis, and people are little affected by a change in a price, the exchange rate, in a market in which relatively few have direct dealings.

Of course, it is not impossible for both these arguments to be valid—the first in countries like Germany, which have recently experienced hyper-inflations and violently fluctuating exchange rates, the second in countries like Great Britain, which have not. But, even in countries like Britain, it is far from clear that a rigid exchange rate is more conducive under present conditions to noninflationary internal economic policy than a flexible exchange rate. A rigid exchange rate thwarts any immediate manifestation of a deterioration in the foreign-payments position as a result of inflationary internal policy. With an independent monetary standard, the loss of exchange reserves does not automatically reduce the stock of money or prevent its continued increase; yet it does temporarily reduce domestic inflationary pressure by providing goods in return for the foreign-exchange reserves without any simultaneous creation of domestic income. The deterioration shows up only sometime later, in the dull tables of statistics summarizing the state of foreign-exchange reserves. Even then, the authorities in the modern world have the alternative—or think they have—of suppressing a deficit by more stringent direct controls and thus postponing still longer the necessity for taking the appropriate internal measures; and they can always find any number of special reasons for the particular deterioration other than their internal policy. While the possibilities of using direct controls and of finding plausible excuses are present equally with flexible exchange rates, at least the deterioration in the foreign-payments position shows up promptly in the more readily understandable and simpler form of a decline in the exchange rates, and there is no emergency, no suddenly discovered decline in monetary reserves to dangerous levels, to force the imposition of supposedly unavoidable direct controls.

# THE OBSOLESCENCE
# OF CAPITAL CONTROLS?

## ECONOMIC MANAGEMENT
## IN AN AGE OF GLOBAL MARKETS

John B. Goodman and Louis W. Pauly

In this article, our principal aim is to address two prior puzzles: First, why did policies of capital decontrol converge across a rising number of industrial states between the late 1970s and the early 1990s? Second, why did some states move to eliminate controls more rapidly than others? We argue that the movement away from controls on short-term capital flows did not result, as regime or epistemic community theories might predict, from the emergence of a common normative framework or widespread belief in the benefits of unfettered capital mobility. Nor has it simply reflected the overarching power of a liberal state. Instead, we contend that it has been driven by fundamental changes in the structures of international production and financial intermediation, which made it easier and more urgent for private firms—specifically, corporations and financial institutions whose aspirations had become increasingly global—effectively to pursue strategies of evasion and exit. For governments, the utility of controls declined as their perceived cost thereby increased.

Still, not all governments abandoned capital controls at the same pace. In order to examine both the process through which these pressures impinged on policy at the national level and variations in the timing of policy reform, we analyze policy developments in four advanced industrial states that relied extensively on capital controls—Japan, Germany, France, and Italy. The first two moved decisively away from capital controls in 1980 and 1981, the latter two, at the end of the decade. These differences can be traced to the interaction between generic types of external pressure and remaining distinctions in domestic structures. Specifically, governments facing capital inflows liberalized sooner than governments facing capital outflows—a conclusion that is not obvious, since capital inflows can be as threatening to national policy-making autonomy as capital outflows. Our analysis at the national level highlights the mechanisms by which such systematic economic pressures were transmitted to unique domestic political arenas. But it also provides a clue as to the increasingly common constraints governments would now have to overcome if they wanted to move back to policies designed to influence and control short-term capital flows.

In theoretical terms, our argument and evidence address a central question in international political economy regarding the relative importance of, and relationship between, international and domestic variables. In the crucial area of capital flows, the two interact in a clear pattern: global financial structures affect the dynamics of national policy-making by changing and privileging the interests and actions of certain types of firms. Once those interests have been embedded in policy, movement back is not necessarily precluded but is certainly rendered much more difficult. . . .

## CAPITAL CONTROLS IN THE POSTWAR MONETARY ORDER

Following World War II, capital controls were an accepted part of the international monetary system. Despite pressure from the United States to allow investment as well as goods to cross borders without governmental interference, the 1944 Bretton Woods agreement intentionally legitimated the imposition of controls on capital movements that were not directly linked to trade flows. The agreement gave the International Monetary Fund (IMF) a mandate to discourage exchange restrictions and other financial impediments to trade but pointedly did not give it jurisdiction over capital controls. Most industrial countries accepted the logic of restoring currency convertibility but jealously guarded their right to control short-term capital flows.

In 1961 member states of the Organization for Economic Cooperation and Development (OECD) formally agreed in the Code of Liberalization of Capital Movements to "progressively abolish between one another" restrictions on capital movements "to the extent necessary for effective economic cooperation." However, the code left significant scope for states to make exceptions for certain types of capital transfers and, more broadly, to take any actions necessary for the "maintenance of public order or . . . the protection of essential security interests" *as defined by the member states themselves.* States were also permitted to derogate from their obligations under the code in the event of payments imbalances that *they* themselves considered severe. As this loosely defined set of exceptions made clear, OECD member states retained the right to reimpose controls whenever conditions warranted. The reason they attached such importance to that right quickly became apparent.

Facing persistent payments imbalances and problematic exchange rate rigidities in the 1960s, virtually all leading industrial states resorted to some type of control on capital movements. Even the United States adopted controls to prevent "disequilibrating" outflows. Similar controls were put in place by other states with external deficits, while states with external surpluses adopted measures to ward off unwelcome capital inflows. Ironically, these controls gave a boost to incipient "offshore" financial markets in Europe and elsewhere. The subsequent growth of Euro-currency banking, bond, and equity markets reflected a number of factors—including the unwillingness of governments to coordinate their associated regulatory and tax policies and the development of new technologies.

The disintegration in the early 1970s of the Bretton Woods system of pegged exchange rates potentially opened the door for a new normative framework to coordinate efforts to influence international capital flows. An intergovernmental forum on international monetary reform, the Committee of Twenty of the IMF board of governors was established in 1972, and a group of technical experts was appointed by the committee to examine the problem of disequilibrating capital flows. They concluded that controls should not become a permanent feature of a reformed system because of their potentially negative impact on trade and investment flows. But since capital flows could continue to disrupt even a more flexible exchange rate arrangement, they recommended the adoption of a code of conduct monitored by the IMF to govern the future use sof controls. In the end, however, their recommendation was not pursued by the committee.

When the IMF Articles of Agreement were finally amended in 1976 to accommodate floating exchange rates, the normative framework guiding international capital movements originally articulated at Bretton Woods remained intact. States retained the right to resort to controls at their own discretion. In sum, at the official level, neither the beliefs concerning capital controls nor the rules governing them changed significantly over the postwar period. The forces behind the wave of policy liberalization that was about to occur were located elsewhere.

## GLOBAL FINANCE AND FIRM BEHAVIOR

Between the late 1970s and the early 1990s, the development of truly international financial markets and the globalization of production undercut the rationale for capital controls. To analyze how these changes affected policies designed to limit capital mobility, it is useful to begin by looking at why such policies were deemed necessary in the first place. In the early 1960s strong theoretical support for the use of capital controls was provided by J. Marcus Fleming and Robert Mundell, who demonstrated that a government could achieve at most two of the following three conditions: capital mobility, monetary autonomy, and a fixed exchange rate. Consider what happens when a government decides to tighten monetary policy and maintain a constant exchange rate. Without capital mobility, the rise in interest rates will simply reduce aggregate demand. With capital mobility, such autonomy is lost, as funds attracted from abroad drive interest rates back down to world levels. A decision to loosen monetary policy would have the opposite effect. Of course, few countries have ever sought to insulate themselves completely from capital inflows or outflows. But throughout the postwar period, many did seek to limit the volume of those flows and thus preserve a degree of autonomy.

During the 1960s a growing number of economists argued that a preferable way to preserve national monetary autonomy was to abandon fixed exchange rates. With flexible exchange rates, a decision to tighten monetary policy might still attract capital, but its principal effect would be on the value of the national currency, not domestic interest rates. In this light, Harry Johnson explained, flexible exchange rates would "allow countries autonomy with respect to their use of monetary, fiscal, and other policy instruments, consistent with the maintenance of whatever degree of freedom in international transactions they choose to allow their citizens."

In practice, the shift to flexible exchange rates in the 1970s did not provide the desired panacea. The Mundell-Fleming analysis (upon which Johnson's recommendation was based) ignored feedback effects between exchange rates and domestic prices. As predicted, a country that sought to stimulate production by lowering interest rates suffered a depreciation of its currency. This depreciation, in turn, raised the price of its imports. If the country could not reduce imports quickly, higher import costs translated into higher prices for domestic production, thereby reducing the anticipated increase in output. Despite the shift to floating rates, many countries therefore still considered capital controls necessary to carve out as much autonomy as possible for their monetary policies.

In the 1970s and 1980s, however, two developments dramatically reduced the usefulness of capital controls. The first was the transformation and rapid growth of international financial markets. Between 1972 and 1985, for example, the size of the international banking market increased at a compound growth rate of 21.4 percent, compared with compound annual growth rates of 10.9 percent for world gross domestic product and 12.7 percent for world trade. Moreover, just as this pool of funds increased in size, technological changes reduced the time it took to transfer funds across borders. Since the early 1970s the daily turnover on the world's exchange markets has risen tremendously. In the midst of the currency crisis in March 1973, $3 billion were converted into European currencies in one day. In the late 1970s, daily turnover around the world was estimated at $100 billion; a decade later, that figure had reached $650 billion.

Just as these changes were occurring, a related development was taking place—an increasing number of businesses were moving toward a global configuration. Multinational enterprises (MNEs) were, of course, not new. What was new was the growth in their number, from just a few hundred in the early 1970s to well over a thousand in 1990. Moreover, for more and more MNEs, the home base was outside the United States. Globalization was also evident in the rapid growth of foreign direct investment. During the latter half of the 1980s, for example, flows of new FDI rose at an annual rate of 29 percent. According to one recent study, more than $3.5 trillion of business assets came under "foreign control" in the 1980s.

These twin changes had dramatic consequences for the use of capital controls. Most importantly, the expansion of financial markets made it progressively easier for private firms whose operations had become increasingly global to adopt strategies of exit and evasion. Evasion had obviously taken place for decades, but the means by which it could be conducted were now multiplied. Multinational structures enabled firms to evade capital controls by changing transfer prices or the timing of payments to or from foreign subsidiaries. The deepening of financial markets meant that firms could use subsidiaries or lend funds on foreign markets. If controls in a country became too onerous, MNEs could also attempt to escape them altogether by transferring activities abroad, that is, by exercising the exit option.

This possibility, in turn, constrained the choices available to governments. Assume that a government maintains a more expansionary monetary policy than the rest of the world in order to stimulate growth and create jobs. Assume further that it recognizes that higher interest rates abroad are likely to attract domestic savings needed to finance domestic investment, and it therefore imposes controls on capital outflows. If MNEs react to these controls by moving certain operations offshore, the domestic savings base essentially shrinks. In this instance, the country finds itself in a worse position than when it started. Clearly, if a government can anticipate this effect, credible threats of exit would deter the imposition of capital controls. To the extent that such threats are indeed credible, they highlight the deepening interrelationship between short-term and long-term investment flows. A government that is truly serious about restricting short-term capital movements would also have to be prepared to restrict offshore direct investments by domestic firms. It would then have to balance the losses (in terms of efficiency) borne by those firms and the national economy against the anticipated benefits of capital controls.

From the perspectives of firms, however, neither evasion nor exit is a costless option. Firms surely prefer to avoid capital controls or to have them removed, rather than having to consider either option. Thus, MNEs and financial institutions might be expected to mobilize against controls and promote policies encouraging international capital mobility. Governments concerned with the issue of national competitiveness might be expected to be especially responsive to such entreaties. They might also be expected to press other governments to liberalize.

Government decisions to abandon capital controls during the 1980s reflected fundamental changes in the markets through which capital could flow. In our examination of specific decisions in the cases of Japan, Germany, France, and Italy, we provide examples of how these changes affected decision-making processes. Not surprisingly, indisputable evidence of evasion and exit on the part of firms is difficult to find—the former because firms have little interest in making apparent their use of loopholes; the latter because it involves, in essence, a kind of structural power. It need not be exercised to have effect. What comes out clearly, however, is the perception by national policymakers that capital controls had become less useful and more costly.

Although similar pressures affected all advanced industrial countries, the speed with which specific governments responded depended upon whether they were experiencing capital inflows or outflows. The four countries we examine in the next section provide examples of each. Japan and Germany, typically recording surpluses in their current accounts and experiencing capital inflows, liberalized in 1980–81. France and Italy, typically recording external deficits and experiencing capital outflows, did not abandon capital controls until the end of the decade. This difference in timing should not be exaggerated, but neither should it be overlooked, for it helps to clarify the way in which the pressures discussed above shaped the development of particular national policies.

Countries that sought to control capital inflows faced different incentives from those facing countries that sought to control capital outflows. The reason lies mainly in the asymmetric impact of capital movements on foreign exchange reserves. Current account deficits, capital outflows, weakening exchange rates, and depleting reserves often go together; when they do, governments must either adjust their policies or adopt controls before the loss of reserves is complete. In contrast, governments facing the obverse situation find it easier to abandon controls since their reserve position is not threatened. This asymmetry can be enhanced for deficit countries committed to maintaining a fixed exchange rate, as was the case for France and Italy in the context of the European Monetary System (EMS).

## THE FOUR CASES

GERMANY  DEVELOPMENT OF CONTROLS.  In the early years of the Federal Republic, current account deficits and a dearth of foreign exchange reserves led to a strict prohibition on all exports of capital by residents. The legal basis for these controls was provided in the foreign exchange regulations of the Allied Occupation. By the early 1950s, however, West Germany's current account turned to surplus and the country's war-related external debts were finally settled. Restrictions on foreign direct investment abroad began to be liberalized in 1952, and residents were allowed to purchase foreign securities in 1956. By 1957 export of capital by residents was generally permitted without authorization. The relaxation of controls on outflows was effectively completed following restoration of currency convertibility in 1958, a policy stance legally enshrined in the Foreign Trade and Payments Act of 1961.

Owing largely to structural pressures on the deutsche mark in the Bretton Woods system of pegged exchange rates, however, this liberalization was not matched by similar progress on capital inflows. These pressures first emerged in the mid-1950s, when West Germany's low inflation rate and growing current account surplus increased the attractiveness of the mark relative to other currencies, notably the dollar. Under the Bretton Woods rules, the Bundesbank was required to enter the foreign exchange market and sell marks whenever the intervention point with the dollar was reached. But, of course, such obligatory purchases served to increase liquidity in the banking system and expand the money supply, thus creating inflation. Capital inflows therefore quickly came to be seen as significant threats to the Bundesbank's goal of maintaining price stability. Periodic expectations of revaluation and the resulting increase in speculative capital inflows dramatically underlined the dilemma.

In this situation, Germany essentially had two options as it struggled to maintain control over its domestic money supply. It could either revalue its currency or impose capital controls. Given the strong opposition of export interests to revaluation, transmitted in the subtle interplay between the government (which had responsibility for exchange rate policy) and the Bundesbank, the central bank's inclination tended in the latter direction. . . .

The transition to floating initially eased many of the pressures on the currency; the Bundesbank therefore began loosening some of its earlier restrictions but not dismantling its control apparatus altogether. Indeed, when confidence in the dollar began to decline in 1977, the Bundesbank again tightened existing capital controls and raised minimum reserve requirements on nonresidents' bank deposits to prevent what it considered an excessive appreciation of the mark. These measures were eased somewhat in 1978, when a shift in U.S. economic policy reduced inflows from abroad.

REASONS FOR LIBERALIZATION. The sudden lifting of controls in 1981 was certainly triggered by a shift in Germany's external accounts. What is striking, however, is that the Bundesbank did not consider it necessary to reimpose capital controls when the current account returned to surplus in 1982 or when the mark once again began to appreciate after the Plaza Agreement in 1985. The reasons for this policy turnaround are several.

Official views on the deutsche mark clearly underwent a dramatic change in the early 1980s. Throughout the 1960s and 1970s, the Bundesbank had, in effect, sought to prevent the mark from becoming a reserve currency largely to protect its ability to conduct an autonomous monetary policy and to deflect pressures for revaluation. Yet by 1983 the Bundesbank had reluctantly accepted the mark's increasing role in the world economy. Financial openness was seen to promise benefits; in 1986 the central bank would even boast that Germany "definitely maintained its international position as a financial center."

The rapid transformation in the Bundesbank's perspective reflected the changing interests of German banks. By the early 1980s, the large West German banks had become extensively involved in external markets. Their international assets (loans), for example, rose from $6.7 billion in 1973 to $73.3 billion in 1980 and $191 billion in 1985. With such rapidly rising international assets subject to world interest rates, banks became concerned about retaining a similar flexibility on the deposit side.

More subtle pressures on official policies also emanated from changing corporate strategies. In the 1970s and 1980s German companies became increasingly multinational and directed larger volumes of their investment overseas. Reflecting this evolution, German foreign direct investment in foreign markets rose from DM 3.2 billion in 1970 to DM 7.6 billion in 1980 and DM 14.1 billion in 1985. The growing internationalization of German business strengthened resistance to the reimposition of capital controls.

In the same vein, financial institutions, which had adapted well to the restrictiveness of the German capital market in the early years of the Federal Republic, gradually became willing to threaten the exit option. The decision, for example, by the Deutsche Bank to buy 5 percent of Morgan Grenfell and move its international capital market operations to London provided the West German authorities with a clear signal that something had to be done to prevent international business from gravitating away from Frankfurt to London.

By the opening of the 1990s, the desire to see Frankfurt more deeply integrated into global financial markets had overwhelmed residual concerns about the implications of capital decontrol. The perennial issue of enhancing the competitiveness of German industry would be advanced by other means, including the expansion of production facilities outside the Federal Republic. The massive financial challenges posed by unification only reinforced the policy movement away from controls. The inflows that had proved so problematic in earlier decades were now deliberately encouraged.

JAPAN   DEVELOPMENT OF CONTROLS.   As in Germany, the priority of economic reconstruction in Japan during the immediate years after World War II entailed tight official controls over both inflows and outflows of short-term capital.

Notwithstanding the first tentative moves toward financial openness, much publicized at the time, an extremely tight regime of controls over most capital movements remained. To be sure, certain inflows of hard currency, mainly U.S. dollars in the form of portfolio investment and foreign currency loans from American banks, were welcomed, but outflows and direct investment inflows were rigorously discouraged. The rationale for this policy stance was obvious. Even twenty years after the war, the country had no foreign currency reserves and was pursuing an ambitious strategy of indigenous industrial development. In effect, the policy amounted to husbanding and rationing scarce national resources. With an export-oriented economic growth strategy in place, the direct beneficiaries of the policy were leading industries selling their products in external markets. Financing was channeled to them mainly through highly regulated banks. Capital controls were key elements in a complex, but bureaucratically organized and directed financial system. In view of its own overarching foreign policy interests, the United States, the only possible challenger to this arrangement, willingly acquiesced.

A string of current account surpluses began to generate increasing volumes of reserves in the early 1970s, and corporate as well as official interest began to shift in the face of impending resource scarcities, domestic environmental problems, and the rise of trade barriers in several foreign markets. . . .

REASONS FOR LIBERALIZATION. Having contributed to tensions in its economic relations with the United States and Western Europe in the early 1970s and again in 1976, exchange rate issues were in the background in 1979 when the Ministry of Finance announced its intention to initiate a major liberalization program to cover inward as well as outward capital movements. The relative ease with which the economy was adjusting to the second oil crisis provided a permissive policy context for this shift. In 1980 it was codified in a new Foreign Exchange and Foreign Trade Control Law, which replaced the concept of capital flow interdiction with the concept of automaticity-in-principle.

It is no coincidence that such a regime was put into place at a time when remarkable changes were under way in the international direct investment strategies of Japanese firms. After decades of slight involvement abroad, Japanese FDI went into a period of explosive growth. Comparable to volumes recorded throughout the late 1960s and early 1970s, net long-term capital movements from Japan totaled U.S. $3.1 billion in 1977. In 1978 that number jumped to $12.4 billion, or 1.5 percent of Japan's GNP. By 1986 it had reached $132.1 billion, or 6.7 percent of GNP. In the face of these flows, and the options of evasion and exit that they implied for externally oriented Japanese firms, the control regime originally enshrined in law in 1949 had outlived its usefulness.

It is clear, however, that well-positioned Japanese intermediaries had the most to gain from the deepening of domestic capital markets promised by the twin policies of decontrol and deregulation, while Japanese manufacturing and financial firms overseas benefited to the extent that such policies defended their positions in foreign markets.

The private pressure for increased openness thereby generated was matched during much of the 1980s by the effects of rising public sector indebtedness, which further encouraged the deepening of domestic debt markets. Even without the added pressure coming from foreign governmental demands for decontrol, by 1990 high volumes of inward as well as outward capital flows translated into a broadening domestic political base for progressive financial liberalization and capital decontrol.

Despite extreme financial turbulence in the 1990s, including a collapse in stock and real estate prices and an associated pullback of Japanese financial intermediaries from foreign markets, few observers expected a movement back to capital controls. The internationalization of Japanese business and the international integration of Japanese financial markets had proceeded far enough to make such an option much less feasible than it had been even a decade earlier. For leading Japanese firms, in particular, strategies of evasion and exit were now embedded in their very structures. That reality gave them significant new leverage over Japan's capital policies.

FRANCE    DEVELOPMENT OF CONTROLS. Controls on foreign exchange transactions in France, although first introduced in 1915, became firmly established only after the Second World War. Like most other

European countries, France initially used capital controls to ensure that its limited foreign exchange be used for domestic reconstruction and development. In later years, controls on capital outflows were kept in place because of persistent current account deficits.

For the socialists as for their conservative predecessors, heavy reliance on capital controls thus resulted primarily from a desire to keep domestic interest rates lower than those generally prevailing in the rest of the world without abandoning the objective of exchange rate stability. Lower interest rates reduced demand for franc-denominated assets and stimulated domestic demand for imports. Together, these two effects increased net capital outflows and placed pressure on the franc. To avoid a precipitous decline of the franc (even if France left the EMS), tighter capital controls were deemed necessary. As the socialist government discovered, however, such controls had to be continuously tightened if they were to be effective. The controls of 1983 placed the French economy in the tightest corset since World War II.

REASONS FOR LIBERALIZATION. In November 1984 Prime Minister Laurent Fabius announced a dramatic new plan to reform the entire financial system. The government planned not only to eliminate credit ceilings and capital controls, but also to create new money, bond, and futures markets. Such wholesale reform had not been expected. Unlike France's decision to remain in the EMS, pressure from its EC partners was not part of the policy calculation; indeed, the announcement of its financial reform package *preceded* the commission's June 1985 white paper on European financial integration.

What drove this new program of financial liberalization? Evasion strategies on the part of individuals and firms were certainly in the background; the famous stories about suitcases filled with foreign currency being carried into Switzerland come to mind. More subtle and ultimately more decisive pressures emanated, however, from the boardrooms of large French firms and financial intermediaries. In the French case, direct threats of exit were muted by the fact that virtually all of these firms were owned or controlled by the state. In this environment, such an option was transmuted into the rising concerns of government officials regarding the competitiveness of those firms relative to their foreign rivals. Jobs and investment that were promised by growth in the service sector, for example, were seen to be leaving France and migrating to less-restricted markets. In a very real sense, especially in financial services, Paris was increasingly seen to be in direct competition with London and Frankfurt. Such perceptions clearly lay behind the subsequent commitment of Finance Minister Balladur to make Paris "the leading financial market in Europe. . . ."

ITALY DEVELOPMENT OF CONTROLS. Restrictions on capital movements were initially put in place in Italy during the First World War. They were refined and tightened by Mussolini during the following two decades. Controls were relaxed in the late 1950s, a period of current account surpluses and currency stability. The "hot autumn" of 1969, however, dramatically altered Italy's economic trajectory. Facing increased labor militancy, the government put into place an expansionary fiscal policy to spur growth and ensure social peace. By 1973 this policy resulted in fiscal imbalances and current account deficits. The lira soon came under speculative attack. Rather than reverse its economic policy and risk unrest, the government responded by tightening capital controls. . . .

Still, government officials viewed capital controls as a means of avoiding hard choices. By the mid-1980s the annual budget deficit had topped 11 percent of GDP and cumulative debt approached 100 percent of GDP. To finance these deficits, the government had long relied on a large domestic savings pool. Household savings in Italy amounted to 20 percent of personal disposable income—the second highest savings rate in the world after Japan. Doing away with capital controls in the face of such deficits meant that domestic savers would be able to purchase foreign assets, forcing the government to offer a higher rate of interest on its own debt.

REASONS FOR LIBERALIZATION.   The elimination of capital controls in Italy did not begin until 1987 and was not completed until 1992. Given the difficulties faced by Italian policymakers, the source of this policy change is particularly interesting. Of the major EC countries, Italy was the only one whose decision was affected by pressure from its partners, particularly Germany, to comply with the EC directive on capital movements. . . .

Still, it would be a mistake to attribute Italy's policy shift primarily to such external pressure, for in Italy—as in Germany, Japan, and France—private pressure for liberalization had become pervasive. Evasion of capital controls, of course, was a national sport, practiced by business executives, government ministers, and even church officials.

More important for the shift in policy, however, was the increasingly assertive position taken by private firms. Financial institutions, for example, had become concerned about the effect of controls on their ability to compete. It was perhaps not surprising that foreign companies opposed capital controls.

Manufacturing firms, like Olivetti and Fiat, also favored an end to controls. As the power of organized labor diminished in the 1980s, these firms became more profitable and competitive in foreign markets. They were therefore also more directly hampered by restrictions on capital movements and concerned about the prospect of not being able to take full advantage of the expanding EC market.

## CONCLUSION

In the early years of the postwar period, governments relied on controls over short-term capital movements for one fundamental purpose—to provide their economies with the maximum feasible degree of policymaking autonomy without sacrificing the benefits of economic interdependence. Controls were a shield that helped deflect the blows of international competition and ameliorate its domestic political effects. In the Bretton Woods system of pegged exchange rates, controls promised to provide both the space needed for the design of distinct national economic policies and the time needed for gradual economic adjustment to a changing external environment. To the surprise of some, they remained essential for many governments even when that system was replaced by managed floating.

Between the late 1970s and the early 1990s, a broad movement away from capital controls was evident across the industrialized world. The rapid growth of liquid international funds and the increasing globalization of production drove this process. Offshore markets eroded national financial barriers, not least by providing ever-widening sources of funding for multinational firms engaged in the process of globalizing their production facilities. In so doing, they enhanced the capability of firms to develop evasion and exit strategies. Governments thus first found that controls had to be tightened continuously to remain useful and then discovered that the resulting or potential economic costs of such tightening soon exceeded the benefits.

To be sure, governments encouraged or at least acquiesced in both the growth of offshore money markets and the international expansion of firms. Yet as our case histories show, governments continued to impose capital controls long after such developments became salient. In this sense, the diminishing utility of capital controls can be considered the unintended consequence of other and earlier policy decisions.

Strategies of evasion and exit on the part of firms, we have argued, threatened to reduce the volume of domestic savings and investment, the promotion of which often constituted the original rationale for controls. Of course, firms could use direct methods for pushing the decontrol agenda, as we saw in the French case where state ownership was a significant factor. But their ultimate influence on policy came from the pressure to evade controls or exit from their national jurisdictions if they were to remain competitive. In the German case, for example, by making moves offshore, the Deutsche Bank effectively made the case that capital controls were inconsistent with the goal of building a strong national financial center.

Other factors have influenced the elimination of capital controls, but our cases suggest that such factors played a secondary role. The principle of international capital mobility, for example, had long been enshrined in the OECD Code on Capital Movements, but until the 1980s virtually every major signatory country had at some point honored that principle in the breach. Similarly, a common European capital market was a key objective of the 1992 program, but the success of this effort was preceded (and made possible) by national programs of capital decontrol in both France and Germany. Fundamental changes at the domestic level also underpinned the apparent success of direct political pressure by other governments. In the Japanese case, for example, American pressure appeared at most to reinforce firm-level pressures associated with the rapid expansion of Japanese financial intermediaries and companies in overseas markets.

Notwithstanding the general movement in the direction of capital liberalization across the advanced industrial world, our cases point to important differences in the timing of actual decisions to decontrol. It was easier for countries facing capital inflows (Japan and Germany) to lift capital controls, than it was for countries facing capital outflows (France and Italy). The difference in timing—roughly a decade—underlines the mechanism by which systemic forces were translated into national decisions. Our cases do not enable us to reach definitive conclusions in this regard, but it seems likely that these differences in timing are correlated with broader variations in domestic political structures. Whether a country is facing chronic capital inflows or outflows may depend upon the structure of the state and the relative strength of domestic interest groups. But the fundamental convergence in the direction of capital mobility noted in all of our cases suggests that systemic forces are now dominant in the financial area and have dramatically reduced the ability of governments to set autonomous economic policies.

Our argument and evidence do not suggest, however, that a movement back toward capital controls or analogous policies to influence the flow of capital are impossible, only that such a movement would be more costly from a national point of view. Indeed, the restoration of controls is not just a theoretical possibility. In the midst of the European currency crisis in September 1992, for example, Spain and Ireland imposed new controls on banks' foreign exchange transactions. Despite the fact that such "temporary" measures did not contravene the letter of a prior agreement to eliminate impediments to capital mobility throughout the European Community, they surely conflicted with its spirit. More generally, continuing instability in global currency markets did subsequently lead the G-7, at the urging of American treasury secretary Nicholas Brady, to commission a new study to explore multilateral approaches to dealing with the consequences of international capital mobility.

If our argument is correct, two theoretical as well as policy implications bear underlining. First, if pressures for capital decontrol are now deeply embedded in firm structure and strategy, any efforts to understand or deal with the political effects of short-term capital mobility would seem to entail dealing with the politics of foreign direct investment. The two issues have long been related, but have also long been viewed as distinguishable for conceptual as well as for policy purposes. The distinction has broken down. The adoption of policies to influence short-term capital flows would now have a clearer impact on long-term investment decisions. Further research on this deepening connection is warranted.

Second, if policy convergence on the issue of capital controls is intimately linked to the development of international financial markets, attempts to understand and manage the effects of short-term capital mobility cannot be divorced from efforts to enhance the cross-national coordination of financial policies. As the negotiators at Bretton Woods recognized in 1944, open and stable markets ultimately depend upon a modicum of shared behavioral norms. Despite deepening interdependence across contemporary financial markets, states retain the right to change their policies on capital movements, either individually or on a regional basis. What remains unclear is their obligation to take into account the consequences of such policies for other states and for the world community. Thus, the time may now be ripe to begin considering new international arrangements to define and demarcate national responsibilities in an age of global markets.

# SECURITY,
# DEVELOPMENT, AND THE STATE

This section examines two related issues: The first issue relates the compatibility of economic development with political and environmental concerns. The second issue relates economic development with the notion of security. Are they two different issues or are they two sides of the same coin?

The selection by Raymond Vernon examines the reasons behind the global movement toward liberalization and privatization. After decades of experimenting with state ownership, governments of all persuasions appear committed to strengthening the private sector. Why is this? He argues that fundamental forces, such as the lack of funds, changes in market structures, obsolescent industries, and the learning process, are the main factors behind the movement toward privatization.

Alison Butler looks at a different question. Economists have traditionally considered the environment to be outside the realm of economic analysis. Moreover, conventional wisdom suggests that environmental protection hinders trade. After laying out the rationale behind environmental protection, she maintains that it is possible to adopt certain environmental standards without distorting trade, provided there are international agreements that are strictly enforced and that industrial countries do not put an undue burden on industrializing economies.

The selections illustrating the political approach analyze somewhat different problems. Michael Klare looks at attempts at redefining security. The concept has traditionally had a military connotation. This view has been challenged in the 1990s. The term has been expanded to incorporate ethnic, social, and economic dimensions because they all affect a country's security. The selection illustrates the point that IPE is no longer confined to its traditional realm of economics, but is closely linked to so-called high politics as well.

Janet Welsh Brown looks at a very important global problem, the relationship between population increases and consequent rises in consumption and their effects on sustainable development. She finds that increases in population will have catastrophic effects on development given the current rates of consumption in the world. In her view, government rather than the market, is the solution. To avoid this tragedy, she advocates a reduction of the high rates of consumption by eliminating subsidies to certain industries in developed countries and halting the inefficient use of renewable resources in developing nations. The author hopes that these combined measures will prompt countries to achieve levels of growth they can sustain for generations to come.

# THE PROMISE OF PRIVATIZATION

Raymond Vernon

In the past half decade, scores of governments throughout the world have announced their intention to dispose of some of the enterprises that they own, by selling them to the private sector in some instances and by liquidating them in others.

## AN ABRUPT SHIFT

The change of mood and policy on the subject of privatization came swiftly: an abrupt shift became visible in the early 1980s and grew rapidly thereafter. Before that period, privatization programs had been rare in both the mature industrialized economies and the developing countries. Indeed, the only programs of much importance were the U.S. government's liquidations and divestitures immediately after the end of World War II of various enterprises created during the war and the Chilean divestitures of the 1970s under President Augusto Pinochet. . . .

Critics of state-owned enterprises commonly took it for granted that the insatiable appetite of such enterprises for cash was due primarily to the inefficiency of their managers and workers, and that the problem could be cured by turning these enterprises over to private ownership. But the facts have proved much more complicated.

Cases of gross incompetence, padded payrolls, and even outright looting of state-owned enterprises have not been hard to find. Flagrant instances under each of these headings have appeared in various countries, including the Philippines, Indonesia, Nigeria, and Zaire. The glaring cases, however, have revealed much more about the basic character of the governments involved than about the efficiency potentials of state-owned enterprises. Where governments have been reasonably competent and responsible, and where comparisons between private enterprises and state-owned enterprises have been possible, the technical performance of state-owned enterprises has not appeared much different from that of private enterprises. Here and there, a strikingly efficient performance by a state-owned enterprise has cast added doubt on the simple stereotype of the public enterprise as a perennial wastrel.

Still, the evidence that state-owned enterprises contributed heavily to the cash deficits of governments in the late 1970s and 1980s has been incontrovertible. Some of the causes of that drain have been obvious. For one thing, state-owned enterprises in developing countries were charged principally with building up the modern infrastructure of those countries, an activity that is, as a rule, highly capital-intensive. The cash needs of the enterprises were increased by the fact that their governments commonly used them as conduits for the distribution of subsidies, such as subsidies for staple foods and transportation to urban dwellers or for electrical power and transportation to rural areas. In addition, in both developed and developing countries, state-owned enterprises were often expected to mount rescue operations for privately owned factories and shipyards that were about to close their doors. In brief, the deficits of the state-owned enterprises were much more easily traced to the policies of their governments than to their own inherent inefficiencies. . . .

The first few years of the 1980s were difficult for practically all countries. Economic growth slowed markedly. As a result, the financial resources of the public sector dried up at the same time that the private sector in many countries found itself in a much easier cash position. In the mature industrialized countries, national electorates proved strongly resistant to increasing their tax burdens as a way of meeting the fiscal problems of the public sector. In the developing countries, following the 1982 debt crisis in Mexico, the international capital markets proved unavailable. The acute needs for cash on the public side suggested an obvious solution: to sell salable public assets to the private sector.

The sudden drying up of resources for the public sector of many countries in the 1980s, however, appears to have triggered deeper and broader reactions to governments' economic policies, reactions that had been building over longer periods of time.

With hindsight, it appears that the high point in the self-confidence of public policymakers in their ability to manage the economy occurred in the late 1960s. Up to that time, macroeconomic modeling was thought to provide a reliable guide for the fine-tuning of the mature industrialized economies, while input-output matrices were thought to afford important guidance for the policies of developing countries.

In the 1970s, however, public confidence in the ability of governments to manage their national economies shrank dramatically, under the impact of floating exchange rates, erratic commodity prices, huge capital flows, and inflation. A generation of young economists rediscovered the virtues of decentralized decision making and the power of the efficient market, a shift facilitated and accelerated by the fact that many were receiving their graduate training in the United States and Great Britain. For many of these economists, the principal question became how to structure markets so that their theoretical virtues could in fact be realized.

## CHANGE AND OBSOLESCENCE

The countries that have announced their intention of launching some kind of privatization program profess to a wide variety of economic ideologies, from undiluted capitalism to collectivism in a dozen forms. But almost all of them allow for the possibility of private ownership of the means of production and for the operation of markets as an essential feature of the economy's functioning.

In such countries, the government's decision to create a state-owned enterprise has typically been an eclectic response to a public need, based on the pragmatic conclusion that the creation of such an enterprise would serve that need more effectively than would any other alternative, such as a new set of regulations, a program of taxation, or a program of subsidies. As a rule, however, the circumstances leading to these decisions have been changing, raising questions about the continued usefulness of the state-owned enterprise.

**THE RISE OF A MANAGERIAL CLASS.** The most obvious illustration of such a change has been the achievement of some measure of industrialization, accompanied by the rise of a managerial class. Developments in Japan from 1868 to 1880 provided one of the most striking cases in the modern era of a government's pragmatically creating a series of state-owned enterprises in order to launch a process of industrialization, then turning these enterprises over to private entrepreneurs when the entrepreneurs appeared ready for the transfer. After World War II, many developing countries created state-owned enterprises for much the same reasons as the Japanese had: at the time many of these enterprises were created, indigenous entrepreneurs were not yet ready to assume the financial risks and assemble the managerial and technical talent required for the purpose; and foreign entrepreneurs were unacceptable as owners of key industries, particularly at the pioneer stage, when such enterprises were likely to be monopolists in the national economy.

As in Japan, however, indigenous entrepreneurs have not been long in acquiring the financial resources and managerial skills needed for a modern industrial state. It has taken only a generation for the newly industrializing countries—the so-called NICs—to generate communities of formidable local businessmen. With the appearance of such entrepreneurs, the pioneer state-owned enterprises have sometimes found themselves in competition with new entrants from the private sector. What is more, in facing that competition, some state-owned enterprises have been handicapped by obsolescent technologies and inflated work forces, handicaps so large that they have overwhelmed the privileges that such enterprises usually enjoyed, such as privileged access to credit. Where such developments have occurred, the possibility of turning the enterprises over to the private sector has become a feasible option, one that has been rendered more attractive to governments by the drying up of sources of cash for the public sector.

CHANGES IN MARKET STRUCTURES. Another factor that has influenced governments to reconsider the role of state-owned enterprise in their national economies is changes in the structure of international markets. A central motivation that led governments to create many state-owned enterprises during the 1960s and 1970s was to try to increase their share of the monopoly rents from their exports of minerals, petroleum, and agricultural products. Developing countries in Asia and Africa, upon attaining independence after World War II, frequently found themselves heirs to systems of monopoly export that had been created by their erstwhile mother countries. Official systems of monopoly export were particularly common in agricultural products. In other products, such as copper and oil, foreign-owned firms typically controlled both the production and the export functions, thereby exercising a dominant role in the economies in which they operated. During the 1960s and 1970s, however, many governments set up state-owned enterprises to take over the functions that previously had been performed by the foreign-owned enterprises.

But the very forces that made it possible for developing countries to consider gaining control of their export industries were undermining the monopolistic possibilities in many of those same industries. In tropical products, like bananas and cocoa beans, leading firms such as Unilever and United Fruit were being forced to share their market dominance with an increasing number of newcomers. In copper, the four or five companies that had dominated world markets for many decades were going through a similar experience. These companies were being obliged to share world markets with a dozen or so new entrants, many of them state-owned. In oil, the Seven Sisters were surrendering significant shares of the world market to a half dozen smaller privately owned oil companies.

The state-owned enterprises that came into existence in the 1960s and 1970s, therefore, were participating in markets that were much more difficult to control than those existing a decade or two earlier. That fact was quickly apparent in some markets, including cocoa beans and copper; eventually, after a bonanza period of five or six years in which the new state-owned enterprises in the oil industry gained huge profits, the weakness in market control devices also became evident in the oil market. The increase in the number of sellers, combined with other handicaps that hobbled state-owned enterprises in any effective effort at international cooperation, weakened the efforts of these enterprises to collect monopoly rents.

As the change in global market structures has become apparent, some governments have begun to consider whether partnerships with foreign firms could recapture some of their shrunken monopoly rents and could increase the stability in the flow of income from their export products. The account of developments in the oil industry that appears in a later chapter portrays the second thoughts that governments have had on this score. In most developing countries, the possibility of entering into a new association with foreign firms in products such as oil, copper, and bananas raises some prickly political issues. But once again, the monetary crisis appears to have created the circumstances in which governments can seriously entertain such possibilities.

**OBSOLESCENT INDUSTRIES.** As a rule, governments have hoped to use their power and resources in the creation of state-owned enterprises to promote the fundamental objectives of growth and development. In actual practice, however, many have found themselves diverting a considerable part of their resources to rescuing the failing operations of the private sector. Sometimes those operations have taken the form of buy-outs, thereby adding to the roster of state-owned enterprises. At other times, the rescue operations have involved the extension of public credit to the private sector; when borrowers have defaulted, governments have found themselves in possession of the defaulting enterprise. Patterns of that sort have been prevalent in various countries of Western Europe, notably in steel, shipbuilding, and textiles. But such rescues have also occurred on a considerable scale in many developing countries, as the private sector has sought to abandon some of its less successful operations.

Governments generally see their role in these operations as one of cushioning a decline. Their aim is to reduce the work force by attrition rather than by layoff, and to give localities some time to adjust to the changes in their economic situation. As long as the government clings to that objective, cash drains are usually unavoidable. What is in contention, therefore, is only the speed of the adjustment process and the duration of the bridging operation. The political forces in most countries usually tip the scale toward prolonging the bridging operation in perpetuity. With the cash squeeze of the 1980s, however, governments have turned with renewed interest to the possibility of accelerating their withdrawal, a step that has usually been counted as an act of privatization.

## UNFORESEEN CONSEQUENCES OF STATE OWNERSHIP

In many instances, what has induced governments to reconsider their policies with respect to state-owned enterprises has not been a change in the external environment so much as what they have learned about the costs and benefits of operating such enterprises. In recent years, some governments have turned to the privatization option primarily because the benefits they had hoped to achieve from the operations of the state-owned enterprise have not materialized.

**THE "COMMANDING HEIGHTS" OBJECTIVE.** Political parties that identify themselves with the social democratic tradition, such as the

Labour party in the United Kingdom, have usually supported an active policy of managing the economy in order to stimulate growth, prevent unemployment, and contribute to an egalitarian distribution of income. To that end, they have seen the state-owned enterprise as an instrument for capturing the "commanding heights" of the economy—that is, the key sectors that could serve to stimulate investment, influence prices, and set wage levels in accordance with official objectives.

The experience of governments in attempting to use state-owned enterprises for such purposes, however, has rarely measured up to expectations. Managers sometimes successfully resist or subvert the directions of the ministers, when those directions seem adverse to the interests of the firm. And when managers respond affirmatively to directions that are not in their firm's best interests, such as an instruction to expand investment in order to stimulate the economy, the consequences are sometimes disastrous for the firm. . . .

CAPTURE BY STAKEHOLDERS. Another phenomenon that has increased the interest of some governments in privatization has been a tendency for many state-owned enterprises to fall under the dominance of one or more of the principal stakeholders, who stand to profit from the existence of the enterprise. In some cases, notably in the operation of urban transport systems and in the production and distribution of food staples, consumers have been the principal beneficiaries, capturing the profits and benefiting from the deficits of the enterprise. In other cases, including public utilities and other monopolies, semiskilled and unskilled labor has often managed to exact a rent unrelated to its contribution, by drawing wages much higher than those for comparable jobs in the private sector. In still other cases, especially capital-intensive installations that have produced for privately owned import-substituting industries, the owners of such industries have been major beneficiaries. Finally, high-ranking civil servants have used their directorships in state-owned enterprises to augment their civil service incomes, while ministers and other politicians have drawn on the resources of such enterprises for various personal and political purposes.

In any economy that has a place for democratic processes, factions struggling to capture the rewards of a government program are a familiar feature of the political landscape. Once one of these groups has come to dominate the policies of any enterprise, however, the support of other groups for continued state ownership of the enterprise is likely to decrease. At the same time, cash stringencies restrain the capacity of the enterprises to serve even the interests of their principal stakeholders. Workers are not paid; customers are not served. Accordingly, the political support for continuing the operations of some of these enterprises declines. Privatization, with its untapped potential for increasing the cash flow to the public sector, thereby takes on added appeal.

Nevertheless, in some countries, stakeholders still see enough benefits from the operations of state-owned enterprises that they will not give up their prize without a struggle. . . .

**BREAKAWAY MANAGERS.** A number of observers have been struck by the frequency with which managers of state-owned enterprises have employed strategies designed to weaken the control of supervising ministries and increase their own scope of action in the conduct of the enterprise. In a few countries, unfortunately, supervising ministries have been so inept as to be unable to oversee the performance of the managers. In most instances, however, managers have had to reckon with the ministries as an inhibiting force.

The tendency of managers to try to escape from the supervision of the ministries has not been universal. Indeed, in countries that have filled management positions from the regular civil service lists, managers often have seen themselves as the passive caretakers of their enterprises, responding to the commands of their political superiors. But manages who have acquired their position through other routes, especially through careers in the state-owned sector, have characteristically sought to distance themselves from their public controllers, using a number of familiar strategies.

The efforts of managers to acquire some autonomy have highlighted the many difficulties that governments face in creating effective systems of public control over state-owned enterprises. Some governments have attempted to impose controls on the enterprises similar to those that would apply to ministries, including *ex ante* approval of expenditures; but such systems have usually stifled the enterprises to which they were applied or else have degenerated into meaningless routines.

Most governments, therefore, have fashioned systems that depend heavily on *ex post* controls. Such systems, however, demand a high degree of effort and expertise on the part of the controllers, ingredients that have been in scarce supply even in the mature industrialized countries. As a result, the systems of control developed by most governments have left substantial opportunities for managers who have been determined to escape the effective oversight of the ministries.

The motivations of managers in resisting government supervision have been quite mixed. In some cases—for instance, where the state-owned enterprise has been a huge earner of foreign exchange for the country—the chief executive officer has enjoyed a status higher than any minister; managers in this position commonly have regarded any measures of accountability to a minister as an affront to their personal dignity. In many cases—perhaps in most cases—the principal motivation has been to perform more efficiently. Managers of state-owned enterprises in France, Italy, Great Britain, and Brazil have often exhibited behavior suggestive of that state of mind. In some cases, too, managers may have been driven by the human desire to run their own show without having to account to others who were less committed and less knowledgeable about the business. In a few instances, no doubt, managers have wished for a freer hand in order to line their own pockets.

One of the strategies that many managers have employed to weaken the power of the minister has been to restructure the enterprise under their control, especially by creating subsidiaries to take on new ventures or to perform functions that previously had been executed within the enterprise. The opportunity of managers to use such a strategy has depended upon the power and effectiveness of the controllers. But the evidence is that in many countries of Africa and Latin America, managers have succeeded in creating large numbers of such subsidiaries without effective monitoring from the ministries.

The advantages to managers of presiding over a network of subsidiaries also have depended upon the nature of the national systems of control. Under some systems, directors and managers of such subsidiaries have been accountable entirely to the parent state-owned enterprise, and connections to the supervising ministries have been tenuous. At the same time, under some systems of financial control, parent firms have had considerable leeway in determining how the profits of the enterprise are distributed between parent and subsidiary, using the familiar device of apportioning overhead costs and transferring goods and services between parent and subsidiary at arbitrary prices. In some cases, too, parent and subsidiary managers have been in a position to mask the subsidiary's financial statements from the scrutiny of the public controllers, thereby increasing the capacity of the managers to conceal profits or losses for an extended period.

It has taken the money crunch of the 1980s to get many governments to review the condition of their state-owned enterprise sectors. In the process, some have discovered that their commitments were larger and more diverse than ministers had realized. That discovery, coupled with the realization that the fashioning of effective measures of control is extremely difficult, has whetted the interests of governments in the privatization option.

# ENVIRONMENTAL PROTECTION AND FREE TRADE: ARE THEY MUTUALLY EXCLUSIVE?

Alison Butler

This paper examines the different ways environmental policy can have international ramifications and their implications for international trade and international trade agreements. A general introduction to environmental economics is given, followed by an analysis of the relationship between environmental policy and international trade. The paper concludes with a discussion of the status of environmental considerations in multilateral trade agreements.

## AN ECONOMIC RATIONALE FOR ENVIRONMENTAL POLICY

The environment is used primarily in three ways: as a consumption good, a supplier of resources and a receptacle of wastes. These three uses may conflict with one another. For example, using a river as a receptacle of wastes can conflict with its use as a supplier of resources and as a consumption good. When either the production or consumption of a good causes a cost that is not reflected in a market price, market failures that are termed "externalities" may exist. Such market failures frequently involve the environment. . . .

**WHY DO EXTERNALITIES OCCUR?**   Externalities exist when the *social cost* of an activity differs from the *private cost* because of the absence of property rights. In the preceding example, because no one "owns" the air, the factory does not take into account the extra washing costs it imposes on the citizens of the town. As a result, more pollution than is socially optimal will occur because the private cost of the smoke emissions to the firm (zero) is lower than the social cost (£290,000 a year). In general, if nothing is done about negative externalities, environmental damage will result as ecologically harmful products are overproduced and the environment is overused.

To eliminate externalities, the divergence between the social and private costs must be eliminated, either by assigning private property rights (that is, ownership rights) or by direct government regulation. The approach taken often depends on whether property rights can be assigned. The advantage of assigning property rights to an externality is that it creates a market for that product and allows the price mechanism to reflect the value of the externality.

**EXAMPLE OF ASSIGNING PROPERTY RIGHTS.** Suppose a chemical factory locates upstream from a small town and emits waste into the river as part of its production process. Suppose further that the town uses the river as its primary source of water. As a result of these emissions, the town must process the water before use. Clearly there is an externality associated with the firm's use of the water—it is no longer usable to the town without cost. If property rights to the river could be assigned to either the town or the firm, then the two parties could bargain for the most efficient level of pollutants in the water.

If property rights are assigned to the firm, the town pays the firm to reduce its pollution. The town's willingness to pay for reduced levels of pollution depends on the benefits it receives from cleaner water. Generally speaking, as the water becomes more pure, the additional (marginal) benefits to the town likely decrease. On the other hand, the firm's willingness to reduce pollution depends on the costs it incurs to reduce pollution by, for example, changing to a more costly production or waste-disposal method. Generally speaking, as the firm pollutes less, the additional (marginal) costs to the firm increase. The amount of pollution agreed upon will be such that the added benefits to the town of a further reduction in pollution are less than the added costs to the firm of the further reduction.

## THE TRADE-RELATED ASPECTS OF ENVIRONMENTAL QUALITY

Pollution can have international effects in two ways. First, it might be localized within national boundaries but, through the impact of environmental policy, affect a country's international trade. On the other hand, pollution may be transported across borders without the consent of the countries affected (so-called transfrontier pollution). These two types of environmental damage have different effects on international trade and, therefore, are discussed separately.

**WHY DO COUNTRIES TRADE?** Countries trade because of differences in comparative advantage. The idea of comparative advantage suggests that, given demand, countries should export products that they can produce relatively cheaply and import products for which they have a relative cost disadvantage. Traditional international trade models ignore externalities such as non-priced uses of the environment.

By not explicitly including the environment as a factor of production, the costs associated with using the environment are ignored. More recent economic models have extended the definition of factors to include *assimilative capacity*, that is, the capacity of the environment to reduce pollutants by natural processes. The degree to which the environment will be affected by its use or by the production of ecologically harmful products depends on its assimilative capacity. The higher the assimilative capacity, the less the environmental damage caused by the emission of a given amount of pollutants. Assimilative capacity can differ across regions and countries and thus is an important factor in determining the effects of environmental use on trade.

Traditional trade models also ignore the non-priced use of the environment as a consumption good. This underestimates the value consumers may place on the environment and therefore the cost of using the environment for other functions. These two factors can be significant in determining a country's comparative advantage.

**WHY WOULD COUNTRIES CHOOSE DIFFERENT LEVELS OF ENVIRONMENTAL QUALITY?** Assimilative capacity is one of the principal factors affecting a country's choice of environmental quality. In general, assimilative capacity is lower in industrialized countries because of the effects of past pollution. Less-industrialized countries often have greater assimilative capacities and thus can tolerate a higher level of emissions without increasing pollution levels. Population density and geography also affect a country's assimilative capacity. For example, the introduction of a polluting industry in a sparsely populated area, all else equal, will likely not affect the assimilative capacity of that area as much as it would in a densely populated area.

Other factors can also affect a country's willingness to accept environmental degradation. For example, poor countries may put a higher priority on the benefits of production (such as higher employment and income) relative to the benefits of environmental quality than wealthy countries. As income levels increase, however, demand for environmental quality also rises. Thus, countries with similar assimilative capacities might choose different levels of environmental quality. As the example below demonstrates, environmental policies that result from differences in countries' preferences and income levels can have significant trade effects.

**ENVIRONMENTAL POLICY WHEN POLLUTION IS WITHIN NATIONAL BOUNDARIES.** How does environmental policy affect trade? Recall that, in the emissions tax example, the higher production costs that resulted from the tax caused the price of the industry's output to increase and the quantity produced to fall. Assume there is a chemical industry in

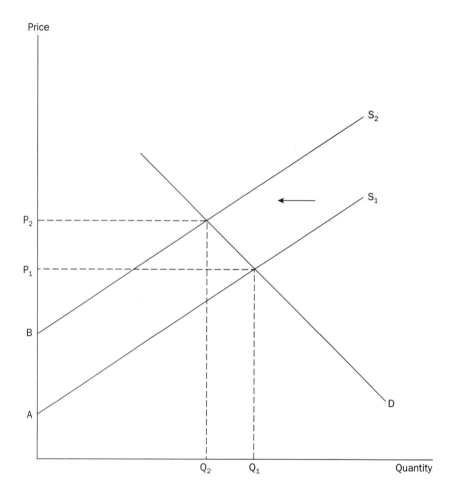

**FIGURE 1**

THE EFFECT OF AN EMISSIONS TAX ON INDUSTRY PRICE AND OUTPUT

another country producing the same product with the same level of emissions. For simplicity, assume that, prior to the implementation of environmental controls, each industry produced just enough to meet its home demand, and the price was the same in both countries. As a result, trade did not occur. Suppose, because of different preferences, income levels or assimilative capacity, it is optimal to impose environmental controls in one country but not in the other. What happens to price, output and environmental quality in the two countries?

The answer depends in part on whether the two countries can trade. If trade does not occur, the effect is the same as in the previous example. As Figure 1 shows, in the country where pollution controls were imposed, the price

THE EFFECT OF AN EMISSIONS TAX ON INDUSTRY
PRICE AND OUTPUT IN A TWO-COUNTRY WORLD

FIGURE 2

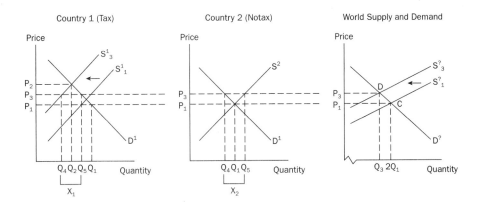

will rise to $P_2$ and the quantity of output will fall to $Q_2$, while in the other country nothing changes. Figure 2 shows the effect of an emissions tax on price and output in the two countries when trade occurs. The reduction in supply of the chemical in the taxed country (Tax) will reduce the world supply of that product, causing the world supply curve to shift upward to the left. At the new world equilibrium D, the price, $P_3$, is lower than the autarkic (no trade) equilibrium price in Tax ($P_2$), but higher than the autarkic equilibrium price in the other country, Notax ($P_1$). At $P_3$, consumers in Notax demand $Q_4$, but firms are willing to supply $Q_5$. The distance $X_2$ is exactly equal to the distance $X_1$, which measures the difference between what firms in Tax are willing to supply at $P_3$ ($Q_4$) and what consumers demand at that price ($Q_5$). As a result, Notax exports the quantity $X_2$ of the chemical to Tax.

What is the effect on other economic variables? Consumption of the chemical falls in Notax, even though output rises. In general, because of the increased production in Notax, there will be an increase in pollution emissions in that country. How much the pollution *level* actually increases in Notax (if at all) depends on the assimilative capacity and the method of production used in that country. Whether the people in Notax are better off at the potentially higher level of pollution that resulted from increased production depends on that country's willingness to accept higher pollution for higher income.

Pollution declines in Tax. If the assimilative capacity is higher in Notax, world pollution will likely be lower after environmental controls are implemented. The effect on world employment is ambiguous and depends on certain country-specific variables. The terms of trade will deteriorate for the country with the emissions tax.

If the new level of emissions in each country is optimal given preferences and income, both countries are better off by trade. The taxed country is able to consume more at a lower price than in the autarkic case, while the value of total output rises in Notax. If measures of national income or wealth accurately reflected environmental damage, they would increase in both countries.

**DOES ENVIRONMENTAL PROTECTION DISTORT TRADE?** One concern is that environmental regulation unfairly discriminates against domestic firms when they compete with firms in a country that has lower environmental standards. In the example discussed above, an externality existed in Tax but, by assumption, not in Notax. As a result, introducing environmental controls eliminated a distortion that previously existed. This changed the flow of trade, but caused all the costs of using the environment, both as inputs in production and as consumption items, to be reflected in market prices. Thus, assuming that environmental quality was not socially optimal before protections were enacted, pollution-intensive sectors in Tax were actually receiving an implicit subsidy from those who had been incurring the external costs of pollution.

The difficulties in trying to determine the optimal amount of environmental quality within a country, as discussed above, are substantial. The optimal level of environmental quality in one country is unlikely to be optimal in another, particularly if the two countries have significantly different income levels. Attempting to impose one country's environmental standards on another by using import restrictions does not allow countries to capitalize fully on their comparative advantage. As discussed later, it is also illegal under current international trading rules.

**ENVIRONMENTAL POLICY WHEN POLLUTION CROSSES NATIONAL BOUNDARIES.** The previous section discussed the international effects of environmental policy when environmental damage is contained within national borders. Many other uses of the environment cause environmental damage across borders, such as acid rain, which results from sulphur dioxide emissions, or worldwide, such as ozone depletion, which results primarily from chlorofluorocarbons (CFCs). Transfrontier pollution may occur in essentially four ways:

1. A firm's production takes place in one country, but pollutes only in another.
2. Both countries have firms whose production processes pollute, but each country's pollution is experienced only in the other country.
3. Pollution occurs as a result of production in one country but the effects are felt in *both* countries.
4. Both countries pollute, and the pollution generated by each is felt in *both* countries.

If property rights are assigned to the town, on the other hand, the firm pays the town to pollute. The firm's willingness to pay for the right to pollute depends on the benefits it receives from polluting. These benefits are directly related to the costs it incurs from using a more costly production or waste-disposal method. Similarly, the town's willingness to sell pollution rights depends on the costs it incurs from additional pollution. The amount of pollution agreed upon is where the additional benefits to the firm of increasing pollution are less than the additional costs to the town of additional pollution.

The Coase theorem proves that the equilibrium level of pollution is the same in the preceding cases. Furthermore, such an outcome is efficient. Thus, when property rights are clearly defined and there is an explicitly designated polluter and victim, the efficient outcome is independent of how the property rights are assigned.

GOVERNMENT REGULATION. Property rights are not always assigned because many uses of the environment are considered public goods. A pure public good is one that has two qualities: First, it is impossible or extremely costly to exclude people from the benefits or costs of the good (non-excludability). For example, even if a person does not contribute to cleaning the air, she still cannot be excluded from breathing the cleaner air. Second, the consumption of the good by one person does not diminish the amount of that good available to someone else (non-rivalry). For example, the fact that one person is breathing clean air does not reduce the amount of clean air others breathe. In this case, property rights cannot be assigned because rationing is impossible.

While few uses of the environment are pure public goods like air, many have enough features of non-excludability and non-rivalry to make assigning property rights virtually impossible. The functions of the environment that are public goods, such as breathable air and clean water, are summarized by the term *environmental quality.*

Regulating environmental quality is difficult because the government first needs to determine the public's demand for environmental quality before deciding the efficient level of pollution. The *free-rider* problem that occurs with public goods makes this determination especially difficult. When people cannot be excluded from use, they have an incentive to understate their willingness to pay for environmental quality because they can gamble that others will be willing to pay. Similarly, if they are asked their preferences and know they will not have to pay, people have an incentive to overstate their desire for a given public good. The degree to which free-riding is a problem depends on the size of the non-rival group affected. The larger the group, the greater the free-rider problem.

For the purposes of this paper, we will assume that to determine the "true" value of public goods, the government measures the costs of pollution reduction and the benefits of pollution abatement accurately. Using a cost-benefit approach, the optimal outcome is where the marginal cost of pollution reduction equals the marginal benefit of pollution abatement.

It is important to recognize that the socially optimal level of pollution is generally not zero. Achieving zero pollution would require an extremely low level of production or an extremely high cost of pollution control. In determining the optimal amount of pollution, both the costs to individuals and industry need to be taken into account.

If pollution is of form 1 or 2, in the absence of an international agreement, the polluting country has no incentive to curtail its polluting activities by implementing an environmental policy. If, instead, pollution is of the form 3 or 4, pollution may be regulated domestically. Without taking into account the pollution in the other country, however, these controls will not likely be optimal internationally. In the absence of a globally optimal international agreement, domestic policymakers have less incentive to take into account the costs imposed on a foreign country than if the costs were borne domestically. Thus, from a global perspective there will be excessive use of the environment.

## NORTH–SOUTH ISSUES

One of the main reasons environmental policy affects trade is because countries are at different levels of industrialization and thus have different income levels, which can cause their optimal levels of pollution to differ. Because the interests between high- and low-income countries may differ, it is important to look more closely at these so-called North–South issues.

Currently the industrialized countries, in general, are greater polluters than less industrialized countries and thus tend to put a relatively greater demand on worldwide assimilative capacity. One concern heard in developing countries is that industrial economies, rather than reducing their own demand for assimilative services, could impose their environmental standards on developing countries without any assistance in paying for them, thereby reducing the opportunity for less-industrialized countries to grow. As one news commentator suggests:

> Developing nations are suspicious that born-again environmentalists in the North will saddle them with commitments to regulate pollution, slow down deforestation, and control population growth, all in the name of sustainable development, yet won't follow through with economic aid to improve their own productivity and employment. Meanwhile, developed nations are reluctant to undertake radical domestic [environmental] policy changes that threaten their own economic growth.

Other types of environmental issues have a particular North–South nature. For example, many of the world's nature preserves are in developing countries in Africa. Currently, trade in elephant hides and ivory, along with other endangered species, are prohibited under the Convention on International Trade in Endangered Species (CITES). At a recent conference on CITES in Kyoto, Japan, several African countries argued that their elephant herds are large enough to be culled without endangering the species. In addition, they argued, revenue generated by the sale of ivory and other elephant products is needed to fund future preservation.

Here, the interest of the industrialized countries, who do not have a native elephant population, is to protect an endangered species. The African countries, however, face a trade-off between the benefits of protecting the species and the loss of revenue associated with the prohibition of trade in elephant products. As a result, less-industrialized countries are putting increased pressure on industrialized countries to help pay for the services they are providing (such as species diversity).

In March 1992, the General Agreement on Tariffs and Trade (GATT), the main body regulating international trade, released a report entitled "Trade and the Environment" that takes a non-traditional approach to North–South problems. One hotly debated issue concerns the protection of the rain forests, most of which are located in Latin America. Industrialized countries have moved to bar wood imports from Brazil and Thailand, for example, as a way to reduce deforestation in those countries. GATT argues that, rather than barring imports of wood products (much of which is GATT-illegal), the industrialized countries should compensate rain-forest countries for providing "carbon absorption services."

Although this approach is novel, its advantage is that poorer countries are assisted with financing environmental protection, so that it does not come at the expense of economic development. This approach also reduces the free-rider problem that enables much of the world to benefit from the carbon absorption services provided by rain forests and the diversity of species provided by countries that are not the primary users of the environment. In addition, the approach directly protects the rain forests, rather than barring certain types of wood products in the hopes that doing so will cause the exporting countries to protect them.

Other approaches taken to improve environmental standards in lower-income, less-industrialized countries include debt-for-nature swaps. Here, foreign debt is purchased by environmental groups and sold back to the issuing governments in exchange for investment in local environmental projects, including the purchase of land that is then turned into environmental preserves.

## CONCLUSION

This article examines the role of environmental policy on international trade. Environmental policy is justified because of the nature of externalities associated with using the environment. When the divergence between the social and private costs of using the environment is ignored, polluting activities receive an implicit subsidy. Environmental regulations may change international trade, but enhance social welfare by removing this subsidy. The optimal amount of environmental protection, however, can differ significantly across countries because of differences in preferences, income and assimilative capacities.

One important concern is that countries will use environmental policies as an excuse to establish protectionist policies. As environmental protection and environmental use take on a more transnational nature and the assimilative capacity is reduced worldwide, new agreements will have to be designed to both protect scarce resources and protect countries from being discriminated against because of how they choose to use their environmental endowments domestically. As the recent GATT report suggested, however, it is possible to protect the environment without distorting trade flows. Thus, free trade and environmental policy are not mutually exclusive but can work together to encourage both economic growth and environmental quality worldwide.

# REDEFINING SECURITY:
# THE NEW GLOBAL SCHISMS

Michael T. Klare

Geopolitical boundaries—notably those separating rival powers and major military blocs—have constituted the principal "fault lines" of international politics during much of the twentieth century. Throughout the cold war, the world's greatest concentrations of military strength were to be found along such key dividing lines as the Iron Curtain between East and West in Europe and the demilitarized zone between North and South Korea.

When the cold war ended, many of these boundaries quickly lost their geopolitical significance. With the reunification of Germany and the breakup of the Soviet Union, the divide between East and West in Europe ceased to have any meaning. Other key boundaries—for example, the demilitarized zone in Korea—retained their strategic importance, but elsewhere thousands of miles of previously fortified frontier became open borders with a minimal military presence. The strategic alliances associated with these divisions also lost much of their prominence: the Warsaw Treaty Organization was eliminated altogether, while NATO was given new roles and missions in order to forestall a similar fate.

## BATTLE LINES OF THE FUTURE

The changes associated with the cold war's end have been so dramatic and profound that it is reasonable to question whether traditional assumptions regarding the nature of global conflict will continue to prove reliable in the new, post–cold war era. In particular, one could question whether conflicts between states (or groups of states) will remain the principal form of international strife, and whether the boundaries between them will continue to constitute the world's major fault lines. Certainly the outbreak of ethno-nationalist conflict in the former Yugoslavia and several other former communist states has focused fresh attention on internal warfare, as has the persistence of tribal and religious strife in such countries as Afghanistan, Burundi, Liberia, Rwanda, Somalia, Sri Lanka, and Sudan.

Nevertheless, traditional concepts retain great currency among security analysts. Although the Iron Curtain has disappeared, it is argued, similar schisms of a geographic or territorial nature will arise to take its place. Indeed, several theories have been advanced positing the likely location of these schisms.

Some analysts contend that the territorial schisms of earlier periods—notably those produced by military competition among the major powers—will be revived in the years ahead. Professor Kenneth Waltz of the University of California at Berkeley suggests that such competition will eventually reappear, with Germany, Japan, or some other rising power such as China building its military strength in order to contest America's global paramountcy. "Countries have always competed for wealth and security, and the competition has often led to conflict," he wrote in *International Security*'s summer 1993 issue. "Why should the future be different from the past?"

More novel, perhaps, is the suggestion that the principal schisms of the post–cold war era are to be found along the peripheries of the world's great civilizations: Western (including Europe and North America), Slavic-Orthodox (including Russia, Ukraine, and Serbia), Japanese, Islamic, Confucian (China), Latin American, and African. First propounded by Harvard's Samuel Huntington in the summer 1993 issue of *Foreign Affairs*, this argument holds that the economic and ideological antagonisms of the nineteenth and twentieth centuries will be superseded in the twenty-first by antagonisms over culture and cultural identity. "Nation-states will remain the most powerful actors in world affairs," Huntington wrote, "but the principal conflicts of global politics will occur between nations and groups of different civilizations." Although the boundaries between civilizations are not as precise as those between sovereign states, he noted, these loose frontiers will be the site of major conflict. "The clash of civilizations will dominate global politics. The fault lines between civilizations will be the battle lines of the future."

Others have argued that the world's future fault lines will fall not between the major states or civilizations, but between the growing nexus of democratic, market-oriented societies and those "holdout" states that have eschewed democracy or defied the world community in other ways. Such "pariah" states or "rogue" powers are said to harbor aggressive inclinations, to support terrorism, and to seek the production of nuclear or chemical weapons. "[We] must face the reality of recalcitrant and outlaw states that not only choose to remain outside the family [of nations] but also to assault its basic values," wrote President Clinton's national security adviser, Anthony Lake, in the March–April 1994 *Foreign Affairs*. Lake placed several nations in this category—Cuba, North Korea, Iran, Iraq, and Libya—and other writers have added Sudan and Syria. But while there is disagreement about which of these states might actually fall into the "outlaw" category, Lake and other proponents of this analysis hold that the United States and its allies must work together to "contain" the rogue states and frustrate their aggressive designs.

While these assessments of the world security environment differ in many of their particulars, they share a common belief that the "battle lines of the future" (to use Huntington's expression) will fall along geographically defined boundaries, with the contending powers (and their friends and allies) arrayed on opposite sides. This, in turn, leads to similar policy recommendations that generally entail the maintenance of sufficient military strength by the United States to defeat any potential adversary or combination of adversaries.

It is certainly understandable that many analysts have proceeded from traditional assumptions regarding the nature of conflict when constructing models of future international relations, but it is not at all apparent that such assessments will prove reliable. While a number of crises since the end of the cold war appear to have followed one of the three models described, many have not. Indeed, the most intense conflicts of the current period—including those in Algeria, Angola, Bosnia, Burma, Burundi, Haiti, Kashmir, Liberia, Rwanda, Somalia, Sri Lanka, and Sudan—cannot be fully explained using these models. Moreover, other forms of contemporary violence—terrorism, racial and religious strife, gang warfare, violence against women, and criminal violence—have shown no respect for geography or civilizational identity whatsoever, erupting in virtually every corner of the world.

## THE THREAT FROM WITHIN

A fresh assessment of the world security environment suggests that the major international schisms of the twenty-first century will not always be definable in geographic terms. Many of the most severe and persistent threats to global peace and stability are arising not from conflicts between major political entities but from increased discord within states, societies, and civilizations along ethnic, racial, religious, linguistic, caste, or class lines.

The intensification and spread of internal discord is a product of powerful stresses on human communities everywhere. These stresses—economic, demographic, sociological, and environmental—are exacerbating the existing divisions within societies and creating entirely new ones. As a result, we are seeing the emergence of new or deepened fissures across international society, producing multiple outbreaks of intergroup hostility and violence. These cleavages cannot be plotted on a normal map, but can be correlated with other forms of data: economic performance, class stratification, population growth, ethnic and religious composition, environmental deterioration, and so on. Where certain conditions prevail—a widening gulf between rich and poor, severe economic competition between neighboring ethnic and religious communities, the declining habitability of marginal lands—internal conflict is likely to erupt.

This is not to say that traditional geopolitical divisions no longer play a role in world security affairs. But it does suggest that such divisions may have been superseded in importance by the new global schisms.

## For Richer and Poorer: The Widening Gap

The world has grown much richer over the past 25 years. According to the Worldwatch Institute, the world's total annual income rose from $10.1 trillion in 1970 to approximately $20 trillion in 1994 (in constant 1987 dollars). This increase has been accompanied by an improved standard of living for many of the world's peoples. But not all nations, and not all people in the richer nations, have benefited from the global increase in wealth: some countries, mostly concentrated in Africa and Latin America, have experienced a net decline in gross domestic product over the past few decades, while many of the countries that have achieved a higher GDP have experienced an increase in the number of people living in extreme poverty. Furthermore, the gap in national income between the richest and the poorest nations continues to increase, as does the gap between rich and poor people within most societies.

These differentials in economic growth rates, along with the widening gap between rich and poor, are producing dangerous fissures in many societies. As the masses of poor see their chances of escaping acute poverty diminish, they are likely to become increasingly resentful of those whose growing wealth is evident. This resentment is especially pronounced in the impoverished shantytowns that surround many of the seemingly prosperous cities of the third world. In these inhospitable surroundings, large numbers of people—especially among the growing legions of unemployed youth—are being attracted to extremist political movements like the Shining Path of Peru and the Islamic Salvation Front of Algeria, or to street gangs and drug-trafficking syndicates. The result is an increase in urban crime and violence.

Deep economic cleavages are also emerging in China and the postcommunist states of Eastern Europe and the former Soviet Union. Until the recent introduction of market reforms in these countries, the financial gap between rich and poor was kept relatively narrow by state policy, and such wealth as did exist among the bureaucratic elite was kept well hidden from public view. With the onset of capitalism the economic plight of the lowest strata of these societies has become considerably worse, while the newly formed entrepreneurial class has been able to accumulate considerable wealth—and to display it in highly conspicuous ways. This has generated new class tensions and provided ammunition for those who, like Gennadi Zyuganov of Russia's reorganized Communist Party, seek the restoration of the old, state-dominated system.

Equally worrisome is the impact of growing income differentials on intergroup relations in multiethnic societies. In most countries the divide between rich and poor is not the only schism that matters: of far greater significance are the divisions between various strata of the poor and lower middle class. When such divisions coincide with ethnic or religious differences—that is, when one group of poor people finds itself to be making less economic progress than a similar group of a different ethnic composition—the result is likely to be increased ethnic antagonisms and, at the extreme, increased inter-group violence. This is evident in Pakistan, where violent gang warfare in Karachi has been fueled by economic competition between the indigenous inhabitants of the surrounding region and several waves of Muslim immigrants from India and Bangladesh; it is also evident in Sri Lanka, where efforts by the Sinhalese to deny employment opportunities to the Tamils helped spark a deadly civil war.

## KINDLING ETHNIC STRIFE

According to information assembled by the Stockholm International Peace Research Institute (SIPRI), ethnic and religious strife figured prominently in all but 3 of the 31 major armed conflicts under way in 1994. And while several long-running ethnic and sectarian conflicts have subsided in recent years, most analysts believe that such strife is likely to erupt repeatedly in the years ahead.

It is true that many recent ethnic and religious conflicts have their roots in clashes or invasions that occurred years ago. It is also true that the violent upheavals that broke out in the former Yugoslavia and the former Soviet Union drew upon deep-seated ethnic hostilities, even if these cleavages were not generally visible during much of the communist era (when overt displays of ethnic antagonism were prohibited by government decree). In this sense, the ethnic fissures that are now receiving close attention from international policymakers are not really new phenomena. Nevertheless, many of these schisms have become more pronounced since the end of the cold war, or have exhibited characteristics that are unique to the current era.

Greatly contributing to the intensity of recent ethnic and religious strife is the erosion or even disappearance of central state authority in poor third world countries experiencing extreme economic, political, and environmental stress. In such countries—especially Burundi, Liberia, Rwanda, Somalia, and Zaire—the flimsy state structures established after independence are simply unable to cope with the demands of housing and feeding their growing populations with the meager resources at hand. In such circumstances people lose all confidence in the state's ability to meet their basic needs and turn instead to more traditional, kinship-based forms of association for help in getting by—a process that often results in competition and conflict among groups over what remains of the nation's scarce resources. This shift in loyalty from the state to group identity is also evident in Bosnia and parts of the former Soviet Union, where various ethnic factions have attempted to seize or divide up the infrastructure (and in some cases the territory) left behind by the communist regime.

Also contributing to the intensity of intergroup conflict in the current era is the spread of mass communications and other instruments of popular mobilization. These advances have contributed to what Professor James Rosenau of George Washington University calls a "skill revolution" in which individual citizens "have become increasingly competent in assessing where they fit in international affairs and how their behavior can be aggregated into significant collective outcomes."[1] This competence can lead to calls for greater personal freedom and democracy. But it can also lead to increased popular mobilization along ethnic, religious, caste, and linguistic lines, often producing great friction and disorder within heterogeneous societies. An important case in point is India, where Hindu nationalists have proved adept at employing modern means of communication and political organization—while retaining traditional symbols and motifs—to encourage anti-Muslim sentiment and thereby erode the authority of India's largely secular government.

## DEMOGRAPHIC SCHISMS

According to the most recent UN estimates, total world population is expected to soar from approximately 5.6 billion people in 1994 to somewhere between 8 billion and 12 billion by the year 2050—an increase that will undoubtedly place great strain on the earth's food production and environmental capacity. But the threat to the world's environment and food supply is not all that we have to worry about. Because population growth is occurring unevenly in different areas, with some of the highest rates of growth to be found in countries with the slowest rates of economic growth, future population increases could combine with other factors to exacerbate existing cleavages along ethnic, religious, and class lines.

Overall, the populations of the less-developed countries (LDCs) are growing at a much faster rate than those of the advanced industrial nations. As a result, the share of world population accounted for by the LDCs rose from 69 percent in 1960 to 74 percent in 1980, and is expected to jump to nearly 80 percent in the year 2000. Among third world countries, moreover, there have been marked variations in the rate of population growth: while the newly industrialized nations of East Asia have experienced a sharp decline in the rate of growth, Africa and parts of the Middle East have experienced an increase. If these trends persist, the global distribution of population will change dramatically over the next few decades, with some areas experiencing a substantial increase in total population and others moderate or even negligible growth.

This is where other factors enter the picture. If the largest increases in population were occurring in areas of rapid growth, the many young adults entering the job market each year would be able to find productive employment and would thus be able to feed and house their families. In many cases, however, large increases in population are coinciding with low or stagnant economic growth, meaning that future job-seekers are not likely to find adequate employment. This will have a considerable impact on the world security

---

[1] James N. Rosenau, "Security in a Turbulent World," *Current History*, May 1995, p. 194.

environment. At the very least, it is likely to produce increased human migration from rural areas (where population growth tends to be greatest) to urban centers (where most new jobs are to be found), and from poor and low-growth countries to more affluent ones. The former process is resulting in the rapid expansion of many third world cities, with an attendant increase in urban crime and intergroup friction (especially where the new urban dwellers are of a different ethnic or tribal group from the original settlers); the latter is producing huge numbers of new immigrants in the developed and high-growth countries, often sparking hostility and sometimes violence from the indigenous populations.

Rapid population growth in poor countries with slow or stagnant economic growth has other implications for world security. In many societies it is leading to the hyperutilization of natural resources, particularly arable soil, grazing lands, forests, and fisheries, a process that severely complicates future economic growth (as vital raw materials are depleted) and accelerates the pace of environmental decline. It can also overwhelm the capacity of weak or divided governments to satisfy their citizens' basic needs, leading eventually to the collapse of states and to the intergroup competition and conflict described earlier. Finally, it could generate fresh international conflicts when states with slow population growth employ stringent measures to exclude immigrants from nearby countries with high rates of growth. While some of this is speculative, early signs of many of these phenomena have been detected. The 1994 United States intervention in Haiti, for instance, was partly motivated by a desire on Washington's part to curb the flow of Haitian "boat people" to the United States.

## ENDANGERED BY ENVIRONMENT

As with massive population growth, the world has been bombarded in recent years with dire predictions about the consequences of further deterioration in the global environment. The continuing build-up of industrial gases in the earth's outer atmosphere, for example, is thought to be impeding the natural radiation of heat from the planet and thereby producing a gradual increase in global temperatures—a process known as "greenhouse warming." If such warming continues, global sea levels will rise, deserts will grow, and severe drought could afflict many important agricultural zones. Other forms of environmental degradation—the thinning of the earth's outer ozone layer, the depletion of arable soil through overcultivation, the persistence of acid rain caused by industrial emissions—could endanger human health and survival in other ways. As with population growth, these environmental effects will not be felt uniformly around the world but will threaten some states and groups more than others producing new cleavages in human society.

The uneven impact of global environmental decline is being seen in many areas. The first to suffer are invariably those living in marginally habitable areas—arid grazing lands, coastal lowlands, tropical rain forests. As annual rainfall declines, sea levels rise, and forests are harvested, these lands become uninhabitable. The choice, for those living in such areas, is often grim: to migrate to the cities, with all of their attendant problems, or to move onto the lands of neighboring peoples (who may be of a different ethnicity or religion), producing new outbreaks of intergroup violence. This grim choice has fallen with particular severity on indigenous peoples, who in many cases were originally driven into these marginal habitats by more powerful groups. A conspicuous case in point is the Amazon region of Brazil, where systematic deforestation is destroying the habitat and lifestyle of the indigenous peoples and producing death, illness, and unwelcome migration to the cities.

States also vary in their capacity to cope with environmental crisis and the depletion of natural resources. While the wealthier countries can rebuild areas damaged by flooding or other disasters, relocate displaced citizens to safer regions, and import food and other commodities no longer produced locally, the poorer countries are much less capable of doing these things. As noted by Professor Thomas Homer-Dixon of the University of Toronto, "Environmental scarcity sharply raises financial and political demands on government by requiring huge spending on new infrastructure."[2] Because many third world countries cannot sustain such expenditures, he notes, "we have . . . the potential for a widening gap between demands on the state and its financial ability to meet these demands"—a gap that could lead to internal conflict between competing ethnic groups, or significant out-migration to countries better able to cope with environmental stresses.[3]

Finally, there is a danger that acute environmental scarcities will lead to armed interstate conflict over such vital resources as water, forests, and energy supplies. Some believe that the era of "resource wars" has already occurred in the form of recurring conflict over the Middle East's oil supplies and that similar conflicts will arise over control of major sources of water, such as the Nile, Euphrates, and Ganges Rivers.

## THE NEW CARTOGRAPHY

These new and growing schisms are creating a map of international security that is based on economic, demographic, and environmental factors. If this map could be represented in graphic terms, it would show an elaborate network of fissures stretching across human society in all directions—producing large concentrations of rifts in some areas and smaller clusters in others, but leaving no area entirely untouched. Each line would represent a cleavage in the human community, dividing one group (however defined) from another; the deeper and wider clefts, and those composed of many fault lines, would indicate the site of current or potential conflict.

[2] Thomas Homer-Dixon, "Environmental Scarcity and Intergroup Conflict," in Michael T. Klare and Daniel C. Thomas, eds., *World Security: Challenges for a New Century* (New York: St. Martin's Press, 1994), pp. 298–299.

[3] Ibid.

These schisms, and their continued growth, will force policymakers to re-think their approach to international security. It is no longer possible to rely on strategies of defense and diplomacy that assume a flat, two-dimensional world of contending geopolitical actors. While such units still play a significant role in world security affairs, they are not the only actors that matter; nor is their interaction the only significant threat to peace and stability. Other actors, and other modes of interaction, are equally important. Only by considering the full range of security threats will it be possible for policymakers to design effective strategies for peace.

When the principal fault lines of international security coincided with the boundaries between countries, it was always possible for individual states to attempt to solve their security problems by fortifying their borders or by joining with other nations in regional defense systems like NATO and the Warsaw Pact. When the fault lines fall *within* societies, however, there are no clear boundaries to be defended and no role for traditional alliance systems. Indeed, it is questionable whether there is a role for military power at all: any use of force by one side in these disputes, however successful, will inevitably cause damage to the body politic as a whole, eroding its capacity to overcome the problems involved and to provide for its long-term stability. Rather than fortifying and defending borders, a successful quest for peace must entail strategies for easing and erasing the rifts in society, by eliminating the causes of dissension or finding ways to peacefully bridge the gap between mutually antagonistic groups.

The new map of international security will not replace older, traditional types. The relations between states will still matter in world affairs, and their interactions may lead, as they have in the past, to major armed conflicts. But it will not be possible to promote international peace and stability without using the new map as well, and dealing with the effects of the new global schisms. Should we fail to do so, the world of the next century could prove as violent as the present one.

# POPULATION, CONSUMPTION, AND THE PATH TO SUSTAINABILITY

Janet Welsh Brown

Is world population growth a problem? Most Americans would answer yes though they do not think of the United States as being part of the problem. The technological optimists among us claim that, theoretically at least, the planet can feed, clothe, and house 10 billion people. But rapid population growth multiplies poverty and environmental degradation, and a laissez-faire attitude about a world population that will double in the next 50 years will assure that for the poor the world over, life will remain harsh.

Does this mean that rapid population growth is a security problem? Not if one equates security with the traditional struggle of major military powers over scarce resources. But if the world pursues the American model of development, with its high levels of consumption, air and water pollution, and damage to the natural resource base, and extrapolates these effects and population growth to 2025 and 2050, some basic physical and biological systems could be at risk of collapse. Less apocalyptic but just as loaded with the potential for human misery is the possibility that in many countries on the upswing, such as Mexico, Egypt, Kenya, or the Philippines, a downward spiral of population growth, debt, inequality, and loss of soil and agricultural production could lead to economic decline and widespread political instability.

There is time—but not a lot—to control pollution and prevent degradation of the natural resource base. Collectively, countries know better ways of assuring development, and a population stabilizing at 10 billion or 11 billion should be able to live humanely on the planet's resources if governments take the difficult steps required to curb excessive consumption and manage resources sustainably—and if the United States takes the lead.

## POPULATION GROWTH NORTH AND SOUTH . . .

Between the Second World War and the 1990s, the world's population increased from 2.5 billion to 5 billion, and the global economy grew fourfold. Most of the population growth occurred in the developing countries, where 80 percent of the world's people live today. Economic activity exploded commensurately, but with the most impressive advances seen in the highly industrialized states of the Organization for Economic Cooperation and Development (OECD). On a tide of postwar, postindependence economic growth and great reductions in mortality, the quality of life of most people everywhere improved—a fact easily forgotten as headlines of wars and natural disasters repeat themselves.

Using a medium-growth scenario, United Nations population projections promise a world of 8.5 billion people in 2025 and around 10 billion in 2050. Ninety-five percent of the growth will be in developing countries, most of it in the very poorest. The populations of some countries, such as Somalia, Pakistan, Nicaragua, and Honduras, will double in as little as 22 or 23 years. Others—Mexico and Egypt, for instance—will double in 30 years. Even China, which has achieved a remarkable decline in fertility and reached replacement-only levels in the early 1990s, will see 17 million people added to its population each year, assuring growth from its current 1.2 billion to 1.5 billion by 2025. India, the second-largest country with 905 million people in 1994, will surpass China in population soon after 2025 because its population is still increasing at 1.9 percent per year. Bangladesh and the Philippines are growing at more than 2 percent annually. (In the next century, half the world's people will live in Asia.) Growth is also rapid in sub-Saharan Africa and the Arab countries. Most population increases in developing countries will take place in cities, and the ranks of the young will swell throughout these countries. Already 45 percent of all Africans are under the age of 15.

What demands does such growth in the developing world put on economies and ecosystems? Food production must more than double in the next 50 years, and the demand for wood, the main fuel in the poorest communities, will also double. (Even now, some cities in African countries are ringed with deforested areas, and in India demand for fuelwood is six times the sustainable yield of India's forests.) Governments must build twice as many schools and clinics, train twice as many teachers and health-care workers, and scramble desperately to keep from slipping backward in the provision of drinking water and sanitation. Twice as many jobs will be needed, just to stay even with population growth. Pressure on land, air, and water everywhere will double, and waste and pollution levels will soar.

No government is adequately prepared for these tasks—especially in the poorer developing countries of Asia, Africa, and Latin America, where rapidly growing populations, poverty, and environmental degradation feed on one another. The poor, who are both victims and agents of environmental deterioration, press upon fragile lands, contributing to a cycle of deforestation, soil erosion, periodic flooding, loss of productivity, and further poverty. With few or no educational and health services, poor sanitation, and low status and meager opportunities for women, the populations of poor countries swell. Despite high infant and maternal mortality, the numbers of the poor will increase and feed migration to the cities, where life is only marginally better and where people face a new set of environmental problems—water and air pollution of debilitating intensity. Some developing countries have broken the cycle. South Korea and China represent two different models for development: they have produced stunning economic growth and reduced poverty and fertility rates, but both are paying dearly in pollution and resource degradation.

The population of the former communist countries is likely to increase only slightly by 2025. In the same period the highly industrialized countries will increase from 1.2 billion to 1.4 billion, and most of that growth will be in the United States. Without immigration, the United States is growing at the rate of 0.7 percent annually, compared with 0.2 percent for Europe and 0.38 percent for Japan. Each year the United States adds 2 million people in births over deaths, plus another million through immigration. This is the equivalent of adding another California every 10 years. And alone among all the highly industrialized countries, the United States has seen its fertility rate rise in the 1990s to two children per woman, after hovering between 1.7 and 1.8 for 17 years.

In the United States, a 1 percent population growth rate means adding almost 3 million people to the population each year. It means further suburban sprawl, longer commutes to work, more pollution, and fewer open spaces. Even though these are real problems, few Americans perceive population growth as a domestic issue. Indeed, only when the differing rates at which societies consume materials and energy are taken into account, and when the relative impacts on the environment of different levels of development, wealth, and technology are calculated, does the seriousness of population growth become clear.

## . . . And Consumption North and South

Relative rates of resource consumption have become an issue internationally only since the North-South negotiations that led to the United Nations Conference on Environment and Development (UNCED) in Rio de Janeiro in 1992 at the "Earth Summit." The 180 nations represented at the conference signed a declaration and work plan that acknowledged the links between economic growth and environmental protection and the need for sustainable development. The OECD countries insisted that population growth be addressed, while developing countries charged that the North's extraordinary per capita consumption of energy and natural resources—including many from the South—drives global environmental problems. As a result, both population and consumption concerns found their way into Agenda 21, the conference's blueprint for a sustainable world.

After UNCED, consumption was examined in relation to resource deple-tion, environmental degradation, and such global environmental problems as atmospheric warming, destruction of the ozone layer, fisheries depletion, and biodiversity loss. The postconference studies have made it clear that the environmental effects of population growth and increasing consumption rates can be tempered by technological improvements that make produc-tion, distribution, and disposal more efficient, by incentives to invest and trade, and by taxes and regulations. Examples include reduction of subsid-ies to resource-hungry industries and tax revisions that make polluters pay and provide incentives for more efficient resource use. Tools such as these are gaining acceptance as countries begin fulfilling their UNCED commit-ments, though not as rapidly as population is growing or certain resources deteriorating.

Current income and consumption disparities stem from a long history of economic domination of Africa, Asia, and Latin America by Europe, the United States, and Japan. Today there is a great divide, based on purchasing-power parity, between the average per capita GDP of the OECD countries ($18,988 in 1991) and that of the developing countries ($2,377).[1] These aver-ages, of course, mask even wider disparities when the rich countries are com-pared with the poorest ones and declining commodity prices are taken into account. Hope of quickly closing the gap is dim, since the new technologies promising greater efficiency and substitutes for scarce materials are owned mostly by northern enterprises.

The rich and the poor take their toll on the environment in different ways: the rich through their high per capita consumption and production of wastes, and the poor through their pressure on fragile lands. In most poor countries a growing upper class consumes on a level comparable to that of citizens of the OECD countries. While the OECD countries have had the greater impact—contributing mightily to global warming and destruction of the ozone layer with their heavy use of fossil fuels and chemicals—the develop-ing countries' production of food and fiber, mining and processing, and dis-posal of wastes have had mostly local impacts on soils, forests, biodiversity, and water.

Thirty years ago, environmentalists such as the authors of *Limits to Growth*, were mainly worried about the depletion of nonrenewable resources (fossil fuels, metals, and other minerals). Technology has since decreased depen-dence on natural resources by providing new materials and making the use of resources more efficient. Today it is clear that it is the so-called renewable resources—soil, forests, fisheries, biological diversity, air, and water—that human society is despoiling and using at unsustainable rates. In the worst

---

[1] Purchasing power parity is a GDP estimate based on the purchasing power of currencies rather than current exchange rates.

cases, the depletion of the resource base may exceed its ability to regenerate, perhaps leading to ecosystem collapse.

Consumption, according to the President's Council on Sustainable Development (PCSD), which was organized in 1993, includes the "end-products, their ingredients and by-products, and all wastes generated throughout the life of a product, from raw materials extraction through disposal. It also means resource use by all kinds of consumers—industries, commercial firms, governments, nongovernmental organizations and individuals." Not surprisingly, consumption rates differ starkly between the industrialized and developing countries.

The 20 percent of the world's population that lives in the highly industrialized countries consumes an inordinate share of the world's resources: 80 percent of its paper, iron, and steel; 75 percent of its timber and energy; 60 percent of its meat, fertilizer, and cement; and half of its fish and grain. Per capita consumption comparisons are even more dramatic: in the OECD nations, each person uses 20 times as much aluminum and 17 times as much copper as a person in the developing countries. As for fossil fuels, so central to development and key to global warming, the industrialized countries use almost 50 percent of the total, which is nine times the average per capita consumption in the developing countries. Historically, the highly industrialized countries are responsible for as much as 75 percent of total world consumption, but the developing countries' share of consumption of most materials and energy is slowly rising and will continue to do so.

The United States, with the world's largest economy, is also the largest consumer of natural resources and the largest producer of wastes. In the last 20 years, personal consumption of goods and services in the United States has risen 45 percent. The country is an especially heavy user of plastics and petroleum feedstocks, synthetic fabrics, aluminum and copper, potash, and gravel and cement. With a few exceptions, most notably oil, 70 percent of the minerals the United States uses are produced domestically, so the primary environmental consequences of production, transportation, and use are also felt there. The United States, with barely 5 percent of the world's population, is the leading contributor of greenhouse gases (about 19 percent) and probably the largest producer of toxic wastes. Although per capita consumption in the United States of most materials is decreasing slightly (the exceptions are paper and plastics), overall consumption continues to rise as population grows. For example, per capita energy consumption declined between 1980 and 1993, but total consumption rose 10 percent with the addition of 32 million to the population.

## IMPLEMENTING SUSTAINABILITY

Although it is not politically popular to admit it, American patterns of production and consumption—admired and imitated by most of the world—are not sustainable. The environmental effects of high natural resources consumption will be multiplied as the developing countries' economic development requires an increasing share of the earth's largesse. And larger populations in both the industrialized and developing worlds constitute another formidable multiplier. The world faces a dilemma—poor countries need to "grow" out of poverty, just as the United States and Europe and Japan seek to "grow" their economies to provide jobs and services expected by the citizenry.

But growth on the American model, or even on that of the more materials-efficient European and Japanese economies, cannot alone forestall an environmental day of reckoning. Remaining tropical forests and all the diversity they house are disappearing at an annual rate of 0.9 percent—equivalent to the loss of a territory the size of the state of Washington annually. According to the UN Food and Agriculture Organization, all 17 major ocean fisheries have reached or exceeded their limits, mainly from overfishing, and 9 are in serious decline. Stabilizing atmospheric concentrations of greenhouse gases will require as much as a 60 percent reduction in emissions worldwide. Current emission levels, even without the growth required in energy use in developing countries, will result in a doubling and eventually a quadrupling of greenhouse gases—bringing long-term global warming, changes in precipitation, and sea-level rise.

If a new kind of security threat is to be avoided and these trends diverted, then a more sustainable model of development is clearly required. As was noted earlier, in 1992 at UNCED, nations from around the world produced Agenda 21, their blueprint for sustainable development. Although loaded with political compromises, the 294-page document is instructive in its detail and comprehensiveness. It includes chapters on energy and marine management, as well as on the status of women and the role of nongovernmental organizations in development. By 1996 the President's Council on Sustainable Development had made international and intergenerational equity part of America's definition of sustainable activity—an activity "that can be continued indefinitely without harming the environmental, economic, or social basis on which it depends and without diminishing the opportunities of future generations to enjoy the resources and a quality of life at least equal to our own."

Sustainable development, by definition, means that each nation has to work out its own plan for economically and environmentally sensible development. Among the highly industrialized nations, the Netherlands has moved with greatest determination, ordering a radical reduction of toxic agricultural chemicals and negotiating long-term agreements between major industries and government that sets ambitious goals for improving energy efficiency. By setting an example at home, and promoting sustainable development in its bilateral aid program, the Dutch have exerted leadership both in the European Union and in worldwide environmental negotiations that is extraordinary for so small a country.

Not all countries waited for UNCED before tackling their unsustainable development practices. Brazil, in the late 1980s, reversed the policies that had encouraged cattle ranching over tropical forest protection. And the Philippines halted logging subsidies that had encouraged transforming steep uplands from forest to farmland, with all the attendant problems. The transition to sustainable development is as difficult in developing countries as anywhere else, as entrenched political elites defend the old models of development that have benefited them. Further changes in the developing countries will depend largely on the policies and practices of the international financial institutions—the World Bank and the IMF—which so far have been reluctant partners in the push for sustainable development.

Equally important is the example set by the highly industrialized countries, which must demonstrate that the transition to sustainable development is technically feasible, affordable, and politically possible. The United States, as the largest economic power, consumer, and polluter, is the key country that skeptics are watching. At present the United States is at a difficult point of transition. The nation has taken many steps to control pollution and degradation over the last 25 years, but few politicians are willing seriously to challenge such sacred cows as America's national addiction to the automobile, its extensive subsidies of water and energy, and its unsustainable harvest of public forests and catch from the seas.

The United States does, however, have many tools and experience in using them. In the early 1980s, state and federal legislation stemmed the loss of coastal wetlands, in part by cutting off construction and insurance subsidies for more than 150 undeveloped barrier islands. States like Florida, faced with a huge influx of retirees and tourists in the 1970s and 1980s, enacted land-use management to control development. Along with the federal government and private conservation organizations, states have also purchased sensitive and wilderness areas to protect them from development. The Clean Air Act provided the incentives for rapidly developing such pollution-control technologies as scrubbers, cleaner coal, and fluidized-bed combustion—advances that the energy industry had claimed would be difficult and costly when the legislation was first proposed.

Prices can also trigger technological improvement. The 1970s oil crisis, precipitated by price hikes by the Organization of Petroleum Exporting Countries, led to major savings in fuel costs when airlines invested in more efficient engines. Banning harmful materials—phosphates from detergents, asbestos, chlorofluorocarbons (CFCs)—has also been achieved at both the national and international levels, despite strong opposition from affected industries.

Unlike in some European countries, fiscal measures have not been effectively used in the United States to restrain the use of private automobiles and subsidize public transport. The only serious gasoline tax proposals ever made in the United States were quickly shot down in 1993, although modest measures such as taxes on petroleum and mineral extraction, recycling incentives, and user fees for waste disposal have been employed at state and local levels for conservation purposes.

## POLICIES FOR CHANGE

It is clear that the poorer developing countries need steady international assistance and incentives to reduce population growth and to shift to more sustainable models of development. Exhorting these countries to pursue such difficult changes will have little effect until they perceive that the OECD nations are practicing what they preach. The United States in particular must provide such an example.

The task force on population and consumption of the President's Council on Sustainable Development has proposed a mix of tools for curbing population growth and consumption in the United States. To reduce population growth, the task force recommends focusing on family planning (specifically on avoiding unintended pregnancies and reducing teen pregnancy) and on immigration. Based on experience in both the United States and other countries that shows reproductive services work best in combination with an attack on related socioeconomic conditions, the task force recommended policies that would reduce poverty and discrimination and improve economic opportunities, especially for poor women. Similarly, the council's recommendations on immigration emphasize not just law enforcement, but also the need to help address, through foreign assistance and trade policies, the conditions in poor countries that give rise to emigration.

A second cluster of PCSD recommendations would help individuals exercise consumer choice—through environmental education and the certification and labeling of products—and also support the reduction of wastes. Public policies to reduce, reuse, and recycle are necessary, as are volume-based garbage fees that produce incentives and practical arrangements for the disposal of household toxic materials. In each case, the role of federal, state, and local governments in procuring and disposing of their own wastes is pivotal. The leverage that governments collectively wield as consumers of goods and services could provide the necessary momentum for fundamental changes in how the whole nation consumes and disposes of goods.

A third set of PCSD recommendations goes right to the heart of economic development interests in the United States. They are the most important to sustainable development and the most difficult to achieve. These prescriptions would affect resource use by eliminating government subsidies to a wide variety of industries and sectors that have come to expect them, and by shifting taxes from labor and investments to consumption—especially consumption of natural resources, virgin materials, and goods and services that harm the environment. Taxpayers are understandably nervous about how such fundamental shifts would personally affect them. Proposals therefore include provisions for "tax neutrality," with new consumption taxes offset by reductions in payroll taxes. Such a basic change in America's national tax system will not come easily or quickly, but state experiments such as promising legislation now in the Minnesota state legislature, backed by an unusual coalition of organizations of taxpayers and conservationists, may demonstrate the way to national legislation.

Although each of these recommendations would save money for government agencies and make United States producers more competitive in world markets, there are real up-front costs for all change. Environmentalists and family-planning advocates argue convincingly that the cost of not making these changes would be much higher, and would compound the problems facing the next generation. Some political leaders are thinking along these lines, but advocacy of belt tightening does not get politicians elected, so the campaign to change economic incentives will have to be couched in terms of efficiency, economy, and higher productivity.

In the past, policymakers in the United States have often been jolted into action by catastrophes. Severe drought-driven crop failure in the southeast in 1988 riveted Congress's attention for the first time on the dangers of global warming, even though the drought could not be directly attributed to it. Hurricanes and the 1993 flooding of the Missouri and Mississippi Rivers revived the national debate on limits on federal disaster insurance. The United States can count on more such crises—a major crop failure, disease, or destruction associated with the weather, or an unmanageable threat to petroleum supplies from abroad—that will crank up the legislative and policy machinery and provide the impetus for a national shift to sustainable development. But American political leaders could also act before avoidable tragedy strikes again and could govern with the ecological and environmental security of future generations in mind.

# VI

# DEMOCRACY AND
# THE FREE MARKET

The final section of this anthology contains two analyses of an important issue: Whither the democratic state? The first selection, written by an influential management consultant, Kenichi Ohmae, addresses the future of the nation–state in the new integrated global economy. He believes that political borders are an accident of history. The global mobility of investment, industry, information technology, and consumers makes today's national governments unnecessary and unproductive. Ohmae believes that region–states will supplant traditional nation–states because that's where "real work is done and real markets flourish." These region–states are geographically-concentrated units, such as Hong Kong and the adjacent region of southern China, or Spain's Catalonia. (What matters are not their borders, but their right size and scale.) Their size and scale, rather than the location of their borders, make them better suited as business units to compete in a borderless, global economy.

The second selection by Stephen Haggard and Robert Kaufman deals with the same issue although it adds the notion of democracy. Naturally for political scientists the interesting question is less the future of the nation–state but more the future of the democratic state. Many countries around the world are facing the twin tasks of fostering economic growth and strengthening democracy. The authors observe that, in most instances, growth came first. Countries laid the foundations for a more sound economy and a fiscally sound state. However, once the economic pie begins to grow, questions of equity become important. The problem now, according to the authors, is to find a way to relieve some of the distributional pressures without sacrificing growth. The answer is to develop an institutionally more responsive and competent bureaucracy to handle these delicate questions before they become serious crises. In contrast to Ohmae, these political scientists not only see a future for national government, but they maintain that it must be further strengthened and adapted to present conditions. Contrasting the two essays will provide students with sufficient insight to begin formulating their own answers to the future of the democratic state.

# THE END OF
# THE NATION STATE

Kenichi Ohmae

With the ending of the frigid Fifty Years' War between Soviet-style communism and the West's liberal democracy, some observers—Francis Fukuyama,
in particular—announced that we had reached the "end of history." Nothing
could be further from the truth. In fact, now that the bitter ideological con-
frontation sparked by this century's collision of "isms" has ended, larger
numbers of people from more points on the globe than ever before have ag-
gressively come forward to participate *in* history. They have left behind centuries, even millennia, of obscurity in forest and desert and rural isolation to
request from the world community—and from the global economy that links
it together—a decent life for themselves and a better life for their children. A
generation ago, even a decade ago, most of them were as voiceless and invisible as they had always been. This is true no longer: they have entered history
with a vengeance, and they have demands—economic demands—to make.

But to whom or to what should they make them? Their first impulse, of
course, will likely be to turn to the heads of the governments of nation states.
These, after all, are the leaders whose plans and schemes have long shaped
the flow of public events. But, in today's more competitive world, nation states
no longer possess the seemingly bottomless well of resources from which
they used to draw with impunity to fund their ambitions. These days, even
they have to look for assistance to the global economy and make the changes
at home needed to invite it in. So these new claimants will turn to international bodies like the United Nations. But what is the UN if not a collection
of nation states? So they will turn to multilateral agencies like the World
Bank, but these too are the creatures of a nation state-defined and -funded
universe. So they will turn to explicitly economic groupings like OPEC or

G-7 or ASEAN or APEC or NAFTA or the EU (European Union). But once again, all they will find behind each new acronym is a grouping of nation states.

Then, if they are clever, they may interrupt their quest to ask a few simple questions. Are these nation states—notwithstanding the obvious and important role they play in world affairs—really the primary actors in today's global economy? Do they provide the best window on that economy? Do they provide the best port of access to it? In a world where economic borders are progressively disappearing, are their arbitrary, historically accidental boundaries genuinely meaningful in economic terms? And if not, what kinds of boundaries do make sense? In other words, exactly what, at bottom, are the natural business units—the sufficient, correctly-sized and scaled aggregations of people and activities—through which to tap into that economy?

One way to answer these questions is to observe the flows of what I call the 4 "I's" that define it. First, the capital markets in most developed countries are flush with excess cash for investment. Japan, for example, has the equivalent of US $10 trillion stored away. Even where a country itself hovers close to bankruptcy, there is often a huge accumulation of money in pension funds and life insurance programs. The problem is that suitable—and suitably large—investment opportunities are not often available in the same geographies where this money sits. As a result, the capital markets have developed a wide variety of mechanisms to transfer it across national borders. Today, nearly 10 percent of U.S. pension funds is invested in Asia. Ten years ago, that degree of participation in Asian markets would have been unthinkable.

Thus, investment—the first "I"—is no longer geographically constrained. Now, wherever you sit in the world, if the opportunity is attractive, the money will come in. And it will be, for the most part, "private" money. Again, ten years ago, the flow of cross-border funds was primarily from government to government or from multilateral lending agency to government. There was a capital city and an army of public bureaucrats on at least one end of the transaction. That is no longer the case. Because most of the money now moving across borders is private, governments do not have to be involved at either end. All that matters is the quality of the investment opportunity. The money will go where the good opportunities are.

The second "I"—industry—is also far more global in orientation today than it was a decade ago. In the past, with the interests of their home governments clearly in mind, companies would strike deals with host governments to bring in resources and skills in exchange for privileged access to local markets. This, too, has changed. The strategies of modern multinational corporations are no longer shaped and conditioned by reasons of state but, rather, by the desire—and the need—to serve attractive markets wherever they exist and to tap attractive pools of resources wherever they sit. Government-funded subsidies—old-fashioned tax breaks for investing in this or that location—are becoming irrelevant as a decision criterion. The Western firms now moving, say, into parts of China and India are there because that is where their future lies, not because the host government has suddenly dangled a carrot in front of their nose.

As corporations move, of course, they bring with them working capital. Perhaps more important, they transfer technology and managerial know-how. These are not concessions to host governments; they are the essential raw materials these companies need to do their work. But they also bring something else. Pension fund money in the United States, for example, might look for decent China-related opportunities by scouting out the possibilities on the Shanghai stock exchange. The prospects thus identified, however, will be largely unfamiliar. Money managers will do their best to provide adequate research, but everyone will admit that relevant knowledge is limited. But if it is a GE or an IBM or a Unilever or a P&G that is building a presence in China, the markets back home and elsewhere in the developed world will know how to evaluate that. They will be more comfortable with it. And that, in turn, expands the range of capital markets on which these companies can draw for resources to be used in China.

The movement of both investment and industry has been greatly facilitated by the third "I"—information technology—which now makes it possible for a company to operate in various parts of the world without having to build up an entire business system in each of the countries where it has a presence. Engineers at workstations in Osaka can easily control plant operations in newly exciting parts of China like Dalian. Product designers in Oregon can control the activities of a network of factories throughout Asia-Pacific. Thus, the hurdles for cross-border participation and strategic alliance have come way down. Armies of experts do not have to be transferred; armies of workers do not have to be trained. Capability can reside in the network and be made available—virtually anywhere—as needed.

Finally, individual consumers—the fourth "I"—have also become more global in orientation. With better access to information about lifestyles around the globe, they are much less likely to want to buy—and much less conditioned by government injunctions to buy—American or French or Japanese products merely because of their national associations. Consumers increasingly want the best and cheapest products, no matter where they come from. And they have shown their willingness to vote these preferences with their pocketbooks.

Taken together, the mobility of these four I's makes it possible for viable economic units in any part of the world to pull in whatever is needed for development. They need not look for assistance only to pools of resources close to home. Nor need they rely on the formal efforts of governments to attract resources from elsewhere and funnel them to the ultimate users. This makes the traditional "middleman" function of nation states—and of their governments—largely unnecessary. Because the global markets for all the I's work just fine on their own, nation states no longer have to play a market-making role. In fact, given their own troubles, which are considerable, they most often just get in the way. If allowed, global solutions will flow to where they are needed without the intervention of nation states. On current evidence, moreover, they flow better precisely because such intervention is absent.

This fundamentally changes the economic equation. If the unfettered movement of these I's makes the middleman role of nation states obsolete, the qualifications needed to sit at the global table and pull in global solutions begin to correspond not to the artificial political borders of countries, but to the more focused geographical units—Hong Kong, for example, and the adjacent stretch of southern China, or the Kansai region around Osaka, or Catalonia—where real work gets done and real markets flourish. I call these units "region states." They may lie entirely within or across the borders of a nation state. This does not matter. It is the irrelevant result of historical accident. What defines them is not the location of their political borders but the fact that they are the right size and scale to be the true, natural business units in today's global economy. Theirs are the borders—and the connections— that matter in a borderless world.

# THE CHALLENGES
# OF CONSOLIDATION

Stephan Haggard and Robert R. Kaufman

As the recent wave of democratization crested in the 1980s, skeptics questioned the capacity of new democratic governments to manage the daunting political challenges of economic reform. It was thought that either reform would undermine democracy by placing undue strains on fragile polities, or democratic politics would undermine the coherence of policy, generating a downward economic spiral.

Concerns about democratic breakdown and policy stalemate remain salient in many parts of the world, particularly the new republics of the former Soviet Union. By the 1990s, however, newly established democratic regimes in many developing countries had initiated deep and wide-ranging economic reforms. The early democratizers of Southern Europe are now firmly ensconced in the European Union, having undertaken important economic adjustments required for their admission. In Latin America, longstanding development strategies have been reversed by fundamental shifts in economic policy: deep fiscal and exchange-rate adjustments, reduction of trade barriers, and privatization of state-owned enterprises. The trade-oriented countries of East and Southeast Asia did not experience crises of the same magnitude, but in the Philippines, Korea, Taiwan, and Thailand, the trend toward political liberalization has also coincided with the initiation of a new round of economic policy changes. And, of course, most of the post-communist democracies of Central Europe have inaugurated massive—and wrenching—market-oriented reforms.

The changes in all these regions and countries have been accompanied by substantial controversy; nevertheless, for good or for ill, they are now a *fait accompli*. The next phase of adjustment raises questions somewhat different

from those faced during the 1980s: not whether democracies can initiate reforms, but how they will meet the new challenges likely to arise as economies
are stabilized. Will they be able to consolidate existing reforms, or correct
course as social and economic conditions change? More important, will they
manage to consolidate democratic institutions themselves?

Three key issues have emerged more clearly as earlier crises have been
brought under control. The first concerns the role of the state in achieving
sustainable growth. The second involves the distributional consequences of
reform and their implications for political conflict. The third, which points to
a particularly difficult challenge, pertains to the accountability of the reform
process. The heads of government who implemented the initial reforms generally wielded substantial discretionary power vis-à-vis economic interests
and representative institutions. How can economic decision making become
less discretionary and more institutionalized?

We begin with the assumption that economic instability and recession
pose serious threats to democratic consolidation. In this essay, "consolidation" is used to refer to processes through which acceptance of a given set of
constitutional rules becomes increasingly widespread, valued, and rou-
tinized. It is important to make a clear distinction between the survival of
democracies and their consolidation. During the 1980s, many new democracies survived severe economic shocks, but their durability was often attributable to factors that did not necessarily imply increasing legitimacy and
acceptance of the "rules of the game."

New democratic regimes benefited in the first place from the decline and
collapse of the Soviet Union and the end of Cold War politics. As perceptions
of the Soviet threat diminished, the United States and European governments
were less willing to back dictatorial clients against opposition challenges, and
more inclined to punish groups seeking to overthrow their constitutional
successors. Even where authoritarian reversals occurred, international pressures played a significant role in preventing the consolidation of authoritarian rule (for example, in Peru), or in forcing a relatively rapid return to
electoral politics (as seen in Thailand and Guatemala).

The early survival of many new democracies was also attributable to aspects of domestic politics that were not necessarily permanent. Economic
difficulties could, for a time, be blamed on the outgoing authoritarian regime
or the incumbent government, rather than on the democratic system itself.

Even where democratic regimes are held in place by these international
and domestic political contingencies, however, weak economic performance
can undermine attitudes and behaviors that are important for democratic
consolidation. In Brazil and Peru, for example, inflation and economic deterioration have had a corrosive effect on political institutions and have been
closely linked to increasing social tension and civil violence. Signs of aliena-
tion are also apparent in the former socialist world, where ex-communists
and right-wing movements are tapping a nostalgia for the old order.

For countries experiencing prolonged economic distress, it is easy to
sketch a stylized model in which constitutional institutions are drained of

their democratic content, even in the absence of formal regime change. Such a cycle would begin with developments already evident in a number of developing and formerly socialist countries: an increase in political cynicism and apathy, a decline in effective political participation, and a failure of the political system to generate stable and representative ruling coalitions. In a later stage, crime, civil violence, and organized revolutionary or antirevolutionary ("death squad") activity would contribute to a gradual erosion of the substance of democratic rule through intermittent repression of opposition groups, emergency measures, and a decline in the integrity of legal guarantees. In a final stage—still short of a formal transition to authoritarian rule—electoral institutions would be rendered a facade. Elected officials would become subject to the veto power of military elites, or constitute little more than fronts for them.

In cases like Peru, of course, such processes eventually led to a reversal of democracy, and we cannot rule out the possibility of setbacks elsewhere. Democratic backsliding could occur in several ways. A general erosion of faith in the capacity of democratic governments to manage the economy would increase the appeal of authoritarian "solutions" to the economic crisis, not only among elites but among the public at large. The erosion of support for democratic institutions would lead to the election of leaders or parties with plebiscitarian or openly authoritarian ambitions, or reduce the perceived costs to the military of intervening. Economic decline might also reverse democratization more indirectly by leading to an increase in crime, strikes, riots, and other forms of civil violence and to the polarization of groups at opposite ends of the political spectrum. Such social unrest and political polarization provide the classic justification for military intervention.

## REDEFINING THE ROLE OF THE STATE

If economic growth is important for democratic consolidation, then current market-oriented reforms necessarily have implications that go well beyond their immediate economic effects. Critics have claimed that such policies are counterproductive from the point of view of both growth and equity—particularly when they are implemented as "shock" packages—and are, by implication, corrosive of stable democratic rule as well. Luiz Carlos Bresser Pereira, Josá María Maravall, and Adam Przeworski make the argument most boldly: "Whenever democratic governments followed neo-liberal tenets, the outcome has been stagnation, increased poverty, political discontent, and the debilitation of democracy."

Many "neoliberal" claims do indeed rest on shaky theoretical and empirical ground. Clearly, the Anglo-Saxon model is not the only viable model of the market economy; many "alternative capitalisms," particularly those that characterize East Asia and the small European social democracies, have been highly successful. Debates over "neoliberalism," however, have frequently become polarized in ways that have obscured and mischaracterized the policies and political options available to new democracies.

First, both "neoliberals" and their critics have often underestimated the significant economic and political constraints under which governments have launched their reform efforts. For many new democracies, reforms typically began as short-term responses to economic crises; as Jeffrey Sachs has put it in a review of his experiences in Russia and Eastern Europe, this was "life in the emergency room." The traumas included high and rapidly accelerating inflation and profound fiscal and balance-of-payments crises. The loss of access to international financial markets was particularly damaging, as constraints on foreign exchange increased dependence on conditional assistance from the international financial institutions and severely limited the range of adjustment options.

Reforms undertaken in response to such conditions were often embedded in an ideological discourse about the virtues or dangers of a "minimalist" state limited to such "basic" functions as protecting property rights and providing certain essential collective goods. In most countries, however, macroeconomic adjustments and privatization programs were motivated less by these broad visions than by the urgent need to confront accelerating inflation and to reduce massive fiscal and balance-of-payments deficits. Trade liberalization is more difficult to understand in these terms, as there are strong incentives *not* to reduce trade barriers in the midst of severe balance-of-payments crises. Yet trade liberalization was also important for establishing the credibility of stabilization efforts and for reassuring foreign investors and international financial institutions at a time when attracting external financing appeared crucial to recovery.

This is not to suggest that there was only one way to adjust to the situation encountered in the 1980s; greater official assistance would have made the task easier for governments committed to reform, and significant technical issues concerning the design and sequencing of adjustment programs remain unresolved. At the same time, short-term crisis management should not be confused with advocacy or adoption of any particular longer-term growth strategy.

It is important to evaluate carefully the net impact that the "neoliberal" adjustments of the 1980s have had on choices available for the long term. Extensive privatization, deregulation, and liberalization may have reduced the availability of policy instruments that have been used successfully elsewhere to promote economic growth. Yet a selective shedding of government commitments can also provide the basis for more effective state intervention in other areas. To the extent that neoliberal reforms have helped to strengthen state finances and establish sustainable balance-of-payments positions, they have arguably expanded the possibilities for states to take a more activist role in the economy in the future.

Some reforms tagged as "neoliberal" have also been aimed explicitly at *strengthening* the state. These include the establishment of a broader tax base, more effective tax collection, and a reorientation of public-spending priorities toward investment and the provision of basic services. The development of commercial law and regulatory capacity are central components of all market-oriented reforms in the former socialist countries. The reform of the civil service and the creation of economic decision-making agencies resistant to particularistic demands constitute useful institutional changes regardless of the economic strategy pursued.

Different views about current reform efforts have often exhibited greater overlap than is commonly acknowledged. "Mainstream" economists have frequently advised caution with regard to the sequence and pace of reforms, and have even expressed skepticism about certain components of the "neo-liberal" package itself, including devaluation, trade liberalization, financial-market liberalization, and privatization. On the other hand, social democratic and "heterodox" critics also emphasize the importance of sound fiscal and exchange-rate policies; they are perfectly aware of the policy failures in the developing and socialist countries during the postwar period, and none would advocate a return to the *status quo ante.*

The convergence of opinion around such issues, however, by no means precludes vigorous contestation over a wide spectrum of policy questions. Among the issues about which political controversy is likely to surface are the efficacy of industrial policy, the provision of education and services, and the adequacy of the social safety net. In countries that achieve sustainable fiscal and balance-of-payments positions, debates over such issues are likely to be of immediate relevance to the policy decisions facing democratic governments. Such debates in turn are likely to improve both the quality and the sustainability of the choices that are made and the legitimacy of the political system as a whole.

## POVERTY AND INCOME INEQUALITY

Even if new democratic governments succeed in reigniting economic growth, they will also have to confront controversial problems of poverty and income inequality. The crises of the 1980s clearly had a devastating impact on low-income groups everywhere. The effects of reforms on these groups have been mixed, but it is clear that at least some measures have exacerbated both poverty and inequality. The demand-reducing effects of stabilization policies and cuts in government spending have had particularly severe consequences for the urban poor and the working and even middle classes, who suffered from cutbacks in subsidies for food, transport, and fuel and the decline in the provision of public services. In the formerly socialist economies, where income disparities were less pronounced and employment was more secure, these effects have been especially marked. At the same time, some reforms, including privatization and financial-market reforms, have provided new opportunities and even windfalls for upper-income groups, further skewing the distribution of income.

Despite these developments, some hopeful elements can be identified in the current situation. In the first place, reforms that succeed in promoting aggregate economic expansion are also likely to ease the plight of the poor. In the past, there was considerable skepticism about the idea that the benefits of growth would "trickle down" to poor households and individuals, and some speculation that economic expansion would actually make these people even poorer. The evidence shows, however, that where growth has been robust, absolute poverty has generally declined, even where the distribution of income remains unequal. Conversely, increases in poverty can frequently be traced to the slow growth typical of the "lost decade" of the 1980s.

Moreover, although some aspects of economic reform have contributed to a widening of income disparities, others may have more positive effects over the long run. In Latin America, Africa, and South Asia, economic liberalization is intended to reverse protectionist practices that for decades had provided monopoly rents for the owners of capital or state-owned enterprises as well as for unionized workers within these sectors. To the extent that such reforms succeed in reversing earlier biases against agriculture, nontraditional exports, and the informal sector, they can contribute to the reduction of inequality as well as the alleviation of poverty, thus enhancing the prospects for democratic consolidation.

The "market-oriented" reforms advocated by mainstream economists and international financial institutions are not necessarily inconsistent with active state efforts to reduce poverty. The World Bank has for some time argued for more effective targeting of antipoverty programs toward the poorest and most vulnerable sectors of the population, such as children and pregnant women, and has increasingly emphasized the role of education and health policy not only in alleviating suffering but in promoting growth as well. Antipoverty programs have been implemented by governments pursuing market-oriented reforms in Ghana, Zambia, Mexico, Bolivia, and Chile (under both Augusto Pinochet and Patricio Aylwin). Even under conditions of recession and fiscal constraint, such programs have had a significant degree of success in cushioning the shocks of structural adjustment.

The fact that the poor can be protected during periods of crisis and adjustment does not mean that they will be, however, and the political equations involved are not altogether encouraging. Some of the most troubling distributional questions center not on the poorest of the poor, but on middle-income employees and formal-sector workers. For most of the postwar period, such groups relied heavily on the public sector to provide opportunities for education, employment, and mobility. Cutbacks in government spending and employment have thus posed significant threats to their income and social status; this is particularly true in the former socialist countries.

The downward mobility of these strata poses two challenges. First, the interests of the downwardly mobile sections of the middle and working classes may conflict with the interests of the very poor, giving rise to serious disputes over the allocation of resources. Clearly, meeting the desperate and pervasive needs of the destitute should be a top priority of governments. Yet blue-collar and middle-class groups are unlikely to support antipoverty subsidies unless they can share in the benefits, and they are likely to oppose them if they entail a reduction in existing services. Because middle-income groups possess greater political and organizational resources than the poorest segments of the population, their economic distress also poses far greater dangers to the stability of newly established democratic systems. In absolute terms, the needs of such groups may be less desperate than those of the very poor. Yet the downward mobility of individuals in these strata, an increasing number of whom are not far from the poverty line, is a powerful impetus to anti-democratic mobilization.

Can the different interests of low-income and middle-income groups be reconciled? If so, under what conditions? One possible solution might be the formation of encompassing coalitions that could press more effectively for the broad provision of educational, health, and other social services, financed through the progressive taxation of wealthier groups. A resumption of growth could increase the political and economic viability of such an alliance.

But the still fragile economic circumstances of Eastern Europe, Africa, and Latin America impose significant constraints on the formation of a coalition of middle-income and low-income groups. Even with substantial external financial assistance, enlarging the scope of public services to reach all of these groups would require either more comprehensive and progressive tax systems than currently exist or a reversion to the macroeconomic populism that has been so costly in the past and is now extracting its price in a number of the former socialist republics.

There is no doubt that efforts to implement comprehensive and progressive tax reforms would encounter strong opposition from powerful upper-income groups as well as daunting administrative obstacles. We cannot, therefore, rule out the possibility of a renewed growth in the popularity of populist ideologies, with its clear implications for both economic expansion and democracy.

## INSTITUTIONALIZING DEMOCRACY

Over the long term, the opportunities that democratic institutions provide for debate and peaceful contestation offer the best hope for finding durable compromises for the social conflicts and economic policy dilemmas described above. But the initiation of far-reaching economic adjustments has often reflected a political logic that is not easily reconciled with the formation of broad-based coalitions and effective representative institutions. To break political logjams during times of pressing economic crisis, heads of government have typically sought to ram reforms through acquiescent legislatures or to legislate by decree; this pattern is particularly evident where very high inflation demands the sudden adjustments known as "shock therapy."

The fact that so many leaders in new democracies have acted autocratically in crisis situations implies that such behavior cannot be explained simply in terms of personal ambition or lack of concern for democratic institutions. We have argued elsewhere that the initiation of reform usually requires a substantial concentration of discretionary political authority to surmount resistance from status-quo interests, collective-action problems

facing potential beneficiaries, and uncertainties surrounding the benefits—
and beneficiaries—of reforms.

An evaluation of such behavior must take into account the constraints
under which leaders operate and the political costs of delaying adjustment.
Where underlying economic conditions are relatively favorable—as they
were, for example, in Spain—it may be feasible to give the right-of-way to the
building of a democratic consensus. Where crises are deeper, however, democratic institutions may suffer as much from the failure to take swift and effective action as from the temporary exercise of discretionary authority.
In many instances, such authority has pressed against constitutional limits;
however, it should not be assumed that strong executive action implies that
the legislature and other representative institutions have abdicated their responsibility for oversight.

If both economic reforms and democracies are to be consolidated, executive authority must eventually be depersonalized and integrated into a
broader framework of contestation and accountability. In the absence of institutionalized consultation with legislators and interest groups, decision
makers are deprived of feedback that may be essential for correcting mis-
takes, and their reforms are more exposed to the possibility of popular backlash and reversal. *Decretismo* in economic decision making also reinforces
broader tendencies toward what Guillermo O'Donnell has called "delegative
democracy," in which elected executives attempt to rule through broad media appeals and personalist movements, bypassing intermediate institutions.
Even where the reform initiatives of plebiscitarian presidents yield positive
economic results, there is substantial risk of a slide into a kind of "soft au-
thoritarianism" in which economic success is used by the ruler to chip away
at constitutional limits on his power.

Certain types of political and institutional arrangements have been suggested as providing a suitable context for this "second stage" of reform. One
possibility is the construction of European-style corporatist frameworks,
within which policy agreements could be directly negotiated among representatives of labor, business, and the state. Such arrangements, however, face
major impediments in the developing and socialist worlds. In Europe itself,
corporatist bargaining has been undermined by the increasing internationalization of financial markets and the corresponding decline of national control
over macroeconomic and exchange-rate variables. Corporatist systems in the
developing world would confront similar international conditions and even
more daunting macroeconomic challenges. They would also have to deal with
far more divisive distributive issues, given the concentrations of income that
exist in these countries.

Another kind of difficulty is posed by the relative weakness of the relevant
players. Effective corporatist pacts rest on the capacity of the most important
economic actors to negotiate binding agreements regarding wages, prices,
and investment. In most countries, however, neither the state, the parties,
nor the interest-group associations are cohesive and strong enough to speak

authoritatively for their memberships and to guarantee some minimal level of compliance.

## CONSTITUTIONAL AND ELECTORAL REFORM

Parliamentarism is a second well-known proposal for encouraging the development of more stable and broad-based decision-making procedures. The core feature of parliamentarist systems is the fusion of legislative and executive authority. "Parliamentistas" argue that this feature allows such systems to provide stronger incentives for political cooperation than do presidential systems, in which executives and legislators are elected separately and serve for fixed terms. Indirect support for these arguments is provided by the problems experienced in many Latin American presidential systems, including the election of outsiders, such as Brazil's Fernando Collor de Mello or Peru's Alberto Fujimori, who lack legislative support; divided government and policy stalemates; and the difficulty of replacing executives who have lost their political backing.

It is possible that, politically speaking, economic adjustment would have gone more smoothly under parliamentary rule. Nevertheless, we are skeptical about the strong claims made for parliamentary alternatives. In societies that have already established presidential constitutions, one of the central problems is getting from here to there. Opportunities for a comprehensive redesign of presidential constitutions are rare. When such opportunities do present themselves, they tend to encounter powerful opposition from groups with vested interests in the existing system, including the incumbent president and the leading aspirants for the office (as exemplified by the defeat of the parliamentary option in the Brazilian plebiscite of 1992).

Even if parliamentary regimes can be established, their effectiveness is likely to depend on how a number of related constitutional issues have been addressed: the organization of electoral districts, thresholds of representation, the relationship between the head of government and the head of state, and specific provisions governing votes of confidence and dissolution of the legislature. Coherent agreements on these questions may not be impossible to negotiate. Nevertheless, compromises with groups that have benefited from existing institutional arrangements may also produce hybrid outcomes that leave lines of accountability unclear and combine the worst of both worlds. Under such circumstances, reform of presidential systems may be a wiser course than a shift to parliamentarism.

Whether regimes are parliamentary or presidential, the organization of the party system has a profound effect on both the coherence of economic policy and the stability of democratic rule. Unstable and fragmented party systems tend to impede the negotiation of sustainable understandings among interest groups and undermine coordination within the state apparatus itself. Where such systems are characterized by high levels of ideological polarization, electoral cycles are likely to destabilize expectations about the future course of policy, as there is greater potential for policy swings between successive governments.

The combination of presidentialism and polarized multiparty competition can be especially devastating, as Scott Mainwaring has argued; the cases of Peru and Brazil illustrate clearly the difficulty that such a combination poses for stable democratic rule. It should be noted, though, that party-system fragmentation also contributed to the breakdown of several parliamentary regimes, including Turkey in 1980 and Thailand in 1991, and posed significant obstacles to the implementation of reforms in Poland.

Party-system consolidation can be encouraged through a number of different institutional reforms: raising the threshold of electoral votes required for legislative representation, reducing the number of representatives per district, reforming nominating and financing procedures, and the like. Party systems, of course, often reflect social and cultural cleavages that will persist even after the implementation of changes in electoral rules. Even so, such changes can make a considerable difference in reducing party-system instability.

As in the case of a shift to a parliamentary system, the politicians who must implement such changes are likely to be the main beneficiaries of the existing system. This is a major problem, but it is not as serious as in the case of wholesale constitutional revision. In the first place, although the positive effects of a switch to parliamentarism are very likely to depend on concurrent reforms of the party system, the reverse is not necessarily the case: reforms of the party system do not depend on broader constitutional changes.

Moreover, party systems need not be reformed all at once; they can be consolidated incrementally through piecemeal changes in electoral arrangements, financing laws, districting, and the like. Politicians benefiting from the status quo may be reluctant to accept even small changes. Still, it may be easier to get backing for partial reforms in a democratic context than to build support for a comprehensive and coherent new design of the constitutional system as a whole.

## ENTERING THE SECOND ROUND

New democracies in developing countries are entering what might be considered a "second round" of economic reform and political institution building. In many countries, the first round was characterized by concerns about economic collapse and democratic reversal, but also by the exhilaration of sweeping changes in political institutions and economic structures. The transformations taking place during the next phase are likely to be more incremental and less dramatic, but no less difficult or crucial for the consolidation of stable capitalist democracies.

The challenges related to economic growth and equity include both strengthening the associational infrastructure of civil society and the construction of a capable and responsive state bureaucracy. Previous efforts at fiscal adjustment and macroeconomic stabilization have arguably laid the groundwork for progress on these fronts, the antistatist rhetoric of neoliberal ideology notwithstanding. The completion of prior reforms, however, provides no guarantee of successful performance of these new institutional tasks. Moreover, we can expect to see increasing contestation over the state's role in promoting economic growth and protecting citizens from the dislocations of the market.

The functioning of democracy will depend on the political institutions that mediate this contestation. Experience in the advanced industrial countries shows that there is a wide variety of political institutions compatible with a market economy and representative government. But the transition to such arrangements remains problematic and reversible. In some cases, a shift to parliamentary rule or social pacts may constitute feasible steps toward the development of viable democratic governance. Such steps are unlikely to substitute, however, for institutional reforms that encourage the evolution of less fragmented party systems capable of aggregating interests and organizing consent.

*Credits Manuscript for Zahariadis,* Contending Perspectives in International Political Economy

**Page 3:** Reprinted from Adam Smith, *The Wealth of Nations,* Chicago: University of Chicago Press, 1976.

**Page 7:** Reprinted from "Imperialism, the Highest State of Capitalism" (excerpts), from *The Lenin Anthology* by Robert C. Tucker. Copyright © 1975 by W. W. Norton & Company, Inc. Reprinted by permission of W. W. Norton & Company, Inc.

**Page 11:** Reprinted from Alexander Hamilton, *The Reports of Alexander Hamilton,* Jacob Cooke, ed., New York: Harper and Row, 1964.

**Page 17:** From "Winners and Losers in the Global Economics Game" by Gerald Epstein, James Crotty, and Patricia Kelly. Reprinted with permission from *Current History* magazine (November 1996). Copyright © 1996 Current History, Inc.

**Page 25:** Excerpts from *U.S. Power and the Multinational Corporation* by Robert Gilpin. Copyright © 1975 by Basic Books, Inc. Reprinted by permission of Basic Books, a division of HarperCollins Publishers, Inc.

**Page 37:** From "Protectionist Trade Policies: A Survey of Theory, Evidence, and Rationale" by Cletus C. Coughlin, K. Alec Chrystal and Geoffrey E. Wood in *Federal Reserve Bank of St. Louis Review* (May/June 1992). Reprinted courtesy of the Federal Reserve Bank of St. Louis.

**Page 51:** From "National Competitiveness: A Dangerous Obsession" by Paul Krug-

man. Reprinted by permission of *Foreign Affairs* (March/April 1994). Copyright © 1994 by the Council on Foreign Relations, Inc.

**Page 59:** From "The Public Choice View of International Political Economy" by Bruno S. Frey. *International Organization,* 38:1 (Winter 1984), pp. 199–223. Copyright © 1984 by the World Peace Foundation and the Massachusetts Institute of Technology. Reprinted by permission.

**Page 69:** From Stephen D. Krasner, "State Power and the Structure of International Trade" in *World Politics* 28 (3), pp. 317–343. Copyright © 1976 by Johns Hopkins University Press. Reprinted by permission.

**Page 79:** From "Power Politics and International Trade" by Joanne Gowa and Edward Mansfield in *American Political Science Review* (1993). Reprinted by permission from the American Political Science Association.

**Page 89:** From "Why State Subsidies? Evidence from European Community Countries, 1981–86" by Nikolaos Zahariadis in *International Studies Quarterly* (1997). Reprinted by permission of Blackwell Publishers, Inc.

**Page 105:** From *Essays in Positive Economics* by Milton Friedman. Copyright © 1953 by the University of Chicago Press. Reprinted by permission.

**Page 113:** From John B. Goodman and Louis W. Pauly, "The Obsolescence of Capital Controls? Economic Management in the Age of Global Markets" in *World Politics* 43 (1), pp. 50–82.